FROM THE HEART
OF THE CREATOR OF LOVE...

REVELATION
A
Love Story

MONICA BENNETT-RYAN

IN HIS NAME
PUBLISHING

REVELATION
A
Love Story

ISBN - 978-0-9807895-3-9

Revised Edition
© 2023 Monica Bennett-Ryan

IN HIS NAME
PUBLISHING

IN HIS NAME PUBLISHING
www.inhisname.com.au

Cover Design

DONIKA MISCHIVENA
www.artofdonika.com.

Photography

BRONWEN RUSSELL
www.bronsdesign.com.au

To him
who sits on the throne
and to the Lamb
be praise and honour
glory and power
forever and ever!

(Rev.5:12-13)

In the center of this image is a man on a horse.
We can't see him clearly yet
but we know he loves us and is on his way back.

CONTENTS

CONTENTS

Rescued and grateful!

INTRODUCTION

Throughout the ages, the Book of Revelation has given millions of people breathtaking visions of hope mingled with the promise of eternal love in a happy-ever-after future. It has filled hearts with glimpses of everlasting joy, peace and contentment so strong it has enabled many to face even the worst persecution. This book explores what they saw and what gave so many such hope.

In contrast, various scholars have tried to link Revelation's many dramatic images and perplexing symbols to historical events in their century. Some have interpreted them as dark omens of Satanic power. Others have viewed them, and many still view them, as prophetic signs riding a hidden timeline that points to the world's end. This book rejects these ways of interpreting Revelation as, at best, an exercise in futility and, at worst, blasphemous deception.

In the following pages, the Book of Revelation is presented as the testimony of a triumphant king, given after his battles were concluded and he was hailed as the victor. This book is about Christ, with *his* story given from *his* point of view as delivered to his servant and friend, the Apostle John. It is written in the language of contrasts and, contrary to popular belief, it shows Revelation is not difficult to understand.

What I find difficult to understand is why so much horror has been attributed to this most awesome of books. It is clear that Revelation glorifies Christ and highlights what he has done for his redeemed, and in that light, the images are not hard to understand, for example:

- The Dragon is 'anti' God himself
- The First Beast is 'anti' Christ
- The Second Beast is 'anti' the Spirit of God
- The Scarlet Harlot is 'anti' the Bride of Christ

Despite the simplicity of the symbolism of Revelation, so much has been added that the original message has become muddied and lost. Confusing concepts have been added that confound the reader and block the truth from being seen. This book removes the additions so that the reader can once again enjoy the beauty and blessings of the Book of Revelation.

One of the additions is the fable of a last days Antichrist figure, who will appear in the flesh and rule all the nations of the world. Total nonsense! According to the Book of Revelation, that belief is so far from the truth it's not even possible. The only 'ruler' in Revelation is Jesus.

It's the same with the Rapture Theory. There is no mention of a rapturous escape from tribulation in the Book of Revelation, or in Christ's teaching, or in his disciple's teaching. No mention at all anywhere in Scripture!

Then there are all the 'additions' from Old Testament prophets, supposedly to explain Revelation's amazing images. A futile exercise! Revelation's images had never been seen before in Heaven or on Earth - not by prophets, patriarchs, disciples or even angels. The images and their meanings were so new that as Christ opened the scroll to reveal them, there was total silence! All Heaven held its breath, waiting to see what no eye had seen and no ear had heard from the beginning of time.

When all the hype, lies, and speculative additions are removed, the simple truth and beauty of Christ's powerful and very personal testimony can be seen. The truth is, the images of Revelation are given so that Christ's redeemed can glory in his conquest of Satan, copy what he has done, and join him in his victory.

All the mysterious symbols, visions and images explain the enormous power and authority of Christ's defeat of Satan in the simplest possible way. They are not complicated or hard to understand. They are simply brilliant!

The most outstanding and enduring message of Revelation is that Christ loves his Bride. He loves her so much that he is willing to die for her! At its base, Revelation is a profoundly deep love story, but what else can we expect from the God who created love, commanded love, lived in love and died for love? Everything he thinks and does is based on love!

Woven through the pages of Revelation is the greatest love story the world has ever known. Each page shows the depth of love and trust between Christ and his Father and how that deep love and trust is mirrored in Christ's love for his beloved Bride. There is so much love to be seen in the Book of Revelation one could spend a lifetime looking into the beauty of that love and never come to the end of the story.

As I explain to you how I see Christ in the most brilliant of books, the last book of the Bible, it is my hope you will see him the way he deserves to be seen; as our mighty conquerer, unrivalled champion, the world's only glorious and victorious Saviour, the hope of our salvation, and the only light that can lead the world out of darkness.

Be blessed as you read,

Monica

Blessed beyond measure!

1

A ROYAL DECREE

The revelation from Jesus Christ, which God gave him...that is, the word of God and the testimony of Jesus Christ. (Rev.1:1-2)

When people today think about the Book of Revelation, usually the first thing that forms in their minds is the concept of a fearsome Antichrist world ruler, his possible One-World Government, and a timely rapture from unbridled Satanic chaos. Many books and movies confirm that fearful scenario, but does the Book of Revelation confirm it? Is this what the Book of Revelation and its many glorious visions teach? The answer is a resounding no!

I will be honest with you upfront and tell you that not one of those three very popular and commonly known concepts can be found in the Book of Revelation. Not one! They are just not there! The word 'antichrist' can't be found at all. That leaves us with a bit of a conundrum. If Revelation is not about any of the above, then what is it about? When the hype is removed, so is the horror, and what remains is a beautiful story. A love story. The testimony of Jesus Christ.

REVELATION IS 'GOOD NEWS'

The testimony of Jesus Christ, penned by the Apostle John and known for centuries as the Book of Revelation, is a story of love. Jesus is love. He created love. He commanded love. He taught love. Everything he did showed his love. His testimony cannot be about anything else but love. When his testimony is viewed through love, all the visions, symbols and images contained within his beautiful testimony lose their mystery and become clear.

Are they scary and frightening? Absolutely not! All the images contained within the Book of Revelation bring us good news and tidings of great joy. They are given to comfort and bless and remind us that no matter how difficult things may become in this world or how many obstacles Christ's enemy may lay before the redeemed, our triumphant Saviour will deliver us from all the devil's schemes and take us safely to his eternal Kingdom just as he has promised.

The confidence we have that we can believe his testimony is the book itself. The Book of Revelation is more than a prophetic glimpse into eternity; it is a royal document.

It's not meant to be confusing or mysterious! It's supposed to be a blessing!

It is the only book of the Bible that contains the personal testimony of the King of Kings, given from his point of view after his battles were fought and won, and he was hailed as the victor. In this royal document, our Saviour and King reveals why he went to war in the first place; to defend his Father's Kingdom and rescue his beautiful future Bride from Satan's power. Everything written shows his enormous love for both his Father and his Bride, for without that love, there would be no battle, no victory, and no testimony.

Christ's personal testimony to John gives us a unique glimpse into the way things changed after he was raised from the dead. It's not meant to be confusing or mysterious–and it's not! It's supposed to be a blessing–and it is! This amazing royal document is a treasure of Heaven, so precious that Christ had to die, be raised from the dead and crowned King over all kings before it could be written and revealed. Let me explain:

- ♥ It's the only book of the Bible that gives a panoramic view of the full expanse of life on Earth from Adam to the end of the world.

- ♥ It's the only book of the Bible that presents Jesus as the *King of kings* and the *Alpha and Omega* and reveals what those splendid titles mean. Not possible before he was crowned King.

- ♥ It's the only book of the Bible that explains precisely who Satan is and how we can expect him to behave. No other book of the Bible does this.

- ♥ It introduces us to Satan's previously unknown cohorts, the beast, false prophet and scarlet woman. Not possible before Christ's death and resurrection.

- ♥ It exposes the predictable tactics they will each try to use in spiritual warfare against Christ's beloved Bride. Not known before the death and resurrection of Christ.

- ♥ It also reveals the traps God has laid out to ensure their evil plans fail every time. Not possible before Christ was crowned King and opened the Scroll of Judgment.

- ♥ It outlines the judgment God had already pronounced on Satan and all his associates before the prophecy was actually written. Not possible before Christ was crowned King and opened the Scroll of Judgment.

- ♥ It unfolds the supreme majesty and power of our glorified Christ. Not possible before his resurrection.

- ♥ It reveals, in minute detail, how God places all Christ's enemies under his feet as promised. Not possible before Christ was handed the Scroll of Judgment.

- ♥ It reveals, in detail, how the Bride of Christ will rule and reign with him during the time of judgment known as the Great Tribulation. Not possible before Christ was crowned King over all kings.

- ♥ It's the only book of the Bible that combines the judgment of the Law of God, written by Moses, with the victory of Christ at Calvary. Mindblowing!

- ♥ It reveals, for the first time in human history, the might of the Holy Spirit and his dominant role as the one who brings judgment to those who reject the great sacrifice of Christ. Not possible before Christ was crowned King and handed the Scroll of Judgment.

- ♥ It's the only Book of the Bible that shows clearly how Father, Son, Spirit and Bride work together in love, harmony and perfect unity. Profoundly beautiful!

- ♥ Finally, it's the only book of the Bible that highlights the absolute authority of Christ, as King of kings and Lord of lords, central to human history, ruler over everyone and everything on Earth and in Heaven, and total victor over Satan and his beasts.

Not one of the above was possible before the death and resurrection of Christ, and each is an extraordinary testament to his victory. This is what Christ wanted his Bride to know.

In short, the brilliant post-resurrection revelation of the majesty of our victorious King, known as the Book of Revelation, is the only book in the Bible that contrasts the ineffective warfare of Satan against the massive, powerful, mighty and invincible brilliance of God and his Christ.

IT'S NOT ABOUT SATAN

This enlightening testimony was written to bring comfort to Christ's Bride, to show that Christ has fulfilled, and will fulfil, everything he told his disciples he would do, and to reveal that everything happening to them, both good and bad, was happening because Christ was keeping his word.

> *Blessed is the one who reads aloud the words of this prophecy, and blessed are those who hear it and take to heart what is written in it, for the time is near. (Rev.1:3)*

Sadly, people with no understanding of the selfless love and grace revealed by this beautiful Royal Testimony have filled the world with stories of fear and horror and deceived the elect into believing this book is about Satan. It clearly is not about Satan! Anyone who reads the above can see it's not about Satan. Revelation is a book of blessings.

The glorious testimony of Christ was written specifically to help believers see things from Christ's point of view. It stands to reason, then, that to understand the intention of the images of Revelation, we need to look at them from the point of view of Christ's victory over Satan.

That's exactly what the wonderful images of Revelation teach us to do; look at the victory of Christ from God's point of view. They're not supposed to be scary or frightening, and they're not! When we look at the images from the same perspective as the Apostle John, from the viewpoint of Heaven, they lose their mystery and become simple parables, so simple even a child can understand and be blessed.

Enlightened by parables!

2

AWESOME IMAGES

The knowledge of the secrets of the Kingdom of God has been given to you, but to others, I speak in parables, so that, 'though seeing, they may not see; though hearing, they may not understand'. (Lk.8:10)

How many times have you heard people say, 'Well, I just don't understand Revelation', or 'It's too complicated, so I don't think about it'.

One of the reasons there is so much confusion amongst believers about this fascinating book is that many biblical scholars, who don't understand Revelation is about Christ, have been trying to interpret the individual pictures of Revelation from the point of view of world history. An absolutely impossible task! That's like trying to convince everyone the world is square when it is clear it's not square and never will be square. It doesn't matter how many scholarly books and articles are written to explain why the world is square; the reality is it will never be square. Likewise, the reality of the Kingdom of Heaven is that it's *not of this world*.

No matter how many books are written to explain the images of Revelation from a worldview, the images are not about this planet. They were written to reveal the testimony of Christ, who is ruling over a Kingdom, *not of this world*.

Most of Christ's teaching on Earth was given through parables. He would encapsulate spiritual truths into stories he knew most people would not understand. Sometimes even his disciples didn't understand, and they would ask him to explain the meaning of the parables, which he never tired of doing. Christ's way of teaching hasn't changed, and throughout Revelation, his teaching style remains the same as it was when he was physically on Earth. He still speaks to the world in parables, knowing most people will not understand what he is saying. Why does he do this? The previous verse tells us why! Every parable is written to reveal knowledge of the Kingdom of God to those who love God and Christ. Parables are never given to reveal knowledge of world events, for they exist to explain the secrets of the Kingdom of God, which are intended to remain hidden from those who don't love God.

Revelation is not about the world. It's about what Christ has done for those who live in the world.

Revelation is filled with parables, images within images, wheels within wheels, yet every parable and image within that amazing book reveals the secrets of the Kingdom. Those who try to interpret Revelation from the point of view of world events miss the whole point of the brilliantly written testimony of Christ. Revelation is not about the world; it is about what Christ has done for those who live in the world.

The thing about parables is that none of them, not one, was ever supposed to be taken literally. Let me explain what I mean by asking just a few simple questions:

- Was there really a *Good Samaritan*, or was he a made-up, story-tale figure?

- Were there really *Ten Virgins* waiting for a bridegroom, or were these women improvised for the sake of illustration?

- Was there really a *Prodigal Son,* or was this story fabricated to explain our heavenly Father's heart?

- Was there really an *Unmerciful Servant*, or was this situation invented to make a point?

The answer to all of these questions is a resounding 'no'. These events did not actually happen. These people did not exist. They were all made up. Each of these stories was created to reveal hidden spiritual truths, and it's the same with the Book of Revelation. There are many interpretations of the images of Revelation, and most of them are vague attempts to prophesy the specific future of our planet and its people. However, we have to ask if that kind of interpretation is possible given the information supplied in the images; information presented to us as the testimony of our Redeemer.

The First Beast

This image shows seven 'lion' heads on a beastly body. It roams around the earth on its four massive feet. The lion heads are also called mountains. So, are there, on this planet, seven mountains which move continually, walking mountains, so to speak? If so, where are they? Isn't this, rather, a picture of the roaring lion Jesus said would be *roaming around seeking whom he could devour?* Is this about literal mountains and literal lions, or is this a parable given by our Saviour to remind us of his teaching?

The Scarlet Women

Greater than these mountains, far greater in size, is the woman who uses these mountains as a chair to sit on. Have you ever seen a woman big enough that she could sit on seven mountains at the same time? Where is this great monster? Surely she would be so big she would blot out the sun? So is this about a literal woman sitting on literal mountains, or is this a parable given for instruction?

The Second Beast

The second beast *looks like a lamb but speaks like a dragon*. Do you know how dragons speak? What language do they use? English? French? Japanese? Have you ever seen a dragon? How can we know how dragons speak if we've never had a conversation with a dragon? Isn't this dragon-speaking lamb merely a pictorial telling of Christ's warning that many destructive false prophets would disguise themselves as sheep in order to deceive the elect? So, is this about real sheep and real dragons, or is it another parable?

The Antichrist

The only physical imagery Christ gives in his testimony to describe the effect of the anti-Christ on the world is that three anti-Christ spirits will *look like frogs* as they set out to deceive all the kings of the earth. Do kings really listen to frogs? That sounds more like a fairytale than the word of God. Or is this a parable?

The Mark of Satan

This mark poses a few questions: Where did Satan get his mark? Who marked Satan? What does a mark on a spirit-being look like? Is it possible to mark a spirit with anything physical? Who has the knowledge and power to put a mark on a spirit? Is this mark something we will see in the natural, or is it another parable?

14

The Woman with Twelve Stars

A pregnant woman, big enough to stand on the moon, clothe herself with the sun, and wrap her head with stars, was confronted by a ten-horned, seven-headed dragon. Was this an actual event in world history? Or is this, rather, a picture which includes all the different elements of the genealogy of Christ from the beginning of time until Christ was raised from the dead? How can this not be a parable?

REVELATION'S IMAGES ARE PARABLES

From the beginning of human history, God used inventive stories to explain invisible spiritual reality. The two trees of 'knowledge' in the Garden of Eden were parables (we can't literally eat 'knowledge'). While he was on Earth, Christ did the same. He used parables to teach spiritual truth everywhere he went, and his way of teaching has not changed.

> *He did not say anything to them without using*
> *a parable. But when he was alone with his own*
> *disciples, he explained everything. (Mk.4:34)*

There is not one image in Revelation that is not a parable of the Kingdom of Heaven, for this has always been Jesus' normal mode of teaching, and that hasn't suddenly changed. However, he still explains the parables to his disciples. Here are a few more examples of images that are clearly parables:

- Are there really four horsemen riding through time?
- Is there an actual sword coming from Christ's mouth?
- Does Hell have physical gates?
- Does Heaven have physical gates?
- Do angels blow actual trumpets?
- Is Jesus knocking on a real door?
- Are our names written into physical books?
- Will angels literally trample people like grapes?

NOT EVERYTHING IS A PARABLE

The parables of the Book of Revelation are mixed with solid reality, and so there are various things mentioned in Revelation that we can see and feel and experience in our lives, not only in the past but in the present as well;

- ♥ The world is something we can see,

- ♥ The Law, written by Moses, is something we can see,

- ♥ Jesus is a historical figure that we can see,

- ♥ The Bride of Christ is something we can see,

- ♥ The anti-Bride is also something we can see,

- ♥ The judgment of the Earth is something we can see.

The real-life concepts written above are not parables or images. Rather, they are the setting behind the images. They are the physical realities of life on this earth and, as such, are the background to everything that happens. Let me explain what I mean by using a picture. Let me put the whole Book of Revelation into a single image.

IMAGES BRING CLARITY

Just imagine that the understandable earthly realities above meld together to form a solid gold crown. Now imagine that each parable-style image in Revelation is a heavenly jewel designed to fit perfectly into that beautifully crafted crown.

It's possible to study the jewels individually and discover some wonderful characteristics. But when you see the completed crown with all its gemstones in place, magnificent and sparkling, you realise the crown itself has a purpose, and that purpose has nothing to do with the individual jewels or the gold used to form the crown. The purpose of the gleaming crown is to draw attention to the wearer of the crown.

That's exactly what we see happening in the Book of Revelation! Christ revealed the supernatural elements of his unseen, heavenly victory to John in a way John's human mind could understand. All the incredibly important holy and eternal events of Christ's victory over invisible things like Satan, sin, death and hell were formed into images that John could relate to. Therefore, what we see through John's eyes, and dotted throughout a backdrop of ordinary and humanly understandable realities, are multiple, unique glimpses into another world, outstanding images that reveal the victory of Christ over the enemies of the Kingdom of God.

The purpose of each of these sparkling images and their background settings is to bring glory to the newly crowned heavenly Royal, the King of kings. Every glittering jewel in his crown is written as an image in Revelation. Everything which gives glory to him for his work in this world, and will glorify him for eternity, is written into those images.

The entire Book of Revelation is like one big and beautiful sparkling crown on the head of our glorious, and victorious eternal King!

The jewels of Christ's glory are so full of beauty that the explanations I am about to give are only a glimpse into their depth. I believe we will spend eternity in awe of the masterly precision and outstanding wisdom of the story of salvation. No one else could do what Christ has done, and no one else is worthy to wear his crown. In a nutshell, that's how I see the Book of Revelation. It is like one big and beautiful sparkling crown on the head of our glorious and victorious, eternal King.

17

Cherished and loved!

3

SEVEN LETTERS TO ANGELS

*He will command his angels concerning you
to guard you carefully; they will lift you up in
their hands so that you will not strike your foot
against a stone. (Psalm.91:11-12)*

The first chapter of the Book of Revelation simply covers John's greeting to the readers of Revelation. It explains what he was doing and where he was at the time he saw this amazing vision, the authority of those who gave him the vision, and the knowledge that the vision he was recording was the testimony of Christ himself. It concludes with a direct quote from the one who told him to write it down, *Don't be afraid! I am the living one. I was dead, but I am alive forever and ever*.

Christ himself speaks to John about the vision and gives him the firm assurance that what he is about to write will bring great blessing to those who hear and believe the accuracy of the testimony which follows. And it doesn't take long for the first amazing blessings to be seen. At the beginning of Christ's actual testimony, in the second chapter's first few words, we see the blessings begin.

Not surprisingly, it is the beloved Bride of Christ who receives the blessings. There are no blessings in the Book of Revelation for anyone else!

SEVEN LETTERS, ONE BRIDE

The next two chapters, the second and third chapters, are the beginning of the testimony of Christ, and they are written purely for the benefit of Christ's future Bride. They contain seven letters John was told to write to angels. Why did John address these letters to angels? This is where we begin to see the blessings.

In recent times people have tried to confine the content of these letters to seven earthly churches, but that is unrealistic, considering the letters are addressed to angels. That they are addressed to angels takes them into the realm of parable.

It must be remembered that Christ only has one Bride, not seven. It must also be remembered that before telling John to write these seven letters concerning his beloved, Christ had just completed the greatest rescue mission the world had ever seen. He had gone to Hell and back to successfully rescue his Bride from the clutches of his arch-rival, the devil. Now, after her rescue, we see him actively putting things in place to ensure she will never be held captive by his enemy again. How blessed is the Bride of Christ! How safe we are in his protection! How secure we are in his love!

These letters reveal both the nature of Christ's protection and the esteem of his future Bride's position, a position he wants all of Heaven to recognise. In writing these letters to angels, Christ shows John it is his greatest desire to see that his betrothed remains safe as she prepares for that great and pending day when they will finally be united in what is described later as *the marriage of the Lamb*.

Through these encouraging letters, our great King reminds all of Heaven that his future Bride is so special to him he has made his angels responsible for her well-being while she remains on the Earth. What an enormous blessing! How loved and protected we are!

Before Christ was born, God commanded his angels to guard him carefully while he was on Earth. Satan knew about this command of God, for he quoted it to Jesus in the wilderness. Now here we see that our Jesus, who has just taken his seat beside his Father on the throne, has passed his personal blessing from God onto us and ordered his angels to watch over his greatly loved Bride while we continue to live on the Earth. What a privilege!

UNASSAILABLE PROTECTION

Even though Christ tells John to write seven letters to angels concerning his Bride, Christ only has one Bride. Therefore these seven letters show the seven ways that Satan, out of hatred for Christ, will try to lure Christ's beloved away from his protection in the hope that she will sin, lose her royal position and forfeit her rewards.

Satan knows Heaven's mighty angels have been given charge over us, just as he knew God had given the angels charge over Christ. As an angel himself, he was well aware it was because of their protection that he couldn't touch Christ directly, and so could only tempt him.

It's the same with us; Satan can't touch those under the protection of Christ. All he can tempt us to do is voluntarily remove ourselves from our Saviour's protection. However, through these seven letters, Christ is letting us know ahead of time what form those temptations will take and how to defend ourselves. How wonderful to be the Bride of Christ!

Despite the unassailable protection of his angels, Christ has not left the protection of his beloved, whom he bled and died for, to angels alone. He has backed up that protection with something even more powerful.

Chapter one of Revelation makes it very clear the Seven Spirits of God are as vital to this testimony of Christ as the authority given to it by his Father. The mighty sevenfold Spirit accompanied Christ as he lived on Earth, died and was raised. Now, at the beginning of the second chapter, we see that Christ sends this same sevenfold Spirit to accompany us as we live on Earth, die and are raised to eternal life. It is no mistake there are seven letters written to angels; there are seven aspects to the protection afforded by the extremely powerful Spirit which Christ has sent to be with us forever.

Satan can't win any fight against the Spirit of God. He can't even win a battle against the angels of Heaven; the last time he tried, he lost and was permanently thrown down from his lofty position. Far stronger than all the angels of God put together, the mighty sevenfold Spirit of God is absolutely unbeatable, and so winning any battle against the Spirit of God is an impossible task for Satan; he won't even try to fight the Spirit of God. If Satan wants to recapture Christ's redeemed, now that we are guarded by all the power of Heaven, he has no choice but to use trickery to try to lure us away from the sure and guaranteed protection of the Spirit of God; protection which comes to us in seven different ways.

SEVEN MIGHTY SPIRITS

When he returned to his Father, Christ was able to send his sevenfold Spirit to his beloved to assist us and help us overcome all the wiles of the devil. The assistance he has provided is not minor; the Spirit of God is and has always been the most powerful force in the universe, so powerful he raised Christ from the dead! The evidence for that statement is seen in the following verse, for Christ did not raise himself from the dead; the mighty sevenfold Spirit accompanied him in his death and resurrection and ensured that he arrived safely in the throne room of God.

> *Then I saw a Lamb looking as if he had been slain standing in the centre of the throne. He had seven horns and seven eyes, which are the seven Spirits of God sent out into the whole Earth. (Rev.5:6)*

There is no more powerful protection Christ can order for his precious Bride than the mighty strength and impressive ability of the sevenfold Spirit who raised him from the dead and accompanied him to the throne room of God. It was this same mighty, sevenfold Spirit who Christ sent into the whole Earth to empower and protect his beloved Bride at Pentecost.

We find out more about these Seven Spirits when we read the New Testament, for each one is a separate part of the victory of Christ and, as we can see in the Scripture above, accompanied him in his death and resurrection. Contrary to popular belief, these seven mighty Spirits are not named in the Old Testament, yet in the New Testament, each is specifically named as a Spirit and identified as having a direct role of service to the Bride of Christ. Their different roles are reinforced and made crystal clear to the Bride in the seven letters of Revelation.

The Seven Spirits of Christ are found in the New Testament.

Each is named as a Spirit and has a specific role of service to the Bride of Christ.

23

These seven Spirits and their roles of service to the Bride are not a new doctrine; they are so familiar to you, you will recognize them as soon as you see them listed. They are:

Spirit of Life

His role is to set us free from the Law. *Through Christ, the Law of the Spirit of Life set me free from the Law of sin and death. (Rom.8:1-2)*

Spirit of Truth

His role is to comfort us and guide us into the truth, which always sets us free. *I will ask the Father, and He will give you another Counselor to be with you forever–the Spirit of Truth. (Jn.14:15-17)*

Spirit of Holiness

His role is to empower the word of God through us and resurrect us on the last day. *... (Jesus), who, through the Spirit of Holiness, was declared with power to be the Son of God by His resurrection from the dead. (Rom.1:3-4)*

Spirit of Adoption

His role is to teach us to take dominion on Earth as the children of God. *For you received the Spirit of Adoption. And by him, we cry, 'Abba, Father'. The Spirit himself testifies with our spirit that we are God's children. (Rom.8:15-16)*

Spirit of Grace

His role is to teach us to revere the great sacrifice Christ made on our behalf. *How much more severely do you think a man deserves to be punished who has trampled the Son of God underfoot, who has treated as an unholy thing the Blood of the Covenant that sanctified him, and who has insulted the Spirit of Grace? (Heb.10:28-29)*

Spirit of Glory

His role is to gently encourage us during times of persecution. *If you are insulted because of the Name of Christ, you are blessed, for the Spirit of Glory and of God rests on you. (1 Pet.4:14-16)*

Spirit of Wisdom

His role is to reveal to us the nature of God in everything so that we can know him intimately. *I keep asking that the God of our Lord Jesus Christ, the glorious Father, may give you the Spirit of Wisdom and revelation so that you may know Him better. (Eph.1:17)*

ONE LITTLE PROBLEM

Satan can never stop the angels of God, or the Spirit of God, from protecting us. Neither can Satan resist the power and effect of the Blood of Christ, the name of Christ or our testimony to Christ, yet in Revelation, we see that Christ writes letters of warning to his precious Bride for her protection. Why is this? Why does Christ's powerfully protected Bride need further protection?

The answer is simple; God gave us free will; therefore, we can walk away from his protection. This means that when all is said and done, only our love for our hero will keep us from being lured away from his unassailable protection by the sneaky temptations of Satan and his agents.

The warnings provided to us by Christ in these letters are all practical and relate to how we live while on this Earth. They are given to help us remember our beloved and how much he loves us so that we, in turn, will remember whom it is we serve, why we serve him, and what we need to do to remain under his protection until the last day.

SEVEN ASTOUNDING REWARDS

Unlike the seven warnings, the seven rewards in the letters are all parables which can't be seen in the physical. They each explain a different aspect of the position we will hold in Christ's invisible Kingdom and the authority which comes with our royal position.

- ♥ Do we actually receive a white stone?
- ♥ Do we literally eat from a tree called life?
- ♥ Do we actually wear snow-white robes?
- ♥ Do we literally wear crowns?

The warnings and rewards of the seven letters are not difficult to understand; they are pretty much self-explanatory. If we choose to live in the protection of our beloved Saviour, we will gain our reward. If we deviate for any reason, we will lose our reward. It's not rocket science! No one needs a degree to work it out. Christ wrote this book for ordinary people.

Revelation of Christ's new kingly position was given in a way ordinary people could understand, educated or uneducated, young or old. As John said in the first chapter, if we take to heart what is written, we will be blessed.

WHAT DOES 'TAKE TO HEART' MEAN?

The most important first step for anyone wanting to understand the glorious *Revelation of Jesus Christ* is that they need to believe what is actually written about Christ. *Taking to heart* simply means believing what we read about Christ is true. God's promise, to old and young alike, is that everyone who learns how to do this one small thing will be blessed by the amazing testimony of Christ, revealed via John, in the most magnificent last book of the Bible.

ALPHA AND OMEGA

The great love Christ has for his promised Bride is shown by the way the Book of Revelation is written. First, we have the 'Introduction', where Christ makes it plain this is his story, that he is the *Alpha and Omega*, the beginning and the end of this high drama. Then we see that his first thoughts are for the security of his beautiful Bride, whom he has just rescued, as he assures her he will keep her safe.

The depth of the love Christ has for his beloved is shown right here, for at the same time, Christ names himself as the Alpha, the beginning; he makes his precious Bride the beginning as well. He places her right beside himself at the very start of his most remarkable testimony. This shows he has no testimony without her, for she is the reason he has any testimony at all, and he is not shy about saying so. What a privileged position he has given us, but that's not all!

His beloved also becomes the Omega with him, for the last two chapters of Revelation are also about the Bride. In those chapters, Christ reveals the glorious beauty of his perfect Bride as she steps into the rewards he has put in place for her from the beginning of time.

What an awesome Saviour!

What a wonderful Lord!

What a beautiful love story!

From start to finish, the thoughts of the King of creation are with his future Bride; he loves her so much he even allows her to have the last word. Amazing! The last word of the Spirit, through the last book of the Bible, is the request from the Bride to her beloved to return quickly. What an incredible Saviour! What a wonderful Lord! What a beautiful love story!

It is fascinating that Christ presented his testimony to John in the way he did, for he was so concerned that his cherished, future Bride be comforted by his words and not worried by the harsh realities which would follow that he began his testimony by giving her the strongest possible assurance he had put everything possible in place for her protection. His first thoughts were for his beloved, and he lovingly assured her he had provided;

- Seven aspects to his Gospel (lampstands), to light her way and help her stay on the right path.

- Seven angels (stars), to cover her and watch continually for any deceit of the enemy which may trip her up as she walks towards her King.

- Seven Spirits, to come to her assistance and steady her if it seems she is about to stumble.

Only once everything was in place, and his greatly loved Bride was encouraged and safe, did Christ reveal to John how the rest of the world, those who had rejected his love and so remained outside his protection, would experience God's righteous judgment for their sin, right up until the last day of Earth's history. That final judgment is what Christ revealed.

THE REVELATION OF JESUS CHRIST

The Revelation of Jesus Christ, which God gave him, to show the world what would soon take place. (Rev.1:1)

In the very first verse of Revelation, we're told that this book is about Christ revealing what God showed him regarding the final judgment for sin that would soon come upon the world. It was only because God loved his children so much that this judgment was deferred until after Christ's resurrection.

There are only twenty-two chapters in the Book of Revelation. The first five reveal Christ's love for his Bride, the strong protections he put in place for us, and the enormous power of his death and resurrection. Then, from chapter five to chapter twenty-one, which is pretty much the rest of Revelation, we are shown what God gave Christ to reveal to us.

GOD'S HOLY SCROLL!

Before Christ went to Calvary, the final judgments for sin had already been written by God into a holy scroll, sealed with seven inpenatrable seals. No one in Heaven or on Earth knew the secret knowledge hidden behind those unbreakable seals. Not Satan nor any other angel, elder, patriarch, or prophet (including Daniel) knew what was written in God's sealed scroll.

> *We speak of the mysterious and hidden wisdom of God, which He destined for our glory before time began. (1 Cor.2:7)*

> *None of the rulers of this age understood it, for if they had, they would not have crucified the Lord of glory. (1 Cor.2:8)*

> *Rather, it is written: "No eye has seen, nor ear heard, no heart has imagined, what God has prepared for those who love Him." (1 Cor.2:9)*

After Christ opened God's holy scroll and revealed its entire contents, he finished with a strong warning. The last chapter of Revelation contains Christ's clear warning not to add to or take from what God had written in his holy scroll.

Yet Christ knew that liars and false prophets would come to try and deceive the elect into adding to His Gospel and God's holy Revelation, and so, even before he opened the scroll, he included in his seven letters seven helpful warnings.

Guided through minefields!

4

SEVEN HELPFUL WARNINGS

Grace and peace to you from him who is, and who was, and who is to come, and from the seven spirits before his throne, and from Jesus Christ, his faithful witness. (Rev.1:4-5)

Like every other picture in the Book of Revelation, the warnings spelt out clearly to the angels given charge over Christ's beloved Bride are parables that speak to every individual, every heart, and every life, and so are as relevant today as when they were first written.

Through these seven warnings, Christ reveals seven sneaky traps laid out by Satan to cause Christ's Bride to forfeit his protection by doing 'good' things that, in reality, betray him. Each one of these traps is placed at the feet of those who love Christ with all their heart, and each involves good works that ultimately deny righteousness. Some of these works are so good in themselves they are commended by Jesus, yet at the same time, those who do them are warned by him to repent because good works alone do not reflect the righteousness which empowered his death and resurrection.

It is interesting that these seven letters of warning just happen to mirror the seven rebukes Jesus gave to the Pharisees while he was on Earth. Some may find that surprising, yet it's not surprising if we believe the word of God confirms itself and fits together like a hand in a glove.

These instructive letters, written by Christ to the love of his life, not only reveal the seven different temptations Satan will use to try to lure us out from under the protection of his angels and his Spirit but also reveal the special blessings promised, by him, to those who love him enough to turn their backs on Satan and overcome these temptations.

Below I have listed the seven warnings and have included a comment on each of the seven rebukes which support each warning. The rewards are listed separately.

EPHESUS - *The Spirit of Wisdom*

I know your deeds, your hard work and perseverance...yet you have forsaken your first love... Repent and do the things you did at first. (Rev.2:1-7)

The temptation revealed here is; to allow the work we do for people to take precedence over our love for our faithful Redeemer. This warning teaches us that when helping people becomes more prominent than encouraging them to develop their own personal relationship with our Saviour, our love for people has taken precedence over our love for God.

It is the role of the *Spirit of Wisdom* to reveal knowledge of the nature of God to us. This is essential to our salvation, for knowing God is, in itself, eternal life. Giving us the ability to know God, along with the capacity to assist others to get to know God, is the whole purpose of this beautiful Spirit.

If we don't allow the *Spirit of Wisdom* to reveal to others the life found in personally knowing Christ, we cause the *Spirit of Wisdom* to grieve and cut ourselves off from the blessings and benefits of his wise revelations.

The promised reward for those who show they love God and Christ more than anything or any person in this world is abundant knowledge of God from the *Tree of Life*.

Lacking in the Pharisees: The *Spirit of Wisdom* protects us from entering into the sin of the Pharisees, who made serving God as a religion more important than knowing God as a Father. Though they religiously studied God's word and knew the promises of God which were available to them and to the people they served, they did not seek the promises themselves, and worse, they did not allow others to seek them or even believe the truth of God's promises.

> *Woe to you, experts in the Law, because you have taken away the key to knowledge. You yourselves have not entered, and you have hindered those who were entering (Lk.11:52)*

The *Spirit of Wisdom* helps us keep our eyes on our beloved Saviour and ensures we share our knowledge of the nature of our Father and his Kingdom as we assist the needy. When we live in the *Spirit of Wisdom,* our righteousness is guaranteed to exceed the righteousness of the Pharisees.

SMYRNA - *The Spirit of Glory*

> *I know your afflictions and your poverty, yet you are rich! I know the slander of those who say they are my people but are not. You will suffer unjust persecution... don't be afraid...be faithful even to the point of death. (Rev.2:8-11)*

33

The temptation revealed here is; fear of suffering persecution for the name of Christ. The purpose of persecution is always to humiliate and shame, and whether it comes through slanderous lies, physical afflictions or relentless ridicule, persecution will always be unjust. It will often come from those who resent our faith and, in some instances, will lead to death, but in every case, God has promised to place a time limit on the length of persecution and simply asks us to remain faithful to him as we endure.

The Spirit of Glory does not bring praise for God but rather amazingly reveals God's praise for us!

The gentle *Spirit of Glory* who comes to lift our heads in these times does not help us praise God but, rather amazingly, encourages us by revealing God's approval of us, and that is why this promise is so special. The high praise of God through the *Spirit of Glory* will always rest on those being persecuted. This is the glory that consumed Stephen's eyes while he was being stoned to death; it's the source of the joy which caused the apostles to sing while they were in chains and is the anaesthetic that takes the sting out of lies, mockery and torment.

This comfort from God is a welcome balm and a precious treasure that cannot be gained any other way than through persecution. So, if in times of persecution we are deceived by Satan into fear, resentment or self-pity for suffering, we will grieve the *Spirit of Glory*, preventing him from being able to speak the high praise of God to us at the time we need him the most.

The promised reward for those who overcome their fear of being persecuted is the total protection of the throne of God and guaranteed immunity from eternal death.

Lacking in the Pharisees: The *Spirit of Glory* protects us from the sin of the Pharisees who, for 'good' religious reasons, approved the persecution of God's people.

> *Woe to you because you build tombs for the prophets, and it was your forefathers who killed them. So you testify that you approve of what your forefathers did; they killed the prophets, and you build the tombs. (Lk.11:47-51)*

The *Spirit of Glory* helps us shun all forms of persecution of others and assists us to endure persecution when it comes to us. When we live in the *Spirit of Glory*, our righteousness will exceed the righteousness of the Pharisees.

PERGAMUM - *The Spirit of Adoption*

> *You remain true to my name. You do not renounce your faith in me...even to death. Yet you have some among you who hold to the teaching of Balaam who taught Balak to entice my people to sin...Repent! (Rev.2:12-17)*

The temptation shown here is; a cowardly reluctance to discipline sin in the church. Even though this church was commended for its courage in the face of external persecution, it was rebuked for not disciplining internal sin.

The example used by Jesus is found in Numbers 22-25, the story of Balaam and Balak. Balak failed to overcome God's people by external force, and Balaam told him they couldn't be overcome while their God protected them. In response, Balak instigated a subtle internal attack on God's people in order to weaken their relationship with their God, so they would then be vulnerable to his waiting armies.

35

He did this by adding additional religious doctrines and rituals into their worship. Using interesting variety and attractive distractions, he deceived the chosen ones into disobeying God's word, thereby weakening their relationship with God and forfeiting his protection.

By using Balak as an example, Jesus is warning us that not rebuking the abomination of false doctrine will lead to desolation; far from making us acceptable to people outside our group, this hypocrisy will weaken our faith, making us vulnerable to even more attack. In other words, if we allow ourselves to be manipulated by a cowardly fear of confrontation of sin within the churches, we choose the acceptance of man over the acceptance of God, which betrays the family name, and grieves the precious *Spirit of Adoption*, causing us to forfeit the dominion given to God's children.

The promised reward, from the *Spirit of Adoption,* for those who overcome this temptation is a white stone (Zech.3:8-9), with a secret name written on it, known only to the one who receives the stone.

Lacking in the Pharisees: The *Spirit of Adoption* protects us from the sin of the Pharisees who, under the guise of conformity to religious protocols, sought the acceptance of man rather than the praise of God.

> *Woe to you because you love the most important seats in the synagogues and greetings in the marketplaces. (Lk.11:43)*

The Spirit of Adoption helps us to seek the praise of God more than the praise of man, which in turn enables us to stand in the dominion given to those who uphold the Name of Christ, a righteousness which exceeds by far the righteousness of the Pharisees.

THYATIRA - *The Spirit of Grace*

I know your deeds, your love and faith, your service and perseverance, but I have this against you. You tolerate Jezebel, who, by her teaching, misleads my servants into sin. Those who do not repent of her ways will suffer with her. (Rev.2:18-29)

The temptation here is; to assume tolerance and Grace are the same when, in fact, they are not even remotely alike. Tolerance insults Grace! The example Christ uses is Jezebel, who was married to Israel's King, Ahab. As the daughter of a foreign king, Jezebel was not one of God's people, nor did she ever claim to be, yet God's people invited her to be one of their leaders. Even though they knew she did not love and worship their God, they tolerated her leadership and followed her. Their deliberate choice to follow someone who not only denied their God but persecuted his prophets made them a partner in her rebellion, idolatry and punishment.

This warning shows that when God's people tolerate spiritual leadership from those whose teaching conflicts with the true Gospel of repentance, we enter into idolatry and make ourselves spiritual whores; saying we belong to Christ while submitting to leadership in the church which does not love and serve our Saviour. In treating the costly sacrifice of Christ so cheaply, we insult God's *Spirit of Grace*.

The promised reward or blessing for those who overcome by meekly seeking their teaching from God's Morning Star is that they *will inherit the Earth and rule it with the authority of Christ.* Revelation 22:16 tells us Jesus is the Morning Star, and we know his teaching is the Gospel of repentance from sin, followed by faith towards God.

37

Lacking in the Pharisees: The *Spirit of Grace* prevents us from living in the sin of the Pharisees, who not only tolerated false teaching but promoted it by accepting additions to the written word and forwarding it on as truth. They trained their new converts to believe the lie so that the new converts would convincingly teach their false teaching as truth and oppose anyone who disagreed with them.

> *Woe to you, teachers of the Law and Pharisees, you hypocrites! You travel over land and sea to win a single convert, and when you have succeeded, you make them twice as much a child of Hell as you are. (Mt.23:15)*

The fiercely loyal Spirit of Grace will never tolerate the trampling of the Gospel and will always empower believers to stand against those in the church who corrupt the true Gospel of Christ and are, therefore, anti-Christ. When we allow the Spirit of Grace to empower us to stand against greed, idolatry and wickedness in the church, our righteousness will always exceed the righteousness of the Pharisees.

SARDIS - *The Spirit of Life*

> *I know your deeds, you have a reputation for being alive, but you are dead... Wake up! I have found your deeds unfinished...remember what you have received and heard, obey it and repent! (Rev.3:1-6)*

The temptation revealed here is; to desire to be seen 'doing' good works in order to gain a reputation for 'doing' good works. It tells us Christ sees good works which look like righteousness but are not done through righteousness, as unfinished and therefore leading to death.

Jesus promises that those who are found worthy will *walk with him, dressed in white*, yet warns that having unfinished good works will mark us as unworthy to wear white. We know what he means by this because Christ taught that any invited wedding guest not wearing the right clothes would be expelled from the wedding feast (Matt.22:11-12).

This warning teaches that if we judge ourselves as good people because we do good things, we could miss out on the reward of eternal life. So, if we rely on good works alone to gain acceptance from either God or man, we could disqualify ourselves from the position of 'worthy to be acknowledged by Christ' as we stand before God.

It is the role of the *Spirit of Life* to set us free from works that lead to death by helping us choose works of righteousness instead. The works of the flesh, both good and evil, are always incomplete. Those who come before God dressed in the works of the flesh will be turned away from the feast and have their names blotted out of the invitation list.

The promised reward or blessing for those who do righteous works is the highest personal protection of Jesus himself, with our names not blotted out but permanently recorded in the Lambs' *Book of Life*.

Lacking in the Pharisees: The *Spirit of Life* prevents us from living in the sin of the Pharisees who, though they may have been regarded as servants of God, were merely doing good works for the sake of appearances and not serving God at all. In the end, like unmarked graves, they had their names permanently removed from living memory.

> *Woe to you because you are like unmarked graves which men walk over without knowing it. (Lk.11.44)*

39

The *Spirit of Life* will always encourage us to 'wake up' to the spiritual purpose of our earthly existence and help us to finish all our good works righteously so that, as happened to the eternally nameless Pharisees, our names won't be blotted out of the Book of Life. When we live in the protection of the *Spirit of Life,* our righteousness will always exceed the righteousness of the Pharisees.

PHILADELPHIA - *The Spirit of Holiness*

I know you have little strength, but you have kept my word and have not denied my name. Since you have kept my command to endure patiently, I will also keep you from the hour of trial that is going to come on the whole world to test the inhabitants of the Earth. Hold on to what you have so that no one will take your crown. (Rev.3:7-13)

Christ did not rebuke his faithful in this church. Instead, he encouraged them. That didn't mean they weren't being tempted to sin; they were. They were being tempted to focus on the weakness of their own little strength instead of the greatness of God's mighty power dwelling within them.

Christ commended his steadfast followers in this church for their patient endurance in upholding the testimony to his name, even through persecution, and their faithful obedience to his commands.

He gently encouraged them to *hold on* to what they had because they were in danger of losing what they had, their eternal crowns, because they were looking at their own personal lack of ability instead of the miraculous, miracle-working power of the creator of the universe.

This warning teaches us that if we focus on our own ability to do works of righteousness, all we will see is our weaknesses, and the temptation to give up will threaten to overtake us. However, if we look at the power of Christ and metaphorically stand aside to allow his power to flow through us, we will see him use our *little strength,* like a mustard seed, to produce a fully grown tree. This is what it means to live in holiness.

> *The Spirit of Holiness will use our little strength, like a mustard seed, to produce a fully grown tree of righteousness.*

The promised reward for those who overcome this way is that they will be kept from the hour of trial and made living pillars of testimony to God's power through mankind.

Lacking in the Pharisees: The *Spirit of Holiness* will prevent us from living in the sin of the Pharisees, who laid heavy religious burdens on God's people to keep them dependent upon their own strength and living by outward signs of holiness rather than on God.

> *And you, experts in the Law, woe to you because you load people down with burdens they can hardly carry, and you yourselves will not lift one finger to help them. (Lk.11.46)*

The *Spirit of Holiness* will always empower the word of God through every believer so that we are able to shake off religious burdens and testify with confidence; 'when I appear weak, look out, for that is when God is strong through me'.

> *I will boast all the more gladly in my weaknesses so that the power of Christ may rest on me. For when I am weak, then I am strong. (2Cor.12:9-10)*

Choosing to allow the Spirit of Holiness to flow through us ensures our righteousness will always exceed the righteousness of the Pharisees.

LAODICEA - *The Spirit of Truth*

I know your deeds that you are neither cold nor hot. So because you are lukewarm, I am about to spit you out of my mouth. You say, 'I am rich and in need of nothing'...you do not realise you are wretched, pitiful, poor, blind and naked. Those whom I love I rebuke and discipline therefore; be earnest and repent. Behold, I stand at the door and knock... (Rev.3:14-22)

The temptation revealed here is; to use physical things to judge eternal, spiritual matters. These people were judging their spiritual needs according to physical appearance, and their judgment proved to be diametrically opposed to the truth. From their point of view, they had every physical thing they needed; that is, nice homes, fine clothes, good jobs, adequate transport, status and position, and so they assumed they were also spiritually sound. They didn't realise their physical prosperity had become a snare that had deceived them into lying to themselves about their spirituality. They were neither hot in their desire to know God nor cold in their rejection of him, and in their lukewarm condition, they couldn't see they were about to be cast away from the presence of God.

This warning teaches that if we look at our worldly circumstances, we can misunderstand our spiritual condition, for our spiritual condition is based on our standing with Christ, not with the world. If we do not heed his call to repent of our misunderstanding, the *Spirit of Truth* cannot 'open the door' to fellowship with Jesus, and the *Spirit of Truth* is grieved.

The promised reward for those who love Christ enough to overcome the cares of the world is that they will be given the highest privilege in Heaven, sharing the throne of Christ.

Lacking in the Pharisees: The *Spirit of Truth* prevents us from living in the sin of the Pharisees, who religiously obeyed the Law in order to have their own needs met and taught others that having their physical needs met meant they were right with God.

> *Woe to you because you give God a tenth of your mint, rue and all other kinds of garden herbs, but you neglect justice and the love of God. You should have practised the latter without leaving the former undone. (Lk.11.42)*

The *Spirit of Truth* opens our eyes to see the shallowness of earthly values and weighs them against the rich treasures, which can only be found in knowing God and loving him with our whole hearts. When we allow the *Spirit of Truth* to keep the door to fellowship with Christ open, our righteousness will always exceed the righteousness of the Pharisees.

BETTER PROMISES

It was Satan who blinded the eyes of Adam and Eve so they couldn't see the traps behind his temptations. It is still his aim to keep us blind, yet here we have Christ, our beloved Saviour, guiding us through Satan's minefields, revealing the hidden traps, laying out a whole world of blessings for those who overcome, and providing rewards for his beloved which are far greater than anything we could hope or imagine. How precious is his love!

Showered with presents!

5

SEVEN UNIQUE REWARDS

Look, I am coming soon! My reward is with me, and I will give to each person according to what they have done. (Rev.22:12)

Christ has promised seven beautiful and generous rewards for those who overcome the temptations revealed in the seven letters of instruction written to angels on our behalf. Revelation explains that these rewards can be experienced, in part, while we are on this Earth but will be fully realised once we are all dwelling in the Holy City of God.

These seven rewards, brought to us by the Spirit of Christ, are not trophies to be displayed for show but are absolutely essential to our Salvation.

- How can we say we know God if we don't know the nature and power of his Spirit?

- How can we live in the Spirit if we don't know how his Spirit lives in us?

- How can we preach the Gospel of Christ if we don't know the character of the one who preaches through us?

- How can we explain the resurrection of Christ unless we know the Spirit who helped Christ break the power of death and Hell?

- How can we guard ourselves against blasphemy of the Spirit if we don't recognise who the Spirit of God is or how he works through us?

Living in the Spirit was never intended to be a mystery, and the seven letters of Revelation show the importance and purpose of Christ's command for us to live in the Spirit. Like Christ, we can't overcome temptation, or even death, without the assistance of the mighty sevenfold Spirit, and we know overcoming is the key to receiving all the spiritual rewards promised to the redeemed. However, Revelation shows that every reward promised to Christ's beloved Bride is brought to her by the Seven Spirits of God. How important it is for us to know the Spirit and the rewards he brings to the Bride.

SPIRIT OF WISDOM

To the one who is victorious, I will give the right to eat from the Tree of Life, which is in the paradise of God (Rev.2:7)

The promised reward for those who overcome the temptation to forsake their first love is the right to eat from the *Tree of Life*. Eating from the *Tree of Life* will give more wisdom, knowledge and revelation of the one we love, but Proverbs shows us those blessings are just the beginning because 'fearing God', 'putting him first', and 'eating from the Tree of Life', are the same thing.

Do not be wise in your own eyes; fear God and shun evil. This will bring health to your body and nourishment to your bones. (Prov.3:7-8)

It is interesting to find, in the previous verse, that the promise of God attached to godly wisdom is healing. Therefore, we can be sure that when we live in our first love, by the power of the *Spirit of Wisdom*, we will be able to bring healing in the same way Christ did when he was on Earth.

Living in the *Spirit of Wisdom* will also ensure we do not become 'worn out' serving the needy; for the ongoing revelation of God, through the *Tree of Life*, will continually bring health to our bodies and nourishment to our bones; in other words, healing!

The promise attached to the Spirit of Wisdom is healing!

Filled with the *Spirit of Wisdom*, Christ imparted knowledge of God and revelation of his Kingdom wherever he went. His teaching was always accompanied by healing. It stands to reason, then, that if we want to heal as Jesus did, we should preach the Gospel of the Kingdom through revelation, which comes to us via his *Spirit of Wisdom*. His teaching in Proverbs to *fear God and shun evil* is a recipe for health, and so, when we do as he says and obey him, his clear reward, both in the Old Testament and in the New, is healing.

> *On each side of the river stood the Tree of Life, bearing twelve crops of fruit, yielding its fruit every month. And the leaves of the tree are for the healing of the nations. (Rev.22:2)*

The *Tree of Life,* which brings healing to the nations, is the same tree Adam and Eve were barred from accessing after the fall, for when knowledge of God was rejected, plague, famine and sword took its place. Now we see that where knowledge of God lives, the curses of plague, famine and sword lose their power. What an awesome reward!

SPIRIT OF GRACE

To the one who is victorious and does my will to the end, I will give authority over the nations–to rule with an iron sceptre and dash them to pieces like pottery. I will also give that one the morning star. (Rev.2:26-29)

The promised reward for those who overcome the temptation to accept any anti-Christ teaching from the church is that they will inherit the Earth and rule it with the authority of Christ in ways that shatter all opposition. This means that those who take their teaching from God's word and Christ's work alone will receive the authority of the Kingdom to tear down everything which raises its head against the knowledge of God, shown through the ongoing testimony of Christ.

The promise attached to the Spirit of Grace is God's sceptre of authority.

The *Spirit of Grace* is very, very powerful. This is the Spirit of which it is said; *it is a dreadful thing to fall into the hands of the living God. (Heb.10:31)*

- ♥ It is the *Spirit of Grace* whose eyes blaze with fire when God is insulted or when the sacrifice of his Son is treated so lightly it is trampled underfoot. (Heb.10.29)

- ♥ It is the *Spirit of Grace* who unleashes the vengeance of God on his enemies. (Heb.10:30)

- ♥ It is the *Spirit of Grace* who holds the iron sceptre of God's royal authority, the rod by which all the nations of the Earth are ruled. (Rev.2:27)

- ♥ It is the *Spirit of Grace* who grants us the key to the authority of the Morning Star. (Rev.2:26)

This authority is more than the right of adoption. It is greater than dominion! This is the ultimate authority, given only to those who have proven themselves loyal to the master, those who have made the master's enemies their enemies. It is the authority of 'the right-hand man'; the one who is able to act on behalf of the master because their hearts are 'one'.

This is the authority Adam and Eve had before the fall! Adam and Eve were made in God's image, but when they chose to be equal to God, they gave away their loyalty to him and, with it, the authority they had received to rule and reign with him on the Earth. They spent the rest of their lives trying to regain their previous position of trust by attempting to work out the minute differences between good and evil, an impossible task which mankind has still not mastered.

Now, thanks to Christ, and through the guidance of the powerful *Spirit of Grace,* we see that 'knowledge of good and evil' has become as irrelevant to God's people as it was before the fall, and in its place, the supreme authority of the fruit of righteousness reigns. What an awesome reward!

SPIRIT OF GLORY

> *I know about the slander of those who say they are my people and are not, but are the synagogue of Satan...Be faithful even to death, and I will give you life as your victor's crown... The one who is victorious will not be hurt by the second death. (Rev.2:9-11)*

The promised reward for those who overcome the temptation to deny Christ under persecution is that they will be praised by God and crowned as victors by Christ himself, and the second death will not be even remotely considered. In other words, eternal life is absolutely guaranteed.

The *Spirit of Glory* is like a healing balm or anaesthetic, which takes the 'sting' out of persecution. This is not something that can be taught and is not something we can 'press into God' to receive. It is not dependent on human ability in any way. It is a tangible, physical 'anaesthetic' which God applies in times of persecution, so real that the pain being experienced literally becomes secondary to the joy set before our eyes like a never-ending banquet.

> *The promise attached to the Spirit of Glory is a victor's crown and guaranteed eternal life.*

Christ tells us that those within the churches, who persecute Christ's Bride, are *of the synagogue of Satan.* He tells us clearly that, though they may be professing Christians, they are of the devil if they persecute believers.

Many true believers will be persecuted, but for those who are, this sure promise of Christ for his beloved Bride is rock solid! When persecution comes, the *Spirit of Glory* will supernaturally cover us so completely we will be able to live above our circumstances in joy so powerful our eyes will remain focused on God and Christ, despite anything Satan and his agents throw at us.

Even without persecution, Adam and Eve lived in the joy of this glory before the fall. God said of them and all creation, *Ah, it is good!* This glory has never been our praise for God; it has always been God's praise for us.

When Adam and Eve sinned, God could no longer praise those he loved; mankind was tainted with sin and unworthy of His praise. This is what the fall was all about; our fall from God's glory. Now we see that, because of Christ, God can praise us once again, but it's only as we go through persecution that we notice our Father praising us.

When we come face to face with the *Spirit of Glory,* our Father's pride and joy in us are revealed, and so persecution loses its power. It was this joy, the joy of the Lord, which saw Christ through his own persecution and death.

The second death referred to in this reward is eternal spiritual death. There is no second death for those who give joy to the heart of God. What an awesome reward!

SPIRIT OF ADOPTION

To the one who is victorious, I will give some of the hidden manna. I will also give that person a white stone with a new name written on it, known only to the one who receives it. (Rev.2:17)

The promised reward for those who value the family name and overcome the temptation to seek the praise of man rather than the praise of God is that they will be given *hidden manna* and a secret name, with full access to everything which can be known about the Seven Spirits of God.

Manna is a form of bread, and Jesus said his bread was to do his Father's will. Being promised *hidden manna* is being promised special access to the will of God, special tasks which are not given to anyone else. These tasks come with full access to the powerful Spirit of God so they can be fulfilled in righteousness, for the promised white stone is described in Zec.3:8-9 as having seven facets or eyes (symbolic of the Seven Spirits), which God uses to remove sin in a single day. As Christ is the only one who has ever removed sin in a single day, the secret name on that stone can only be given to those who love and serve Christ.

The promise attached to the Spirit of Adoption is assignment to special tasks.

The *Spirit of Adoption* will empower us to *go in his name* with the confidence and ability to fulfil the unique tasks God gives each of his willing servants to do; under his guidance and with the comfort of his full approval.

As the Bride of Christ is made up of both men and women, so both men and women are given this authority by God himself. In Genesis, we see that before the fall, 'taking dominion' was the combined role of both the sons and the daughters of God; *Let us make mankind in our image that they may rule...so God created mankind...male and female, he created them (Gen.1:26-27).* However, after the fall, the sons ruled over the daughters instead of over the Earth, and dominion over the Earth was lost to both of them. Christ undid the effect of the fall. Now, through Christ, his redeemed, both men and women have been restored to pre-fall condition and are able to once again take dominion together, as one, in Christ's name.

> *As the Bride consists of both men and women, so both men and women are given this authority by God.*

It is the role of the mighty *Spirit of Adoption* to assist Christ's beloved Bride, both men and women, to overcome our fear of confrontation of sin in the church, so we can stand in the full authority of the name of our mighty Christ and literally take the Kingdom of God with us, wherever he sends us. What an awesome reward!

SPIRIT OF LIFE

The one who is victorious will be dressed in white. I will never blot out the name of that person from the Book of Life but will acknowledge that name before my Father and his angels. (Rev.3:5)

The promised reward for those who overcome the temptation to settle for good works rather than righteousness is that they will never lose their salvation, and it is the *Spirit of Life* who is in charge of this reward...

- The *Spirit of Life* is life itself. He is the *breath of life* who gives life to everyone.

- The *Spirit of Life* carries the *eternal life* promised to all who look to Jesus for salvation.

- The *Spirit of Life* is in charge of the *book of life*, with the authority to blot out names for eternity.

- The *Spirit of Life* is also described as the *river of life* which runs through the centre of the Holy City (Rev.22:1), showing us the *Spirit of Life* is central to everything in Heaven and on Earth.

- The *Spirit of Life* is the one who ensures God's Kingdom will come, and his intention will indeed be done *on Earth as it is in Heaven.*

For those who 'wake up' from the delusion of religion and the deceitfulness of good works which do not involve righteousness and grasp the truth of the life to be found in Christ, the reward is life itself.

Religion and good works are no substitute for the massive blessing of having the *Spirit of Life* flow through us on a daily basis. All we need to do to live in this remarkable privilege is make sure we are not just living by the standards of man, 'appearing' to be God's servants but are 'being' his servants, for real.

The promise attached to the Spirit of Life is a white robe and personal presentation at court.

The promised reward is the high privilege of being clothed in the sparkling white robes of righteousness, followed by personal presentation to God by our beloved.

The reward of the *Spirit of Life* is an exceedingly powerful tool of righteousness. With it, wherever we go, we take Kingdom life with us. If people receive our message of righteousness, they receive life; if they reject our message, God marks them for judgment.

Adam and Eve learned this lesson first-hand. They went from 'life' to 'judgment' in less than a day. Now, through the *Spirit of Life,* we see people transform from 'judgment' to 'life' in less than a day. What an awesome reward!

SPIRIT OF TRUTH

To the one who is victorious, I will give the right to sit with me on my throne, just as I was victorious and sat down with my Father on his throne. (Rev.3:21)

The promised reward for those who overcome the temptation to judge spiritual things according to natural understanding is that they will be given the highest privilege in Heaven, sharing the throne of Christ and being privy to every decision he makes.

What an incredibly powerful, amazing promise! This is an authority greater than dominion. It is greater than the King's sceptre. This is the highest authority of all, the authority of the throne of God.

To understand the overwhelming authority Christ is offering us and the mighty privilege we are being given through this spiritual reward, we need to look at the way Christ describes himself when he addresses the Church at Laodicea.

These are the words of the Amen, the faithful and true witness, the ruler of God's creation. (Rev.3:14).

It is the Amen, the faithful and true witness, the word of God himself, Jesus Christ, who is the ruler of God's creation, all God's creation, not just the Earth.

In the beginning, God's children, both male and female, were given dominion over the Earth, but we were never made rulers over all God's creation, for this involves everything created by God in Heaven and on Earth, including the sun, moon, stars, galaxies and God's angels. When we gave away our dominion to Satan, he received dominion over the Earth and became *prince of this world,* but that was the pinnacle of his power and the limit to his authority. He was never in a position to be the *ruler of God's creation.* The rulership of God's creation is the heart of the throne of God, the source of his authority and power to create, so it has always remained within God's control, untouched by Satan.

No wonder the wind and waves obeyed Christ, no wonder water became solid under his feet, no wonder the fig tree shrivelled, no wonder Heavenly bands of angels were ready to spring to his defence at the first sound of his word. Outstanding miracles are commonplace for the creator of the world, the ruler of God's creation.

The promise attached to the Spirit of Truth is the authority to call down miracles in Christ's name.

This offer to share his throne is an overwhelming privilege of trust because the throne of God is made up of the praises of God's people. That little bit of understanding makes this reward mind-blowing!

55

The authority of the throne of Christ can only go to those who have proven to God that they will not steal his praise for themselves; therefore, this supreme authority can only be given to those who are willing to lay aside their own lives and possessions, their own desires, their own achievements, their own ambitions and their own reputations, and genuinely count all of them as nothing, preferring to give God credit for everything they do.

This overwhelming authority can only go to those who have learned how to dodge the praise of man so completely that all glory for everything they do goes directly to the throne of God. Once this lesson is learned, the authority of the royal throne of God is waiting. What an awesome, awesome reward!

SPIRIT OF HOLINESS

To the one who is victorious, I will make a pillar in the temple of my God. Never again will they leave it. I will write on them the name of my God and the name of the city of my God...and I will write on them my new name. (Rev.3:12)

This is one of the most precious promises of all. Christ himself promises that, for those who faithfully endure, he will open a door in front of them that no one can shut, he will keep them from the hour of trial that is coming on the whole world to test its inhabitants, and he will make the false teachers, who burden them with lies, come and bow before them and acknowledge that Christ loves them.

In this letter, Christ says to his faithful ones; *I know your deeds. I know that you have little strength, yet you have kept my word and have not denied my name.* Knowing they feel weak and small, Christ encourages those who love him by telling them they will not lose their reward.

Christ personally urges them to hold on to what they know to be true, despite the lies they witness and the unrighteous burdens they are forced to carry. He reveals the reason they have been so burdened and rejected is because Satan wants to take away, or 'steal', their crowns.

The promise here is that those who overcome feelings of being small or insignificant by choosing to believe that God's power is made perfect in their weakness and who simply trust in the name of Christ rather than their own ability will see God move in ways that astound them. They will understand what it means to *stand still and see the glory of God (Ex.14:13)*.

The invincible Spirit of Holiness will place all the power of Heaven behind the desires of the righteous.

Anyone who is victorious in this way, on this Earth, will be made living testimonials of continual praise to the power of the holy name of Christ in God's new temple. On them will be written the name of God, the name of his new Holy City, and the new and holy name of Christ; until everyone acknowledges they are not only loved by Christ but are intimately familiar with the power and purpose of his name. They will never be forced to leave God's temple, as the unholy will be forced to leave; instead, as strong pillars, Christ will make them pivotal to the temple, holding everything in place and witnessing to the reason for the temple's existence.

Adam and Eve were supposed to be the pillars of mankind, holding everything in place and witnessing to the reason for mankind's existence on this Earth. When they chose to be God's equals instead of his servants, they forfeited their relationship with holy God and, no longer holy themselves, were forced to leave paradise.

Now, because of Christ, Paradise is open to those who trust him, and the door to it will never be shut. Even when we die, this wonderful promise remains true. When we are dead, we are at our weakest and cannot help ourselves at all, but that is when the power of God becomes most evident. Though we are dead, the *Spirit of Holiness* will raise us from the dead in the same way he raised Christ from the dead (Rom.1:3-4)

Because of this beautiful promise, no matter how weak, small or imperfect others may tell us we are, when we simply 'stand still' and allow the *Spirit of Holiness* to bring God's word and the name of Christ to life in the flesh, through us, we will witness God's holy power at work in ways which will astound our detractors. What an awesome reward!

INCREDIBLE PROMISES!

There is so much beauty, generosity, power, and protection promised to Christ's precious Bride in these seven rewards, and yet the most amazing thing is that these rewards will not be experienced only after the marriage feast in eternity but will also apply in part while we are still on this Earth, waiting for our King to return. Those already living in the Spirit will know exactly what I mean; for living in the Spirit brings with it unspeakable freedom, peace, joy and faith, but on top of that, our beloved plies us with rewards upon rewards, blessings upon blessings, so we can only be overwhelmed by the deep love and endless generosity of our gentle hero and his eternal Father. Who would not want rewards and blessings? Who would not want to live in the Spirit? Who would not want to overcome?

Who would not want to live in the Spirit?

Who would not want to overcome?

Our hero loves us so much he redeemed us from the clutches of his enemy, the devil, took us to a safe place and surrounded us with the most powerful protection his Kingdom could provide. He offered us position, power and majesty beyond our dreams, yet he did not treat us as his prize and keep us as prisoners but offered us the freedom to walk away from his protection at any time. Neither did he use his abundant gifts as bribes to coerce. Instead, he laid them out before us and simply asked us to choose to accept them from his hand. How gracious is our Saviour! How wonderful is his deep and eternal love!

All the above is laid out for us and explained in detail in the first three chapters of Revelation. Our beloved went to great lengths to let us know that, no matter what would follow or how challenging things may become for us in this world, he had put everything in place for our safety, and all we had to do to remain safe was accept the security and power of the position he had already offered.

These seven outstanding letters, dictated by our loving hero to his friend John and written to angels on our behalf, each show very clearly that overcoming is not only the key to gaining promised rewards in the future but vital to living now in a world buffeted by the trouble, or tribulation, caused by the ongoing problems of Satan-inspired sin.

Saved from trouble!

6

RIGHTEOUS TRIBULATION

Do not think that I will accuse you before the Father. Your accuser is Moses, on whom your hopes are set. (Jn.5:45-47)

Despite the assurance of the word of God and the proven love of Christ, when tribulation is mentioned, most believers cringe. Popular theology has made the word 'tribulation' sound so horrible nobody wants to look too closely at what to expect. At the same time, every evil thing that happens in the world is accepted with a shrug of the shoulders and a dismissive attitude, 'Oh well, I guess Tribulation has begun, and we can't do anything to stop the evil'. How confusing! How far from the mark! How can we know what tribulation is if we don't take a close look at Scripture?

The most effective way to know what tribulation actually means is to look at the way Jesus described tribulation. He did not call it 'evil'. Instead, he called it 'punishment', describing it as *a time of punishment in fulfilment of all that has been written (Lk.21:22)*. In fulfilment of all that has been written? What was he talking about? What was written?

Jesus went on to explain what he meant, and he spoke plainly. *Do not think that I will accuse you before the Father. Your accuser is Moses, on whom your hopes are set* *(Jn.5:45)*. What did he mean? What does Moses have to do with tribulation? Isn't Moses Old Testament?

Moses wrote the Law, and Jesus showed through his teaching and through his personal example that tribulation is just the name given to the receiving of the punishments for sin, written about in the Law of Moses. Nothing has changed! Tribulation is still about the punishment of God for sin, written in the Law of Moses.

> *Tribulation is the punishment of God for sin written in the Law of Moses.*

Most people these days, because of false teaching, believe tribulation has nothing to do with the judgment of God; they believe it has somehow been delegated to Satan, while God's judgment is being saved up for one huge and final judgment day. This belief is totally untrue! This subtle deception promotes the lie that Satan is up close and personal, while God is a vague and distant judge in some faraway time; it is the exact opposite of the teaching of Christ.

False teachers who promote this incorrect impression of tribulation have a lot to answer for; their teaching has demoralised believers. It has made us ineffective because we no longer know how to tell what is coming from either the hand of God or the hand of Satan. We no longer know how to stand up for righteousness because we have forgotten how righteousness works. Instead of standing with Christ to 'fight the good fight', believers give in to evil, believing that all the horror they see is 'tribulation'. How terrible! Tribulation has never been evil, and evil still needs to be overcome.

The truth is, we are not waiting for Tribulation to begin, for tribulation has been with us from the beginning of human history. Scripture shows that 'the judgment of God for sin' and 'tribulation' are one and the same. Tribulation is merely the judgment of God in action in a way that can be seen. This is why Jesus also said, *In the world, you will have tribulation, but don't worry, I have overcome the world (Jn.16:33).*

Though there will indeed be a final judgment day, the daily judgment of God for sin (tribulation) has been in operation for a long time. It actually began with Adam and Eve in the Garden of Eden, when God commanded them, *do not eat from that tree.* As soon as they disobeyed and ate from the forbidden tree, they entered into the punishment of God for sin and, from that time on, lived in constant tribulation, setting the pattern for every following generation.

This is why Jesus said; *in the world, you will have tribulation* because tribulation is simply the normal outworking of the ongoing judgment of God for sin, and everyone in the world has been and will be affected by the consequences of sin, whether they believe in God or not.

The whole purpose of the advent of Christ was to save us from the judgment of God, that is, to save us from tribulation. Tribulation is the reason Jesus died for us! This is the foundation of our faith; yet, amazingly, though the Gospel is an old, old story, for some unfathomable reason, false prophets have been able to infiltrate the Body of Christ and successfully deceive his beloved in this area. They have presented Tribulation as something vague and evil. It is not! Jesus went to the cross to save us from tribulation.

Tribulation is the reason Jesus died for us at Calvary!

Despite the widespread grip this false teaching has on the Body of Christ, the reality is, the Gospel hasn't changed, and this is it in a nutshell; God's unwavering love for mankind found a solution to the suffering produced by the judgments of his holy Law. Without breaking his word, interfering with his Law, replacing it, or taking anything away from it, God simply added an amendment that would cause the suffering to cease. That amendment was the Blood of Christ.

Christ died to save mankind from the judgment of God written in the Law of Moses, and his death was so effective that now those covered by his Blood are protected from the ongoing judgment (tribulation) still being brought to the world by God's Law.

This is not new doctrine! This is old doctrine! This is the doctrine that has been believed for nearly 2000 years but was recently replaced by false 'end-time' teaching. The unshakable truth is God's Law has *always* been the only measure of judgment for sin. Moses put the Law of God into writing, and Christ has told us there is no other Law that God will use to judge mankind for sin, and that includes all the judgments of God until the end of time.

God's Law has always been the only measure for judgment of sin.

God's judgment for sin has never changed and will never change. Neither have his punishments. The judgment of God for sin was written in detail by Moses, and the punishments are clearly described as 'curses' for disobedience. These curses make up everything that can be known about tribulation, and therefore, it should be no surprise that the curses written in Deuteronomy 28 foretell and explain the 'tribulation' curses described in the Book of Revelation.

Until Heaven and Earth disappear, not the smallest letter, not the least stroke of a pen, will by any means disappear from the Law until everything is accomplished. (Matt.5:18)

The great love of God for mankind is seen in his decision to send Christ to the world to save us from the judgment of his unstoppable Law. He was so grieved by the ghastly predicament facing his beloved children that he was prepared to send his one sin-free Son and heir to a horrible death in order to bring about the only possible solution to the miserable bondage of sin and consequential tribulation perpetuated by his own holy Commandments.

If there had been another way, Jesus would not have had to die, but he did die! In one single, sacrificial act of ultimate love, God's Christ executed the most significant and effective rescue mission mankind will ever know, and now nothing in Heaven or on Earth can undo what Christ's death has permanently achieved.

When Jesus took the curses of the Law onto himself at Calvary, he overcame the judgment of God for sin, and in doing so, he overcame tribulation. This is what our salvation is all about; the Blood of Christ has saved us from the tribulation brought about by the righteous judgment of the Law of God for Satan-induced sin.

Released from fear!

7

THE BEGINNING OF THE END

The elder asked, 'These in white robes, who are they, and where did they come from?' I answered, 'You know, sir!' Then he said, 'These have come out of the Great Tribulation; they have washed their robes and made them white in the Blood of the Lamb'. (Rev.7:13-14)

Since the beginning of time, not one person has been able to avoid tribulation, for tribulation is just another word for trouble, and since the death of Christ, no one has been able to avoid what is known as the Great Tribulation.

Strong's Concordance describes the root word of tribulation as meaning to press, squeeze or afflict. In other words, tribulation, generally speaking, means *the pressure of being squeezed by affliction.* In modern vernacular, this type of distress is commonly known as 'stress', which is a commonplace and unavoidable human experience.

When the simple but true meaning of tribulation is understood, the panic associated with it dissipates, and fear loses its hold.

Tribulation or trouble has always existed. There has always been stress in this world. Every generation has felt its effect. Every person who has ever lived has been squeezed by affliction simply because stress is the consequence of sin. If we are not suffering under the consequences of our own sins, we will still be suffering under the consequences of other people's sins. Either way, every person on Earth does, and will, suffer stress as a normal experience. So why, then, are the last days known as a time of great distress or Great Tribulation?

THE GREAT TRIBULATION

The time described in Revelation as the Great Tribulation is nothing more than a description of the tribulation experienced after the death and resurrection of Christ, as opposed to the tribulation experienced prior to his death and resurrection, which was just normal tribulation. Great means more widespread, not more horrible! It is described as great simply because the death and resurrection of Christ caused the outworking of tribulation to triple.

Before Christ died, people could only be judged by God for one thing, the sin of breaking God's Law. The stress of living with the consequences of sin alone was bad enough for God to send Christ to redeem the world. However, since Christ paid the price for sin, people are now judged for three things; sin, rejecting the sacrifice of Christ and rejecting his Spirit. No one is immune from the effects of these judgments.

Anyone who rejected the Law of Moses died without mercy on the testimony of two or three witnesses. How much more severely do you think a man deserves to be punished who has trampled the Son of God underfoot...and insulted the Spirit of Grace? (Heb.10:28-29)

There are some who teach that the judgment of the Law of Moses only applies to the Jews, but that's not true. Pharaoh did not believe in the Law of Moses, and that was the exact reason the judgment of God fell on him and destroyed his kingdom.

The judgment of God has always applied to the whole world; however, as we have seen, since the death and resurrection of Christ and the coming of the Spirit, its effects have increased. In the same way, the Old Testament Law of Moses applied to those who didn't believe in God, so the effects of the death and resurrection of Christ, and the coming of his Spirit, also apply to those who don't believe.

The truth is not complicated; rejecting the sacrifice of Christ, blaspheming the Spirit, and breaking God's Law, carry consequences and those consequences, known as 'Great Tribulation', are written plainly.

Some also teach that the tribulation of the last days will last only seven years. That is just impossible and shows a complete ignorance of Scripture. The concept that end-time tribulation will last only seven years is ridiculous when we consider people have been living in tribulation since the world began, and the saints of Christ, in particular, have been buffeted by the effects of Great Tribulation on and through the people around them, since the death and resurrection of Christ nearly 2000 years ago.

Furthermore, since the Great Tribulation began, sin and evil have increased as the population of the world has increased. As a result, many saints have suffered intense persecution for their faith, many are suffering now, and many will suffer in the future. That's the very reason why the Spirit of God was poured out on believers at Pentecost; so that he could be our helper in times of trouble (tribulation).

A MEMORABLE DATE

Quite apart from the obvious logic of the previous comments, Scripture itself slams the futuristic seven-year Tribulation theory and eliminates the need for guesswork by providing an actual 'start date' for the beginning of the end of days. It not only gives a start date but a specific time of day as well; 9 o'clock in the morning!

> *In the last days, God says, "I will pour out my Spirit on all people...and everyone who calls on the Name of the Lord will be saved".*
> *(Acts 2:17)*

On the day of Pentecost, at nine o'clock in the morning, the Apostle Peter stood up and, in his famous speech (above), told everyone the last days had begun. He reminded people of the words of the prophet Joel, who foretold the beginning of the last days. He explained that the pouring out of the Spirit of Christ on all who call on his name for salvation was proof they had entered the last days. To him, the physical signs which showed the last days had begun were evident in the unmistakable wind and fire miracles that ushered them in, but the absolute proof came when they were all filled with the Spirit, exactly as prophesied by Joel. This is all past tense!

The outpouring of the Spirit of Christ has been happening since that momentous day nearly 2000 years ago. It was the ultimate sign, given by God, to show the last days had begun. This means we are not 'waiting for the last days to begin', as some false teachers tell us, but have been living in the last days, the days of the latter rain, since that famous day when Christ began pouring his mighty Spirit into all those who call on his name for salvation; that is, men and women, sons and daughters.

The last days were marked as the beginning of a time of great blessing and great distress, that is, a time which would bear the name 'Great Tribulation'. That is exactly what Revelation explains from start to finish; how the whole concept of judgment will play out in favour of the precious Bride of Christ simply because Christ died to save us and protect us from the distress of the judgment of God for sin.

GOD IS LOGICAL

Revelation's judgments, or curses, are not frightening for those who love Christ, for they are logical. They are as reasonable and understandable as the Ten Commandments.

The judgments of the Law of Moses for murder, stealing, adultery, and all other sins were written in a logical manner. Sins were literally listed and explained, one after the other, but that did not mean those sins would always happen in the order in which they had been listed or that God would judge those sins according to the order in which they had been written down. They were listed, one after the other, for clarity, not sequence. Though they were written in a way that could be understood and taught, what they showed us was that God's complete judgment would be at work all the time; it would never sleep, never tire, and never miss a sin in any individual life–forever.

God's law never sleeps, never tires, and never misses a single sin in any individual life – forever!

In the same way, the Law of Moses was written logically, the individual judgments of Revelation are also written logically, side by side, so they can be understood and taught, yet that does not mean they will happen in the order in which they have been written down.

The jewels, or images, dotted throughout the judgments of Revelation are just as logical. They are simply the amendments God has made to his Mosaic Law through the death and resurrection of his faithful Son, which now set us free from the ongoing judgment of his unstoppable Law.

Scattered throughout the final, end-time outworking of the judgments written in the Law of Moses, we can now see the protection afforded to Christ's beloved Bride because of his victory at Calvary. What a wonderful Saviour!

The images scattered throughout the end-time judgments describe the completed victories which Christ won while he was dying on the cross - victories that protect us from the judgment of God's Law. The judgments written by Moses will continue until the last day, but the permanent victory of Christ, now attached to the outworking of the Law of Moses, will protect his precious Bride from that unstoppable judgment.

God's Law is now all wrapped up in the victory Christ won at Calvary!

Revelation is a profoundly unique and brilliant book. There is no other book of the Bible capable of doing what it does. It shows us clearly that the entire ongoing judgment of God for sin is now all wrapped up in the victory Christ won at Calvary. It is indeed finished! How it must have blessed God's heart to be able to finally trumpet his Son's victory across the Heavens, and to the world, in this unique way.

The parables of Revelation are parables of the completed work of Christ. They testify to his victory. This is not in the future; it is done; it is history. These jewels are set into his crown; they are fixed, they are gleaming, they are perfect, and they are not going to change.

The only thing we, as part of the background setting for these jewels, are going to see happening on the Earth is the ongoing outworking of the judgment of God for sin. This, too, hasn't changed.

It was the judgment for sin, written by Moses, which Jesus faced at Calvary. It is that same judgment, written by Moses, that the world has been experiencing for a long, long time and will continue to experience to the end of days. The major difference in judgment, shown to us through the Book of Revelation, is that none of the judgments of the Law of God, written by Moses, can now fall on the redeemed. We are completely safe!

This safe position is beautifully and powerfully confirmed when Christ opens the Scroll of Judgment, and his four mighty horsemen burst out to begin the final judgments. What an incredible blessing!

Inspired and helped!

8

FOUR FABULOUS HORSEMEN

I saw in the right hand of him who sat on the throne a Scroll with writing on both sides and sealed with seven seals. And I saw a mighty angel proclaiming with a loud voice, 'Who is worthy to break the seals and open the Scroll?' (Rev.5:1-2)

Who are these four mighty horsemen of Revelation? Some say they are Satan's envoys, riding out at his command, the epitome of everything evil. Many books have been written and films made, which fill us with fear and leave impressions of horror that are not easily shaken. Over the years, various scholars have tried to match their so-called evil to current world events. Hollywood attributes them with the same persona as the grim reaper, and so, for many people, they are associated with doomsday and the end of the world.

Some Christians believe they should pray for God's protection from the four horsemen and the plague, famine and sword they bring, while others don't seem to be aware of their existence, despite going to church all their lives.

The majority of believers, however, consider the four horsemen, like the rest of the Book of Revelation, too confusing, too fanciful, or too hard to understand. They choose to ignore them because they can't work their images out or because what they read for themselves doesn't fit with what they've been told they represent.

While various experts try to explain Revelation as a history book from the past, attempting to seek its meaning in the ruins of the seven cities where believers once met, others try to read it as a prophetic road map of a future that doesn't yet exist, while yet others try to explain every current event as a fulfilment of this prophetic vision.

Many people try to impose fluid spiritual images onto a rigid physical world.

It doesn't work!

I can't put Revelation into any of those pigeonholes. I firmly believe that most of the confusion encountered when reading the enthralling Book of Revelation comes because some, often very sincere people, try to force broad and invisible Kingdom concepts into visible, earthbound realities. In other words, they try to impose fluid spiritual images onto the rigid limits of a physical world. It doesn't work! It can never work!

No matter how hard many people may try to fuse the realities of the Kingdom of Heaven with the realities of life in this world, the two just don't mix. for jewels will always be jewels, and gold will always be gold. The firm reality of the Kingdom of God is that it is *not of this world,* and the problem many Christians have in trying to understand the parables of the Kingdom is that they describe an invisible world that can only be realised in full after we leave this planet.

The evocative images of Revelation are not, and cannot be, confined to what can be seen, felt, touched or experienced on this Earth but expertly explain realities that cannot be seen. They brilliantly describe for us:

- an invisible Kingdom,
- an invisible God,
- an invisible Spirit, and,
- an invisible foe.

AN UNSEEN REALITY

The magnificent images that dot the pages of Revelation are parables, awesome, incredibly brilliant parables. As a whole, they clearly reveal concepts of life and death, love and fear, truth and deception, knowledge and foolishness, and hope and despair, together with the eternal consequences of Law, sacrifice and reward. All these concepts are invisible!

- How else could God explain to us the existence of the unseen and ongoing warfare between Christ and Satan and between good and evil, other than through parables?

- How else could God explain to us the unseen concepts of sin, blasphemy, spiritual death, and the attempted deceiving of the elect?

- How else could God reveal the glory, authority and awesome power he has given to his faithful, conquering Son since his resurrection?

None of these things can be measured in the physical, for they are all totally invisible, and without an explanation, we would not be able to understand them at all. However, when put into simple parables, their depth of meaning can become so clear it can take our breath away!

The parable of the four horsemen, I believe, is the most brilliant parable ever written, and even though I have a lot to say about it, what I am about to tell you still doesn't do the image justice. What can I say? It makes my heart sing!

What a forceful image is the vision of those four impressive horses of Revelation. What a visual smorgasbord of movement, richness, colour, might and purpose. What a stunning testimony to the glory achieved by Christ because of his death and resurrection. It is more than intense! The greatest prophetic parable, explaining Christ's total victory at Calvary and his new role of unchallenged King is seen in the strong and unforgettable imagery of those four unstoppable 'Horsemen of the Apocalypse', charging through time!

> *What a stunning testimony to the glory achieved by Christ because of his death and resurrection!*

The striking visual appearance of those four imposing horsemen defies the logic of time. It presents to us a living, quivering, vibrant picture of the past, present, and future, all rolled into one. In a single instant, it reminds us of who Christ is, what he has done, what he is currently doing, and what he intends to do right up until the last moments of human history. It sweeps us up, places us with Christ in all his glory, and allows us to witness his final, crushing defeat of Satan.

This parable shows the immense authority of our mighty, conquering Saviour, the truth of his word, the perfection of his justice and the finality of his decisions. It is an image so packed with movement and meaning it fills everyone who considers it with awe and wonder and leaves a colourful impression which is not easy to ignore, whether the intended message is understood or not.

MORE DEPTH THAN ANY PAINTING

This image speaks long and loud of the glory that belongs only to Christ as it reveals the beauty of his character and the sovereignty of his Heavenly position. These four amazing horsemen unveil the nature of our glorified Christ as they zealously manifest:

- the strength of his power,
- his absolute might,
- his kingly authority,
- his unswerving purpose,
- the wisdom of his choices,
- his unstoppable will,
- his submission to his Father,
- his unity with the Spirit,
- his love for his beloved Bride and
- the fulfilment of every word he has ever spoken.

Just thinking about what this parable means can leave one breathless and lost for words! How does one describe, in the simplest possible form, every invisible victory won by Christ from Adam to Eternity? God is a genius! He has chosen to do it through the imagery of four legendary horsemen!

These four particular horsemen represent the majesty of Christ and the weapons he will use to bring about the total defeat of the enemy who has dared to raise his head and his hand against the almighty and all-powerful God of all gods. They show how Christ intends to place all the enemies of God under his feet, including sin, death, Hell, plague, famine, sword and, of course, Satan and his beasts.

There are three significant events that take place before these four mighty horsemen appear. These three things shed further light on the reason for the appearance of the horsemen and reveal who is sending these horsemen out into the world. These events involve:

1. The person with the authority to open the Scroll,

2. How the judgments are opened, and

3. Whom it is who calls the horsemen forth.

WHO HOLDS THE SCROLL?

First, we see it is the *Lion of the Tribe of Judah* who steps forward to receive the Scroll to open; that is, one Scroll sealed with seven seals. God is not bringing these judgments, for he gave the Scroll to Jesus. Satan is not bringing these judgments, for he was not the one found worthy to open the Scroll of Judgment, and the Scroll was not given to him.

This is significant because it shows that all the judgments contained in the Scroll, and described in the rest of the Book of Revelation, are in Christ's hands and not in Satan's. This teaches us that every judgment, from this point forward, comes through the hands of our risen and glorified Christ and through him alone.

HOW ARE THE SEALS OPENED?

Even though the *Lion of the Tribe of Judah* steps up to receive the Scroll from the hand of God, the Scroll is not opened by him; it is opened by the resurrected *Lamb of God.* In Heaven, when Jesus first volunteers to take the Scroll from the hand of God, he steps forward in his role as the *Lion of the Tribe of Judah*, then, as everyone in Heaven waits for the Lion of Judah to come forward to take the Scroll, suddenly the scene changes! The Lion becomes the Lamb!

As the Lion moves forward to accept the Scroll from God, the hand that receives it is the hand of the risen Lamb. In an instant, Jesus has changed into the mighty risen *Lamb of God,* who is surrounded by four living creatures, one of whom has the face of a lion. These four living creatures never leave Jesus' side. It is their job to do his will and to see his will is done, yet it is the risen *Lamb of God,* not the four living creatures, who opens the Scroll. The Lamb opens the seals!

It was so important to God and the Apostle John that Jesus' role be defined clearly, that the first four judgments, which reveal each of the four horsemen, are introduced with the words *the Lamb opened the seal.* That the Scroll is in the hand of Christ, and it is Christ who opens each of the Seven Seals shows, without doubt, that these four horsemen are completely within the control of Christ at all times.

WHO CALLS FORTH THE HORSEMEN?

There are four living creatures who continually surround our glorified Christ. Their individual characters are visually described through the nature of the animal they depict. Does this mean they physically embody these animals? No! It doesn't mean that at all.

Their four descriptions merely highlight their invisible personality traits. Just as the *Lion of the Tribe of Judah* was a major part of Christ's role on Earth, so now we see that 'lion' is only one of his strengths, for there are also three others which God deems equally important; the persona of an ox, the persona of a man and the persona of a flying eagle.

The fact that these four prominent aspects of Christ's nature surround *the Lamb that was slain* shows that each of these personality traits was a significant part of his role on Earth and of his great sacrifice.

The first living creature was like a lion, the second was like an ox, the third had a face like a man, and the fourth was like a flying eagle. Each of the four living creatures had six wings and was covered with eyes all around. (Rev.4:7-8)

In the Scripture above, we see that the first living creature looks like a lion, the second like an ox, the third like a man, and the fourth like a flying eagle. Their bodies are covered with eyes. These descriptions are symbolic, for it is easy to see that:

- The lion represents Christ's role as Messiah, kingly Saviour and Protector,

- The ox represents Christ's role as a strong and powerful burden-bearing Servant,

- The man represents Christ's role as a human with free will, or choice,

- The flying eagle represents Christ's role as dependent on being led by the Spirit.

Eyes always represent the Spirit. *The Lamb had seven horns and seven eyes, which are the seven Spirits of God. (Rev.5:6).* That these creatures are covered in eyes shows they are Spirit through and through; in other words, they represent the invisible Spirit of Christ. The role of each of these living creatures is defined more precisely when the Lamb opens the first four seals, for it is not the Lamb who calls forth the horsemen but the four living creatures who command the horsemen to come forward. Furthermore, each of the living creatures calls forward a designated horseman. Awesome!

The four living creatures call forward the four horsemen!

When the Lamb opens the first four seals on the Scroll of Judgment he holds in his hand, we notice that each of the four living creatures is a partner to one of the horsemen. That is, the second living creature calls forward the second horseman and the third living creature calls forward the third horseman. We know this because of these Scriptures; *When the Lamb opened the second seal, I heard the second living creature say, 'Come! (Rev.6:3). When the Lamb opened the third seal, I heard the third living creature say, 'Come!' (Rev.6:5).* Therefore, because Scripture is so clear, it's easy to follow and understand the roles of these four superb horsemen:

1. The conqueror/lion calls forward the rider who holds the bow and crown.

2. The strong, obedient servant/ox calls forward the rider who holds a large sword.

3. The man of free choice calls forward the rider who holds the scales of justice.

4. The spirit-led/eagle calls forward the rider who holds the keys to death and Hell.

It is evident that the roles of each of the four mighty horsemen are directly tied to the personalities of the four living creatures who glorify the Lamb and proclaim his worthiness to open the Scroll of Judgment. This is because the judgments of the four horsemen also glorify Christ and proclaim his worthiness to begin the judgments. Furthermore, these Scriptures teach us that judgment would not be possible at all without the death and resurrection of the *Lamb of God* and that the judgments themselves could not happen without the total support of the throne of God.

Sheltered and safe!

9

HOLY JUDGMENT

I watched as the Lamb opened the first of the seven seals. Then I heard one of the four living creatures say, in a voice that sounded like thunder, 'Come!' (Rev.6:1)

There has been much fear and confusion in the Body about the judgments of the last days. Many of God's children have been so thoroughly deceived into believing these judgments are about the supposed power of Satan that it is hard for them to accept they have been deceived and turn away from the lie. But Christ loves his Bride, and he is waiting with open arms for those who have been deceived to return to him, their first love, so that he can wipe away their tears and wash them in the truth of his word.

The truth of his word concerning end-time judgment is very, very clear. Those who are 'in Christ' have been redeemed from the effects of the end-time judgment, written in the Book of Revelation. This is what our Salvation is for, and this is what it means to be saved. Freedom from judgment is the 'hope of our salvation' and the reason for everything Christ has done for his beloved Bride.

To understand how sheltered and safe the Bride is from end-time judgment, it is vital we understand how judgment works through the four incredible horsemen and the four living creatures who control them, for unless we do, we cannot possibly begin to understand any of the judgments of Revelation. This is because every Godly curse of plague, famine, and sword, which unfolds until the return of Christ, is brought about by these four powerful horsemen who, along with God's holy angels, have the authority to execute every single judgment mankind can experience on this Earth. All the judgments of God for sin revealed in Revelation come from the hand of Christ through these magnificent and obedient horsemen and through God's holy angels. What has not been taught, though, is that these four spectacular horsemen also have the power and authority to protect Christ's beloved Bride from the unstoppable effects of the ongoing judgment of the Law.

These four horsemen have the power to protect Christ's Bride from the unstoppable effects of God's judgment.

FOUR LIVING CREATURES

Another thing which has not been taught is that the four gentle living creatures, who appear with Christ on the throne, rule with him, and accompany him everywhere he goes, also manifest the four major aspects of his victory at Calvary, which is easily seen in their faces; for Jesus was;

- First, a brave and conquering Lion/Messiah,
- Second, an obedient, burden-bearing Ox/Servant,
- Third, free to balance Life against Law as Man/God,
- Fourth, guided by faith through the Eagle/Spirit.

86

These four living creatures reveal the four major aspects of the victory of Christ, and their descriptions bear a striking resemblance to the four spiritual laws mentioned in the New Testament. There are only four laws, written as laws, in the New Testament. They are different to the Old Testament Laws because they are spiritually discerned rather than physically seen. These four laws help us to understand further the function of the four living creatures and the purpose of the horsemen they control. The four spiritual laws are:

- The law of love (Jms.2:8)
- The law of liberty (Jms.2:12, Gal.5:1)
- The law of life (Rm.8:2)
- The law of faith (Rom.3:27)

Filled to the brim with the Spirit of God and speaking *with a voice like thunder*, which is the voice of God, these four living creatures exist to give testimony to the victory Christ achieved at Calvary, and yet their testimony to him was lacking! These four living creatures could not provide testament to the judgment of those who would reject the sacrifice of Christ right up until the end of days. That judgment was the reason these creatures, on behalf of the Lamb and with the authority of God, called forward the four horsemen.

When the four horsemen are sent out by the living creatures, we see that the first horseman fulfils the *law of love*, as he assists us to love our Messiah, who gave his life for love. The second horseman fulfils the *law of liberty*, as he encourages us not to be yoked to bondage but to Christ. The third horseman fulfils the *law of the Spirit of Life*, as he weighs law against life and helps believers to choose life, and the fourth horseman fulfils the *law of faith,* as he assists us to abandon our own works and be led by the Spirit.

What a magnificent picture of loving unity and submission this is! God, his Spirit, and Christ, all working individually and as one. Perfect unity! Perfect harmony! Jesus does not have to defend himself against those who reject his sacrifice. The Spirit defends him, and the voice of God speaks through the Spirit, in the living creatures, to command the horseman to bring glory to the work Christ has already finished. How beautiful! How glorious!

THE WHITE HORSE

*The Lamb opened the first of the seven seals...
I looked, and there before me was a white
horse! Its rider held a bow, and he was given a
crown, and he rode out as a conqueror bent on
conquest. (Rev.6:2)*

The resurrected Lamb opened the first of the seven seals, and the judgment of God for all the sins of the world began. When did this happen? Will it happen in the future? Should we be looking for it to happen soon? Absolutely not! This seal was opened nearly 2000 years ago.

Jesus has already conquered, for sin, death, Hell, and Satan are all under his feet and have been there for a long, long time. The judgment for all the sins of the world, not just some of the sins of the world, but all of them, was placed onto Christ at Calvary. *Behold the Lamb of God who takes away the sins of the world (Jn.1:29).*

This belief is the cornerstone of our faith. If we believe that all the judgment for the sin of the world was placed onto Christ at Calvary, then we must believe this was when the final judgment of God for sin began. This is past tense; therefore, this event in Heaven is not about to happen, nor will it happen in the future; this judgment is already finished.

The only reason Christ was able to open the Scroll of Judgment in the first place was because he had successfully conquered, and now we see that the Spirit of the conquerer is still bent on further conquest. This time, however, Christ does not have to go into battle himself because his victory was so thorough and complete that all he needs to do now is send his Spirit to finalize his victory, mop up, so to speak, or put in place the new order which his victory has already won.

When the Lamb opened the first seal, and the living creature, with the face of a lion, called forward the first horseman, the Spirit of the conquering hero who came forward, was the lion-hearted Spirit of our crowned, victorious Messiah, an accomplished conqueror, bent on further conquest, who will not rest until he places every last one of God's enemies under his scarred feet.

> *The First Horseman will not rest until he places all God's enemies under Christ's scarred feet.*

THE RED HORSE

When the Lamb opened the second seal, I heard the second living creature say, 'Come!' Then another horse came out, a fiery red one. Its rider was given power to take peace from the Earth and to make men slay each other. To him was given a large sword. (Rev.6:3-4)

The Lamb opened the second seal, and the second living creature, the creature with the face of an ox, commanded *Come!* And the rider on the second horse appeared. How do we know the second living creature has the face of an ox? They are listed in order as first, second, third and fourth.

*The first living creature was like a lion, the
second was like an ox, the third had a face like
a man, and the fourth was like a flying eagle.
Each of the four living creatures had six wings
and was covered with eyes all around. (Rev.4:7-8)*

The fact that these beautiful living creatures have
been listed in order, and they are also identified as calling
the horsemen in that same order, shows that the character
and role of each living creature are deliberately linked to the
character and role of the horseman he calls forward.

The character and role of the second living creature is
a perfect example of this; the gentle, meek and lowly nature
of the burden-bearing ox/servant, who takes our burdens on
himself and gives us the freedom of rest in return, is an exact
mirror image of the second horseman.

*Come to me, all you who are weary and
burdened and I will give you rest. Take my yoke
upon you and learn from me, for I am gentle
and humble in heart, and you will find rest for
your souls. (Matt.11:28-30)*

The second horseman is given the authority to take
peace from the Earth. He has the power to turn people against
each other and make them slay one another. This is not strange
or even harsh! When we look at how we can gain peace and
rest from our meek and lowly servant Lord, we can see how
those who refuse to be yoked to him will lose peace and rest
in greater amounts until their burdens totally consume them.

Those who refuse to cast their cares on the Lord will
become so tired of their burdens they will begin to hate those
who give them to them and those who will not help them
carry them.

Eventually, they will hate their lives and themselves and others so much that peace will totally elude them, and they will begin to lash out in word and deed and finally slay one another. This is not hypothetical, nor is it beyond the realms of reason; it is the natural outcome of a simple spiritual principle. There is no rest for the wicked!

What we see here is typical of the judgment of God, for it always has two sides. Whether hot or cold, good or evil, dark or light, cursing or blessing, Heaven or Hell, in judgment, there are always two contrasting opposites. Jesus himself, who brought the greatest peace, also said...

Do not think that I have come to bring peace to the Earth. I did not come to bring peace but a sword. For...a man's enemies will be the members of his own household. (Matt.10:34-36)

Christ only has one sword, but it has two sharp sides (Rev.2:12). One side has the power to bring life, while the other has the power to bring death. The large sword which has been given to this second mighty horseman has two sharp edges, and it is fairly obvious that those who love and obey the word of God will be saved by it, while those who despise his word will be killed by it.

When the Lamb opened the second seal, and the living creature with the face of an ox called forward the second horseman, the Spirit of the obedient servant was sent forward to take peace from all those who would not cast their cares on the Lamb.

The Second Horseman has the power to remove peace from all those who will not cast their cares on the Lamb.

91

The burden-bearing Spirit, who rides out, is the Spirit of the glorified Christ, who is able to bear all the burdens given to him, but will also allow chaos to consume those who ignore the price he paid for their freedom, choosing instead to carry the full weight of their own burdens themselves.

THE BLACK HORSE

When the Lamb opened the third seal, I heard the third living creature say, 'Come!' I looked and there before me was a black horse! Its rider was holding a pair of scales in his hand. Then I heard what sounded like a voice among the four living creatures, saying, 'A quart of wheat for a day's wages, and three quarts of barley for a day's wages, and do not damage the oil and the wine!' (Rev.6:5-6)

It is more than amazing to me that so many who say they believe in Jesus attribute the works of Christ to the devil. These horsemen are one such example of that particular blasphemy. These righteous riders cannot possibly belong to Satan! All we have to do is read what is written to see they are servants of Christ, and this particular horseman, the rider on the black horse, provides the ultimate proof it is Christ, and Christ alone, who is bringing judgment to the Earth through these horsemen.

When the Lamb opened the third seal, the third living creature, the one with the face of a man, said, *Come!,* and the rider on the black horse appeared, holding a set of scales, a symbol of measurement. This measure, in the hands of the *man,* is human choice because it is our personal choices which will be weighed in this balance; to bring the judgment of the Law or the deliverance of righteousness.

It is here, also, that we see absolute proof these judgments are coming from Jesus and not from Satan, for suddenly, a voice gives a direct command! The voice that gives this command comes from the one who is standing among the four living creatures. There is only one person this can possibly be, and that person is the *Lamb of God,* whom the living creatures continually surround and glorify. It is Jesus himself who commands the 'curse' that food should become a precious and expensive commodity. It is Jesus who commands the 'blessing' that the oil and wine be spared.

In one breath, Christ gives a perfect example of his awesome authority to both curse and bless and to both condemn and spare; therefore, the scales held by this third horseman represent the authority of Christ to separate the sheep from the goats. This is not the work of Satan; this can only be the work of Christ. Christ is totally in control of the actions of the rider on the black horse, who is not a rebel but a trustworthy partner. Believers need to understand these images and the holy work of Christ. We need to work with him as his Spirit brings these judgments to the world and not work against him.

> *The Third Horseman has the power to weigh the choices of mankind and judge between the sheep and the goats.*

When the Lamb opened the third seal, and the living creature with the face of a man called forward the third horseman, the Spirit of the man/God that came forward was the only one given authority from the Lamb to weigh the choices of mankind. The judging Spirit who rides out is the Spirit of the righteous, glorified Christ, who holds the perfect justice of God in his hands, and weighs everyone in the same balance according to their own choices.

THE PALE HORSE

The Lamb opened the fourth seal...I looked, and there before me was a pale horse! Its rider was named Death, and Hades was following close behind him. They were given power over a fourth of the Earth to kill by sword, famine and plague, and by the wild beasts of the Earth. (Rev.6:7-8)

The big question here is, 'Who has control over death and Hell - Satan or Christ?' Those who say 'Satan' have forgotten about the absolute victory of our great hero and King, whose death and resurrection proved he now, alongside God, holds the keys to death and Hell.

So again, this image is not about Satan. It is about Christ and his power to command death and to send those who rebel against God to Hell.

When the Lamb opened the fourth seal and the fourth living creature, the creature with the face of an eagle, commanded *Come!,* the rider on the pale horse appeared. This creature symbolizes the fullness of the Spirit of God, for an eagle is not like other birds; it does not flap its wings or use its own strength to rise up in order to fly. Instead, it sits on a rock with its wings outstretched and waits to be lifted by the wind. It allows itself to be empowered by the wind, become one with the wind, and move with the wind and not against it. The fourth living creature is described as the face of a flying eagle because, like an eagle on the wind, Christ is empowered by God, moves with God, works with God and is one with God. This is the nature of faith, for our action of waiting for God to move and then moving with him is evidence that we believe. *Faith without works is dead (Js.2:17).*

The hero of Calvary holds the keys to death and Hell, but freedom from death and Hell is only one side of the authority given to this last horseman. These keys not only have the power to free people from death and Hell but also condemn people to death and Hell as well. This has always been the dominion of God, for he has always had authority over life and death. He, alone, has always chosen who will live and who will die. There has never been anyone on this Earth, or in Heavenly places, with the power to interfere with God's sovereign authority over life and death, and that includes Satan. Christ himself had to die and be raised from the dead before he could share God's power over life and death. Satan has never had and never will have the power to bring life or command death.

The Fourth Horseman has the authority and power to bring eternal life or eternal death depending on a person's faith in Christ.

Satan has never had the authority to consign anyone to Hell. Throughout biblical history, it has always been God who has judged mankind and decided between life and death, and now Christ has been given the same authority. This fourth horseman is absolute proof Christ is using his new kingly authority to bring finality to the rebellion of all the enemies of God, and that includes Satan and all his agents.

Throughout history, Satan's only victory has been to deceive God's children into sin so that God would have to punish us. How horrible for God! Nevertheless, the power of life and death has always remained firmly in his hands. To believe that this fourth horseman is Satan is not only great and foolish blasphemy, but it is also a belief that shows enormous ignorance of the word of God and the saving work of Christ.

The faithful Spirit, who rides out on the pale horse, has proven beyond doubt that he is totally in control of death and Hell, and he rides with God's full authority. He guarantees life to those who believe in the work of Christ and guarantees death to those who don't believe.

Why is this horseman given power over a quarter of the Earth? Simply put, a quarter is his share! It must be remembered this is figurative language. These horsemen are not literal, for the whole picture is a parable. Therefore, this statement points to the fullness and completion of the judgment of God. This rider is one of four horsemen, and as four quarters make a whole, this Scripture shows that these four spiritual horsemen will bring the total judgment of Christ, through the Spirit of God, in its entirety, including the judgment of Satan.

SATAN'S FATE IS SEALED

Satan has already been judged and sentenced. He was judged before Revelation was written, and the judgments in Revelation are against him. Jesus spoke in the present tense when he told his disciples; *Satan now stands condemned.* For us, nearly 2000 years later, that is definitely past tense.

> *When he (the Spirit) comes, he will convict the world of guilt in regard to sin, righteousness and judgment...in regard to judgment because the prince of this world now stands condemned. (Jn.16:8-11)*

Though he was condemned before Christ died, his actual judgment was so thoroughly begun and finished in the death and resurrection of Christ that by the time Christ left Hell, Satan was utterly defeated.

Satan's judgment has been documented, in great detail, in the Book of Revelation. He has already been judged, and his sentence has already been determined down to his last minute of freedom. His sentence could not have been dictated in such intricate detail to the Apostle John, and written as the eternal word of God, if Satan had not already been judged, found guilty, condemned and sentenced.

That is why the Royal Testimony of Christ is so remarkable; Satan's judgment was pronounced in Heaven by God, recorded in an eternal document by Christ, shared with Christ's Bride on Earth through his faithful Spirit, and is therefore not going to change. Satan is thoroughly defeated!

Now that we know Satan can have nothing to do with the plague, famine and sword of the end-time judgments, which are actually against him and all his works, it is time to find out who really brings final judgment. According to Jesus' own words, the only one with the delegated authority of both God and Christ to bring final judgment to the world is the all-powerful Spirit of God. The same Spirit Jesus told us would come to us at Pentecost.

These four mighty horsemen, who complete the judgment of God, are the only spiritual force that left Heaven after the resurrection of Christ. Shock of shocks! These four mighty horsemen, who represent the Spirit of God, are the same mighty force that arrived on Earth at Pentecost.

As believers, we should never underestimate the awesome and overwhelming power of the mighty Spirit of God. Jesus may not have come to judge the world, but his faithful Spirit did. He is here to judge!

Cheered and supported!

10

ECHOES OF EZEKIEL

Unless I go away, the Counsellor will not come to you, but if I go, I will send him to you. (Jn.16:7)

Christ redeemed his Bride from the clutches of his enemy, the devil, through his death and resurrection, but redeeming her was not enough. He also needed to ensure she would remain safe after she was redeemed. To keep her safe, he needed to send to her the most powerful guardians that existed anywhere in creation, the same combined spiritual force that had just raised him from the dead.

He could not release that mighty protecting force until he returned to his Father's Kingdom, and it was for this purpose he was so anxious to leave his precious Bride, even if only for a short time, and return to his home. He needed to receive permission from his Father to send guardians to her side. Once he received his Father's blessing, he immediately sent his sevenfold Spirit to protect his beloved. The sending of the Spirit was of great importance to both Christ and his Father, and Revelation is the only book of the Bible which records Heaven's view of that most important event.

God did not leave Heaven at Pentecost! Christ did not leave Heaven at Pentecost! The only sending recorded in Heaven after the resurrection of Christ was the sending of the mighty, judging Spirit, and typically, God chose to use a parable to describe that unique and invisible event. Revelation explains in the clearest possible detail that the only spiritual force which left Heaven directly after Christ's resurrection, and with God's full authority, was a group of four Spirit-saturated and God-commissioned horsemen.

It's not unusual that these four mighty horsemen should be used to represent the sending of the Spirit to mankind. In the Old Testament, there are various references to these four horsemen. Sometimes they are represented slightly differently, but they are still the same four horsemen.

FOUR HORSES AMONG THE MYRTLES

On one occasion, four mighty horsemen were sent out from the throne of God to report on the state of the world:

> *During the night I had a vision and there before me was a man riding a red horse! He was standing among the myrtle trees in a ravine. Behind him were red, brown and white horses.*
>
> *I asked, 'What are these, my lord?' The angel who was talking with me answered, 'I will show you what they are.' Then the man standing among the myrtle trees explained, 'They are the ones the Lord has sent to go throughout the Earth.'*
>
> *And they reported to the angel of the Lord, who was standing among the myrtle trees, 'We have gone throughout the Earth and found the whole world at rest and in peace.' (Zec.1:8-10)*

These four horsemen, standing in a grove of myrtles, are servants of the *man* riding one of them, and it is this Heavenly man who answered Zechariah's questions and explained to him whom this group of four horsemen represented. There has only ever been one Heavenly *man* recorded in Scripture, and that man is Christ. It is patently obvious from this Heavenly man's answers that these four horses were sent out from the throne of God to judge the hearts of mankind on God's behalf, for he said; *they are the ones the Lord has sent to go throughout the Earth.* It is also obvious from his answers that these horsemen remain completely submitted to the will of God. The only surprise is the report they bring back to God about God's people is good!

Four horses and their riders were sent out from the throne of God to judge the hearts of mankind.

Given the reputation which has been attributed to the four horsemen of Revelation, this is not what anyone would expect from four powerful horsemen sent out to judge the hearts of mankind, yet this gentle response serves to show the nature of the horsemen and their role as servants of God.

FOUR CHARIOTS LED BY FOUR HORSES

The prophet Zechariah saw four chariots being pulled by the same four horses we see in Revelation. These horses are the same colours as the previous horses, and they are sent out in four different directions to cover the whole Earth. The stated purpose of these four horse-driven chariots is to bring rest to the concerned heart of God. The mission of these four chariots and of the four horsemen of Revelation is exactly the same. They are both sent out into the world to judge mankind and so bring peace to the heart of God.

> *I looked again, and there before me were four chariots coming out from between two mountains - mountains of bronze!*
>
> *The first chariot had red horses, the second black, the third white and the fourth dappled– all of them powerful!*
>
> *I asked the angel who was speaking to me, 'What are these, my lord?' The angel answered me, 'These are the four Spirits of Heaven, going out from standing in the presence of the Lord of the whole world.'*
>
> *'Look, those going toward the north country have given my Spirit rest in the land of the north.' (Zec.6:1–8)*

These four chariots, pulled by horses with exactly the same colours as the horsemen of Revelation, are expressly named: *the four Spirits of Heaven,* and this shows that their four identical counterparts revealed in the Book of Revelation have always been and are still directly representative of the awesome, obedient and powerful Spirit of God.

EZEKIEL SAW THE SPIRIT OF GOD

In the book of Ezekiel, we have a detailed description that echoes the coming of the Spirit of Christ at Pentecost. The entire first chapter is given to describing a mighty rushing wind, filled with fire which brings forth four living creatures with four distinct faces. The faces of these creatures are listed as; *the face of a man, the face of a lion, the face of an ox and the face of an eagle (v10)*. This detailed description is more than similar; it is exactly the same as the description of the four living creatures of Revelation.

Beside each of these creatures was a set of *wheels within wheels,* covered in eyes, which moved when the creatures moved and would never leave their side. Ezekiel explained that the reason they moved as one was because the Spirit of the living creatures was in the wheels.

> *When the living creatures moved, the wheels beside them moved, and when the living creatures rose from the ground, the wheels also rose. Where ever the Spirit would go, they would go…because the Spirit of the living creatures was in the wheels. (Ez.1:19-20)*

These Scriptures show that the four living creatures, the same creatures who call forth the four horsemen of Revelation, have no other purpose than to represent the powerful Spirit of God. They are the Spirit of God!

There are many images throughout Scripture that confirm the roles of the four horsemen, like the *Four Craftsmen* (Zec.1:18-21) and the *Four Winds of Heaven* (Dan.7:2). As we have seen, some of the prophetic descriptions show the Spirit's role in Heaven, and some show his role on Earth. This is not surprising, as the word of God confirms itself over and over again. The only difference between the various appearances of the four horsemen in the Old Testament and their appearance in the New Testament is that now their appearance is not temporary but permanent. This time,

A mighty rushing wind, filled with fire brought forth four living creatures; the same four creatures we see in Revelation!

they have been ordered by Christ, with the blessing of God, to remain with his faithful Bride until *the end of days. (Matt.28:29)*

A SPIRITUAL EXPLOSION

When we consider the awesome authority which was released from Heaven at Pentecost, it is beyond breathtaking; it is mind-boggling! The sheer power of this single image of four mighty horsemen is a constant reminder of the strength and purpose of the mighty Spirit of God and his authority to bring judgment, both to those who believe and to those who refuse to believe. Like the Book of Deuteronomy, which shows God's judgment has two sides, blessing and cursing, so we see the same two-sided judgment flowing all through the Book of Revelation. It is never one-sided, for just as God brings tribulation for those who choose sin, he also brings protection, power, might, strength, truth, wisdom, glory and, above all, holiness, for those who love the Lamb. These living creatures and their four wonderful horsemen, who bring the judgment of God to the Earth, are beyond magnificent; they are God!

> *These four mighty, judging horsemen and their four living creatures are beyond magnificent; they are God!*

A REAL AND PRESENT HELPER

He said to me, 'Son of man, stand up on your feet, and I will speak to you.' As he spoke, the Spirit came into me and raised me to my feet, and I heard him speaking to me. (Ezekiel 2:1-2)

We can learn a helpful lesson from Ezekiel's encounter with God and his spectacular Spirit. His experience shows what we can expect from Christ and his Spirit and how the relationship between the Spirit of God and the Bride of Christ is supposed to function in reality.

Ezekiel describes a mighty rushing wind filled with fire which ushers in the Spirit. Then he gives a detailed description of the appearance of the Spirit that is ushered in; a four-faced, continually moving Spirit. This is *exactly* how the Spirit of God is described in the Book of Revelation.

From there, Ezekiel's gaze moves beyond the Spirit to the throne of God and then to the one above the throne, who looks like a man. This *man* above the throne gives the four-faced Spirit the authority to act. Again, this is *exactly* what happens in the Book of Revelation. The man above the Throne (Christ) gives the four-faced creatures, who represent the Spirit, the authority to send forth the four horsemen, and when they are sent out, they arrive on Earth in a mighty rush of wind and sin-consuming fire.

What Ezekiel describes echoes what believers can also experience today, for, remarkably, our relationship with the Spirit and with Christ works the same way it did with Ezekiel. The four-faced Spirit helped Ezekiel in *exactly* the same way as the Spirit helps the Bride today. We've all heard about the signs that accompanied the coming of the Spirit, the mighty rushing wind filled with fire, and we know the importance of that encounter. However, some people want to know more about who this Spirit is, and so they search and begin to see, but as they do, something else begins to happen; something wonderful! Those who look deeply into the gentleness and power of the Spirit of God begin to see more of the magnificent glory of our resurrected Christ.

Those who look deeply into the gentleness and power of the Spirit of God begin to see the magnificent glory of our resurrected Christ.

THEN IT BECOMES PERSONAL

At first, Ezekiel couldn't handle what he was seeing, the glory was too much for him, and he fell face down on the ground. While he was lying prostrate, the voice of the *man* above the throne commanded him to stand on his feet so he could speak face-to-face with the one seated on the throne. As soon as the voice of the man above the throne spoke to Ezekiel, the Spirit with four faces came and helped him do what he had just been commanded to do; he helped Ezekiel to his feet. In other words, the voice above the throne told Ezekiel to stand on his feet, and the Spirit came and helped him to stand up.

What a mighty and awesome description of the role of our 'helper'!

Here is the role of the Spirit of God in a nutshell. As it was with Ezekiel, so it is with us; God's word gives us the authority to follow Christ, and when Christ tells us specifically what he wants us to do, his Spirit immediately comes to us and enables us to obey. This doesn't just happen once but over and over again. This mighty and awesomely powerful Spirit chooses to be our helper. Amazing!

After he was raised to his feet, the voice on the throne (God), not the man above the throne (Christ), gave Ezekiel detailed verbal instructions and then commanded him to eat the words he had been given.

As soon as those words of God were spoken directly to Ezekiel, the Spirit came forward and handed Ezekiel a scroll filled with words on both sides. Ezekiel didn't even have to eat the scroll himself, for when he opened his mouth, the Spirit fed him the scroll. What a strong and comforting description of the role of our 'helper'.

The four-faced helping Spirit, who assisted Ezekiel, is *exactly* the same four-faced helping Spirit who came to us in a mighty rushing wind, filled with fire, at Pentecost. It is this same Spirit who is described, by the Apostle John, as helping the Lamb unfold the meaning of another Scroll, also written on both sides, the Scroll of Judgment in Revelation. It is this same Spirit who called forth the four mighty horsemen to assist us to now do what our resurrected Lord, and glorious King of kings, has commanded us to do.

HIS COMMAND - HIS SPIRIT - HIS WORK

Knowing how helpful the Spirit of God is, it is not surprising that Christ advised his disciples to wait until they had received power from on high before going out to fulfil his commission (Lk.24:49). His command hasn't changed, and he still expects believers to wait on him before we try to do the four very powerful things he has commanded us to do.

Preach the Gospel

This is what the first horseman teaches us to do! As we proclaim the Kingdom of God and uphold the name and testimony of its King, we preach the true Gospel. Any rejection of our preaching is witnessed by the Spirit of God in us, and those who reject the testimony of the Son of God literally judge themselves unworthy of protection from judgment.

Cast out Demons

This is what the second horseman teaches us to do! As we help people cast their cares on him, we use the sword of his word to cast out the demons who try to prevent them from knowing God. Those who resist the freedom offered by Christ, and hold on tightly to their burdens, will suffer the consequences of their personal choices with no protection from God's judgment on this Earth, in this life.

Heal the Sick

This is what the third horseman teaches us to do! As we lead people to repentance, away from Law and into life, we see them miraculously healed of all the curses they had invited into their lives through sin. Those who choose not to break away from the curse of the Law will, through their own choice, have no protection from the outworking of the curse of the Law in this life.

Raise the Dead

This is what the fourth horseman teaches us to do! As we use the keys which freed Christ from death and Hell, we watch the Spirit do his supernatural work through us, which may include raising some people from untimely death. Those who choose life through Christ will receive eternal life, while those who choose to reject Christ will receive eternal death.

HERE TO JUDGE

The judgment of God is a sharp two-edged sword. One side brings life, and the other brings death. No believer ever has to fear the rejection or the persecution of man, for the highly protective Spirit of God is witnessing everything that happens to us, and he *will* judge those who reject the word of God through us! Every judgment described in Revelation until the last day of Earth's history is brought about by these four fantastic horsemen and is led specifically by the rider on the White Horse. This is confirmed in chapter 19 of Revelation, where the description of the rider on the White Horse is shown as a combination of all the horsemen put together.

The Spirit of God will judge those who reject the word of God spoken through God's servants.

Here again, we see that the Spirit, represented by all the horsemen, is the Spirit of Christ himself, described as:

- First, charging forth as a multi-crowned *King of kings,* on a white horse, to bring final judgment. (Rev.19:12)

- Second, wielding the sword of the second horseman (the word), which is coming from his mouth. (Rev.19:15)

- Third, using the justice of the third mighty horseman as the basis for his judgments. (Rev.19:11)

- Fourth, enacting the deadly finality of the fourth horseman as he treads the wine press of God's wrath, making all his judgments permanent. (Rev.19:15)

This great and mighty parable shows Christ in all his triumphant Glory, but it is a parable. These images explain invisible spiritual events, which cannot be imparted to us any other way than through concepts familiar to life on Earth:

- Does Jesus literally ride a white horse across eternity?

- Are his clothes literally covered in blood?

- Is a real sword protruding from his mouth?

- Do his eyes literally blaze with fire?

- Are his feet really made of bronze?

The four spiritual laws which the four living creatures and their four horsemen represent, love, liberty, life and faith, cannot be judged by physical standards. Unlike the breaking of the Ten Commandments, which everyone can see, no one on Earth can see the breaking of the laws of love, liberty, life or faith. These laws belong to the Kingdom of Heaven, and that Kingdom is *not of this world*. These four laws guide the four splendid horsemen as they bring final judgment for the breaking of the visible Law, written by Moses.

JOHN KNEW WHAT HE WAS SAYING

The Apostle John was saturated with Scripture. When he wrote the Book of Revelation, he was well aware of the previous references to the four horsemen, the four winds of Heaven, the four craftsmen, the four chariots and the four Spirits of Heaven and their combined roles throughout history. He was not only raised with knowledge of the Scriptures from an early age but was taught personally by Christ, who took his disciples through the Scriptures and showed them how they related to him.

> *What he wrote about the four horsemen did not conflict with anything he had previously read or learned.*

What he wrote about the four horsemen did not conflict with anything he had previously read or learned. Rather his vision confirmed the twofold mission of the four *Spirits of Heaven,* who are sent to judge the hearts of mankind and bring terror to those who seek to destroy God's precious people.

> *Then the Lord showed me the Four Craftsmen. I asked him, 'What are these coming to do?'*
>
> *He answered, 'The horns you see are those that scattered Judah so that no one could raise their head, but the Craftsmen have come to terrify them and throw down these horns of the nations who lifted up their horns against the land of Judah to scatter its people. (Zec.2:20-21)*

Further, John was writing to Hebrew Christians, who were well-versed in Scripture and would have understood the reference and meaning of the four horsemen.

GREAT COMFORT

The believers of John's day were under tremendous persecution, and so when they read his prophetic words, which revealed the role of the four-faced Spirit and his horsemen, they would have been greatly encouraged. His words would have reminded them of the strength, power and impressive ability of the Spirit of God, who had been sent from Heaven to dwell within them, assist them, lead them, and work through them because of the great love Jesus has for his beloved.

With such encouragement, they would have found it a lot easier to forgo judging their persecutors, knowing that the Spirit of God would judge more efficiently than they ever could. The message is the same today. We are still loved by our Saviour and blessed by the mighty power and gentleness of the supernatural helper he has sent to dwell with his Bride until the end of time.

The Book of Revelation is a book of encouragement and blessing. Nowhere in its pages is there any reason presented that would cause those who love Christ to be afraid. On the contrary, there is every reason for us to be cheered to greater love because of the abundant help and support this precious testimony promises.

Breathless with awe!

11

SILENCE IN HEAVEN

Father in Heaven, holy is your name. May your Kingdom come; may your will be done; on Earth, as it is in Heaven. (Matt.6:9-10)

So far, in chapter one of the Book of Revelation, we have seen the announcement of a Royal Decree from Heaven, followed in chapters two and three, by a list of protections and provisions afforded to the Bride of the King. Then, in chapters four and five, we were taken into the innermost throne room of Heaven, where we witnessed God, and all of the angels, saints, and elders, waiting for the great hero to return from his battle at Calvary. We listened as all of Heaven erupted into joy as he arrived, was crowned King, and was finally handed the official Scroll of Judgment by his Father. In chapter six, we watched as Christ took the Scroll into his scarred hands, opened the first six seals, and read the agenda for judgment, which would be executed, in full, by his four glorious horsemen. Now we are about to witness what Christ will do next. And what he is about to do when he opens the seventh seal is so gripping, so engaging, and so deeply profound that all of Heaven holds its breath.

It must be remembered that nothing is going to happen on Earth unless it happens in Heaven first, for one thing is absolutely sure. God's will *will* be done on Earth, as it is in Heaven. And in Heaven, Christ is King, and Satan is totally defeated! Satan was defeated at Calvary, and since then, he and his beasts have been kept on a very tight leash.

It's like this; just imagine Satan is a beast with seven heads and four legs, and he's walking beside Jesus. Compared to Jesus, he is very short; he only comes up to Jesus' ankles. He is bound by an unbreakable red leash that is held firmly in Christ's hand, and he is being forced to heel. He has no freedom to do anything against the will of his master. This is not fantasy! This is how Satan looks from Heaven's point of view. Satan is under the feet of Christ!

The power of Heaven is in Christ's hands, and the judgment of the people of the Earth is in Christ's hands. The judgment of Revelation is simply the ongoing judgment of God for sin, and that judgment will never change. Revelation simply converts the already written word to pictures.

WHAT DO THE PICTURES MEAN?

There is no other book of the Bible that gives us so many powerful, accurate and insightful accounts of what is happening in that invisible world we call Heaven. Through the testimony of Christ, we are able to see into the heart, mind and throne room of God in a way that was never possible prior to his death and resurrection, and what we see there is astounding! The images Christ presents in regard to judgment are beyond spectacular; they are breathtaking! So breathtaking that when they were revealed, there was silence.

There was silence in Heaven for about half an hour (Rev.8:1).

114

Can you imagine what that would have been like? All praise ceased! All activity ceased! No movement! No sound! Total silence! Why? What could halt the continual worship of God for even a second? What could cause silence so great that even a blink could cause an echo? What could possibly have been so profound?

JUDGMENT WAS ABOUT TO BEGIN!

The righteous Lamb had been judged, and now it was his turn to judge! The judgment of the Lamb was so awesome that all of Heaven held its breath. So what did the angels see that was so amazing? This is what they saw...

- An angel was asked to go and get John. The angel took John into the throne room of God and showed him the splendour of Heaven itself. (Rev.4:1-11)

- While there, John noticed another mighty angel calling for someone worthy to come forward and open the Scroll of Judgment, but no one came forward. John wept and wept because, in all of Heaven, no one was found worthy to open the Scroll. (Rev.5:1-4)

- Then the elders leant over to comfort John and confided in him that he should not weep, as the *Lion of the Tribe of Judah* had triumphed and was able to open the Scroll. (Rev.5:5)

- While they were speaking, a Lamb, looking like it had been slain, appeared at the centre of the throne. The Lamb stepped forward to take the Scroll of Judgment from the hand of God. (Rev.5:6:8)

- John watched as the population of Heaven suddenly erupted into praise, declaring the Lamb's worthiness to take the Scroll because he had, with his Blood, purchased kings and priests for his God. (Rev.5:9-10)

- Then multitudes of angels from all over Heaven gathered around the elders and encircled the throne and the Lamb, singing in their loudest voices, *Worthy is the Lamb who was slain.* (Rev.5:11-12)

- After that, all living creatures in the skies, the earth, the sea, and under the earth joined with the elders and angels in singing praise to the Lamb until all Heaven was filled with loud and glorious praise! (Rev.5:13-14)

Amidst this cacophony of praise, the Lamb opened the first six of the seven seals on the Scroll of Judgment. What the first six seals showed was an agenda for the main judgment, which was about to begin. They served to show:

- who would bring the judgment (the four horsemen),

- what form it would take (blessing or cursing),

- who would receive blessing (the righteous),

- who would receive cursing (the unrighteous),

- what would happen to Satan and his beasts, and

- how the judgment would look from Heaven's view.

Then, once everyone in Heaven and on Earth knew what was about to happen, it was time for the risen Lamb to open the seventh seal.

> *When he opened the seventh seal, there was silence in Heaven for about half an hour.* *(Rev.8:1)*

While they watched the Lamb, the voices of praise died away. He had begun to open the final seal. Heaven had just swung from extraordinary praise–to absolute silence! What happened next filled the rest of Revelation and concluded with a strong warning by Christ not to add to what was revealed.

AN EXTRAORDINARY SIGHT

There are only three final judgments written in the Book of Revelation, and they all come from the Scroll in the hand of Christ; they are *The Seven Seals, The Seven Trumpets* and *The Seven Golden Bowls*. There are no other judgments!

All of God's judgments for sin are contained within these three judgments, yet, and this is an awesome wonder; *The Seventh Seal* is the last judgment we can see listed on the Scroll. There are no others! There are no signs of any others!

What about the other two judgments, *The Seven Trumpets* and *The Seven Golden Bowls*? Well, this is what was so spectacular and one of the reasons everyone in Heaven suddenly became silent. The opening of *The Seventh Seal* was extraordinary in that it ushered in the beginning and the end of the other two final judgments and showed that they all happen at the same time!

The Seventh Seal opens like a flower to reveal, for the first time in Heavenly history, the other two final judgments of God hidden within. This is a new event! In the same way that all the layers of beauty held within a flower are hidden until the flower opens, so here we see that all the judgments of God which come from the hand of Christ are hidden within *The Seventh*

> *The Seventh Seal opens like a flower to reveal the other two final judgments hidden inside.*

Seal and cannot be seen until *The Seventh Seal* is opened. This is why Heaven held its breath! These other two newly revealed judgments are hidden within and are part of the full judgment of *The Seventh Seal*. We know this because they all begin and end together! They all begin and end in exactly the same way! Are they open now? Yes! We can see them at work.

When he opened the seventh seal...I saw seven angels...and seven trumpets were given to them. Another angel who had a golden censer came...and the angel took the censer, filled it with fire and hurled it onto the Earth and there came peals of thunder, rumblings, flashes of lightning and an earthquake. (Rev.8:1-5)

When *The Seventh Seal* was opened, seven angels with seven trumpets appeared, along with an angel holding a golden censer filled with prayer. When an angel took the censer, filled it with fire and hurled it onto the Earth, there came *peals of thunder, rumblings, flashes of lightning and an earthquake (Rev.8:5)*.

The opening of *The Seventh Seal* was the beginning of the judgments of *The Seven Trumpets* and *The Seven Golden Bowls*. They all begin and end together. How is this possible? This is another parable that points to something earth-shatteringly brilliant: another reason why all Heaven gasped!

Have you ever wondered why Jesus is called the *Alpha and Omega*, or how he could be both the beginning and the end at the same time? These judgments show how! These judgments, which begin and end at the same time, explain why he holds that amazing title and show that he is the only one who is entitled to hold it. Revelation exalts Christ's testimony, and here, it shows clearly that God's final judgment for sin is in his hands, not in Satan's.

Christ was the only one found worthy to bring these final judgments because each judgment precisely echoes Christ's personal suffering and death at Calvary. All the judgment of the Law of God for the sin of the world was begun and finished in the cross of Christ. This is why he is *Alpha and Omega*, the beginning and the end.

A MIRROR IMAGE OF CALVARY

We have seen that the judgments of *The Seven Trumpets* and *The Seven Golden Bowls* begin with the opening of *The Seventh Seal*, but how do we know they end together? Do they each also end with *peals of thunder, rumblings, flashes of lightning and an earthquake?* Yes, they do!

- ❤ At the end of the judgment of *The Seven Trumpets,* we see that God's temple in Heaven is opened, and within his temple is seen the Ark of his Covenant. *Then there came flashes of lightning, rumblings, peals of thunder, an earthquake and a severe hailstorm. (Rev.11:19.*

- ❤ At the end of the judgment of *The Seven Golden Bowls*, the seventh angel poured out his bowl into the air, and out of the temple came a loud voice from the throne saying, *It is done! Then there came flashes of lightning, rumblings, peals of thunder and a severe earthquake. (Rev.16:17-18)*

Can you see the correlation between the judgments of Revelation and the judgments experienced by Christ? First, we see that when the judgment of *The Seven Trumpets* is completed, the temple in Heaven is opened, revealing the holy of holies, where the Ark of the Covenant is kept. Then we see that when the judgment of *The Seven Golden Bowls* is completed, the voice of God cries out, *It is done!* Those two events are a mirror image of what happened at Calvary, and they show that Calvary is the blueprint for all the judgments of Revelation, for when Christ had completed his sufferings on the cross, he cried out, *It is finished!* At that moment, *the curtain of the temple was torn in two* from top to bottom, exposing the holy of holies, *the Earth shook, and rocks split apart*. Then, after that, the tombs opened, and the righteous dead were raised to life. (Matt.27:50-53)

TWO BUBBLES IN TIME

Let me lay out the two events side by side, like two bubbles in history. It will make it easier to see the identical nature of the judgments of both Calvary and Revelation.

THE JUDGMENT OF CALVARY

The out-poured Blood of Christ freed his redeemed from the consequences of our sins, enabling us to be kings and priests for our God.

When Christ died, the curtain in the Temple was split in two, and the Holy of Holies, the resting place of the Ark of the Covenant, was exposed.

The last words that Christ uttered as the judgment of Calvary was coming to an end were, *It is finished!*

Christ was praying through Psalm 22 as he was dying, which began, *My God, my God...* and ended with *It is done!* During this prayer, we see that Christ asked God to rebuke the lions, beasts and other enemies that were tearing him apart.

When the judgment on Christ at Calvary was complete, the sky darkened, lightning flashed, the Earth trembled, and there was a great earthquake.

Only after the full force of the entire judgment of God, for sin, was completed was Christ raised to enter into new and eternal life with his Father.

THE JUDGMENT OF REVELATION

Christ was worthy to open the seals on the Scroll of Judgment because, by his Blood, he purchased kings and priests for his God.

When the judgment of *The Seven Trumpets* was finished, the Holy of Holies in Heaven was opened, and the Ark of the Covenant was revealed.

The last words that God will utter, as the last judgment of the world is coming to an end, will be, *It is done!*

In the chapters that describe the three final judgments, we see how God answered Christ's prayer and rebuked the roaring lion, his beasts and other enemies, who were totally overcome by Christ's death and resurrection.

When the judgment of Revelation is complete, the sky will darken, lightning will flash, the Earth will tremble, and there will be a great earthquake.

Only after the full force of the final judgment of God is completed will we be raised to enter into new and eternal life with Christ and our Father.

Calvary is the established blueprint for everything happening in end-time judgment! This is the reason Jesus was the only one in Heaven or Earth who was found worthy to open the Scroll of Judgment. The judgments of Revelation are an exact replica of the judgments placed onto him at Calvary!

These judgments have never been in Satan's hands. Not for a minute! Christ was the only one who had first-hand experience of the judgments about to be proclaimed. This meant he, alone, was worthy to proclaim them.

This lofty position of being the only one in all of creation found worthy of bringing these judgments is what makes Christ *King of kings* and *Lord of lords*. It is the reason he holds those splendid titles and why those titles can belong to no other.

Calvary is the blueprint for everything happening in end-time judgment!

From start to finish, Revelation is all about Jesus. The assurance we have been given by the King of judgment, who himself was judged according to the Law of Moses, is that all judgments written in the Scroll of Judgment reflect the established judgments written in the Law of Moses.

> *Do not think that I will accuse you before the Father. Your accuser is Moses...for he wrote about me. (Jn.5:45-47)*

If it weren't for God's loving rescue mission, not one person would be able to survive the judgments for sin written in God's holy scroll. However, because of Christ, believers have our sins washed away by the Blood of the Lamb and, therefore, will not experience the same judgment that will be experienced by those who have rejected his protection.

THE MOST PROFOUND MYSTERY

The origin of this Scroll of Judgment is the most profound mystery of all. It is truly mind-blowing! And it is why Christ warned so strongly that no one should add to it.

> *Let us make mankind in our own image. So God created mankind in his own image, in the image of God he created them; male and female he created them. (Gen.1:26-27)*

Before creation, everything that could possibly go wrong on Earth was already understood by the Godhead. Despite knowing what could go wrong, they still chose to create mankind in their own image. At that time, everything they knew about mankind's fall, rescue and ultimate eternal reward was written into a royal document, a holy scroll, and sealed with seven unbreakable seals.

No one in Heaven or Earth knew the secret knowledge written by the Godhead into this ancient scroll. No angel, including Satan, no elder, patriarch, prophet, or anyone who lived before Christ knew what was written in God's sealed scroll.

Many people claim that Daniel or some other Old Testament prophet knew what was written in the scroll, and so could explain it, but that's not even close to the truth. The knowledge hidden in that ancient scroll had never been shared with anyone, which is why Satan didn't know ahead of time what would happen to him when he crucified Christ.

> *We speak of the mysterious and hidden wisdom of God, which He destined for our glory before time began. None of the rulers of this age understood it, for if they had, they would not have crucified the Lord of glory. Rather, as it is written: "No eye has seen, no ear has heard, no heart has imagined, what God has prepared for those who love Him". (1 Cor.2:7-9)*

Christ had to be born a man, die, be raised from the dead, be crowned King of kings, and be made ruler over the nations before he was regarded 'worthy' to reveal to mankind the contents of that ancient sealed scroll. And when he began to open it, what was about to be revealed was so anticipated and so revered the event was met with absolute silence. The ancient mystery that no eye had seen or ear heard, the Godhead's best-kept secret, was finally about to be revealed to everyone! This is why John called his prophecy, 'The Revelation of Jesus Christ".

THIS IS WHAT CHRIST REVEALED

It is mind-boggling that some Christians today believe they can flippantly add to the contents of this most precious scroll anything they want to add. No wonder Christ gave such a strong warning against adding to what was carefully included in this ancient scroll. It is a warning that needs to be heeded.

Though some have spoken of the holy judgments of Revelation as the vicious and unstoppable works of Satan, they are not and will never be Satan's judgments. Satan had no idea what was written in God's holy scroll and would not have killed Christ if he had known how the judgments written in that scroll would fall on him and his followers.

What is written in the scroll confirms that there will never be any other judgment for sin except the Law written by Moses. Significantly, this is where we see for the first time how the Commandments of God are amended by the victory of Christ. Though God's righteous judgment of sin is unstoppable, the blood of Christ shelters the redeemed like an umbrella in the rain.

Over the next few chapters, I will explain in detail what the three judgments of God are and how Christ protects us from each of them. Our King has saved us, and because of him, we are completely safe! We are not only safe; we are loved!

Amazed by reason!

12

THREE CURSES OF LAW

I will send the sword, famine and plague against them until they are destroyed from the land I gave to them and their ancestors. (Jer.24:10)

It is important to understand the curses placed on mankind, by God, for disobedience to his written Law. When we read through the curses, we can see clearly that these judgments are everywhere. They are not being stored up for one last and final judgment day. They are all around us all the time.

It is also easy to see that these curses are the same curses so picturesquely described in the Book of Revelation. This is because there has only ever been one Law given for the judgment of sin. That Law hasn't changed!

All the curses, or judgments, of the Law of God written by Moses are divided into three clear applications; famine, plague and sword. These three curses are commonly referred to throughout the Old Testament as the embodiment of the full judgment of God for sin. They are clearly laid out in Deuteronomy 28, and though the following might hold a lot of information, please bear with me. This is important!

The first 14 verses of Deuteronomy 28 cover the blessings of God. Then from verses 15 to 46, we see a general overview of all the curses which will come upon people for the breaking of God's Law. After that, from verse 47 to the end of the chapter, the curses are repeated and divided under three distinct themes. The descriptions are long and detailed, which shows that God did not want anyone to be in doubt about the cause and effect of any of these curses.

> *Every believer should know what these curses are and how Christ saved us from each of them.*

These curses are the precise reason Christ died for mankind. Every believer should know what these curses are and how Christ saved us from each of them. How can we give thanks to God for the redemption of Christ or live confidently in his victory if we don't know what we've been saved from or what judgments (curses) his Blood has covered?

FAMINE - *Duet. 28:47-57*

> *Because you did not serve the Lord your God with joy and gladness of heart, for the abundance of everything, <u>therefore you shall serve your enemies, whom the Lord will send against you in hunger, in thirst, in need of everything,</u> and He will put a yoke of iron on your neck until He has destroyed you.*

The above statement (v47-v48) is a generalisation, or 'subject heading', which sums up the cause and effect of the curse of famine. Hunger, thirst, and being in need of everything is a result of not being grateful to God for his provision in times of plenty, with joy and gladness of heart.

The next verses (49-57) detail the steps people will experience in their downward spiral to the greed of selfish ambition once the curse of famine begins. These verses, straight from Scripture, may be hard for some to understand, so I have paraphrased them on the next page for clarity.

The Lord will bring a nation against you from afar, from the end of the Earth; as swift as the eagle flies, a nation whose language you will not understand.

It will be a nation of strong countenance, which does not respect the elderly nor show favour to the young.

And they shall eat the increase of your livestock and the produce of your land until you are destroyed.

They shall not leave you grain or new wine or oil; they shall not leave you the increase of your cattle or the offspring of your flocks until they have destroyed you.

They shall besiege you at all your gates until your high and fortified walls, in which you trust, come down throughout all your land,

And they shall besiege you at all your gates throughout all the land which the Lord your God has given you.

Because of the suffering that your enemy will inflict on you during the siege, you shall eat the fruit of your own body, the flesh of your sons and daughters whom the Lord your God has given you, in the desperate straits in which your enemy shall distress you.

The sensitive and very refined man among you will be hostile; toward his brother, toward the wife of his bosom, and toward the rest of his children whom he leaves behind.

So that he will not give any of them the flesh of his children whom he will eat because he has nothing left in the siege and desperate straits in which your enemy shall distress you at all your gates.

The tender and delicate woman among you, who would not venture to set the sole of her foot on the ground because of her delicateness and sensitivity, will refuse to the husband of her bosom, and to her son and her daughter, her placenta which comes out from between her feet and her children whom she bears,

For she shall eat them secretly for lack of everything in the siege and desperate straits in which your enemy shall distress you at all your gates.

In Modern Language

Suddenly, swiftly, out of nowhere, selfish people will swoop on you. These people will not understand you, and you will not understand them, not just in terms of speech but also in lifestyle, psychology and morality. You will become frustrated because you 'can't get through to them' or 'can't make them understand', and they will resist every effort you make to break through the 'walls' of their resistance. This inability to communicate will lead to isolation and selfishness, as people seek to satisfy their own needs while ignoring the needs of others.

They will have no respect for the wisdom and frailty of age, and they will have no compassion or patience with young children.

They will take everything you have; they will eat you out of house and home.

They will take the best of the fruit of your labour and spend it on their own pleasures. They will take everything you have and leave you with nothing, or worse; they will leave you in debt.

They will attack your possessions and destroy the things you have carefully looked after. They will find everything you own, even those things you thought were well hidden and will destroy them.

Normally loving men and women will become bitter and turn away from each other and from their children. They will become unwilling to share anything they have with the members of their family.

Brothers will turn against brothers, sisters against sisters. Fathers will cease supporting their children and begin living off them instead. Mothers will cease nurturing their young and start using their young to gain nurture.

Trust will not exist either between husbands and wives or between parents and children.

As time goes by, communication within the home will cease to exist, as everything will be done in secret so that no one else can 'take away' what they have.

PLAGUE - *Duet. 28:58-61*

If you do not carefully follow all the words of this Law, which are written in this book and do not revere this glorious and awesome name–the Lord your God–the Lord will send fearful plagues on you and your descendants, harsh and prolonged disasters, and severe and lingering illnesses. He will bring upon you all the diseases of Egypt that you dreaded, and they will cling to you. The Lord will also bring upon you every kind of sickness and disaster not recorded in this Book of the Law until you are destroyed.

The curse of plague is self-evident and easy to understand. All sickness, disease, illness, infirmity, deformity and genetic or hereditary disorder is a direct result of this curse of God on those who do not revere his glorious and awesome name, and on their children, and their children's children down to four generations.

The Lord will plague you with diseases until he has destroyed you from the land you are entering to possess.

The Lord will strike you with wasting disease, with fever and inflammation, with scorching heat and drought, with blight and mildew, which will plague you until you perish.

The Lord will afflict you with the boils of Egypt and with tumours, festering sores and the itch from which you cannot be cured.

The Lord will afflict you with madness, blindness and confusion of mind.

Plagues are not limited to the physical bodies of people but can also include things like drought, mildew and scorching heat. Unlike earthquakes and volcanic eruptions, which produce sudden disasters, plagues start small and do more damage over time. They also result in symptoms of sickness; scorching heat, for example, affects the physical well-being of a person and can lead to heatstroke, which has symptoms of illness such as nausea, skin blistering and confusion of mind.

Who Brings These Plagues?

The question has to be asked, 'Who will afflict people with these things, Satan?' Many people believe Satan is behind all sickness and disease, but apparently, that is not correct, for, in the Law of Moses, it is written very clearly over and over again that the Lord, and author of curses, will do the afflicting. Plague is the outworking of his righteous judgment for sin. This is not my word; this is the word of God.

Is this misunderstanding why so many in the churches can't get healed, because they have been falsely taught that Satan brings all sickness? It is obvious from these Scriptures that these curses are the result of sin. From the above verse, we see that all forms of disease, not just physical but spiritual and psychological as well, are a result of this curse of God (tribulation) on mankind. Further, it is easy to see that this curse is in effect now and has been in effect for a long, long time, for it is still being worked out in various ways, not just in the lives of individuals but in nations as well.

As the end of days draws near, the full range of physical, spiritual and psychological disorders will increase to the point where the only people free from these diseases will be those who are forgiven and healed by faith in the Name of Jesus Christ and so saved from the curse of God for sin.

SWORD - *Duet.28:62-68*

You who were as numerous as the stars in the sky will be left but few in number because you did not obey the Lord your God. Just as it pleased the Lord to make you prosper and increase in number, so it will please him to ruin and destroy you. <u>You will be uprooted from the land you are entering in to possess. The Lord will scatter you among the nations, from one end of the Earth to the other.</u> (Deut.28:62-64)

The curse of the sword is evidenced by the shattering and scattering of continents, kingdoms, nations, peoples, families, businesses, tribes, communities, reputations and influence so that those who were once large in number are dramatically reduced in size and become fractured, fragmented and isolated from each other, thoroughly ruined, and forced to move on to 'greener' pastures.

The scattering and fragmentation are forced by major emotional and financial upheavals, such as marriage breakup, death, war, terrorism, or by sudden disasters, such as earthquake, volcanic eruption, tsunami, flood, avalanche, fire, etc., and includes loss of life as well loss of home, city or nation. Sadly, that is only the beginning of this curse, for verses 64 to 68 show what will happen to people after their sudden upheaval.

There you will worship other gods—gods of wood and stone, which neither you nor your fathers have known.

Among those nations, you will find no repose, no resting place for the sole of your foot.

The Lord will give you an anxious mind, eyes weary with longing, and a despairing heart.

You will live in constant suspense, filled with dread, both night and day, never sure of your life. In the morning, you will say, 'If only it were evening!' And in the evening, you will say, 'If only it were morning!' because of the terror that will fill your heart and the sights that your eyes will see.

The Lord will send you back in ships to Egypt on a journey I said you should never make again.

There you will offer yourselves for sale to your enemies as male and female slaves, but no one will buy you.

In Modern Language

After surviving overwhelming trials, things will change dramatically, to the point where what is left of a family will be transported to a new nation, new town, or new community and introduced to a new set of customs.

In that place, in order to be accepted, a new way of life may require new beliefs so that faith in God is watered down or replaced by an acceptance of other gods. Worse, because of devastation, such as loss of family, homes and personal effects, faith in God may be lost entirely and replaced with worship of things like memories, possessions and survivors.

Reminders of the horror, death, destruction and scattering will consume the minds of the survivors, and fear of sudden disaster will dog their steps.

133

Day and night, their hearts will be filled with regret, remorse, sorrow and countless variations of 'if only'.

Because of their fear of sudden disaster, they will not be able to settle into their adopted home but will be restless, wanting and searching for something more, but not sure what 'more' is.

Stress, anxiety, fear, dread and a sense of constant suspense will become a normal way of living, and life will hold no peace.

After living for a long time without peace of mind, paranoia will set in, and those who are consumed with fear will imagine life would be better somewhere else, anywhere else, that making themselves slaves to their worst enemy would be better than the life of torment they are living.

So, they will take action and try to be reconciled with their enemies, only to be rejected and suffer total and complete humiliation and disgrace.

This curse affects body, spirit and soul, for we see that first, the physical is destroyed, which, in turn, impacts the spirit and then the mind.

A NEVER-ENDING STORY

These three curses are still in effect in the world, and while the world exists, they will never stop working. It doesn't take a genius to see that as populations increase, so does sin. The trouble is, as sin increases in the world, the consequences of sin, that is, the judgment of God for sin, also increase.

These curses are the trouble or tribulation Jesus said everyone who lived in the world would face. They are the reason he died and the reason he could say; *in the world, you will have tribulation (trouble) but do not worry, for I have overcome the world.* The tribulation he was talking about is exactly what believers have been saved from, the plague, famine and sword curses of the Law of Moses.

> *These curses and the tribulation they bring are the reason the Gospel of Repentance is Good News!*

These curses of God for sin and the tribulation they bring are the reason the Gospel of Repentance is Good News. It is also the reason that the Good News of Christ at Calvary and his commission to heal the sick needs to be shared with those in trouble (tribulation).

The saddest thing about the false, modern-day 'end-time' teachings is that those who believe tribulation is reserved for the future can no longer share the power and authority of the Gospel of Repentance with those currently experiencing tribulation. Yet, the Gospel is their salvation!

Overwhelmed by love!

13

THREE CURSES OF CALVARY

Do not think that I have come to abolish the Law or the Prophets; I have not come to abolish them but to fulfil them. (Matt.5:17)

The Gospel is Good News because Jesus overcame the curses of the Law of Moses by taking the punishment for the breaking of the Law onto himself. As we go through curses again, you will recognise them in everything that happened to Christ at Calvary.

The death of Christ fulfilled everything the Law required, for his temptations in the wilderness and his suffering at Calvary were condensed to reflect the famine, plague and sword curses of the Law, introduced to the world through the sin of Adam and Eve.

When we put the Scriptures together, we see that the three temptations of Adam and Eve, the three judgments of the Law of Moses, the three temptations of Christ in the wilderness, the three sufferings of Christ at Calvary, and the three end-time judgments of Revelation, all reflect each other and fit together perfectly, like the pieces of a puzzle.

FAMINE – *Deut. 28:47-48*

Famine is reflected in hunger and is a direct result of not serving the Lord joyfully during times of prosperity, for God promised hunger, thirst, nakedness, and poverty would be the result of not serving him joyfully in times of plenty. *The lust of the eyes (1Jn.2:16)* is easy to see in this curse.

> *Remember how the Lord your God led you all the way in the desert... He humbled you, causing you to hunger and then fed you with manna... to teach you that man does not live on bread alone, but on every word that comes from the mouth of the Lord. (Deut.8:3)*

Does this sound familiar? God led the Israelites into the wilderness so they could learn that man does not live by bread alone, and here we have Jesus going into the wilderness to learn the same lesson. The first temptation of Christ in the wilderness was put to him because of hunger. Jesus' response is famous. He quoted the above verse of Scripture; *Man does not live by bread alone, but on every word that comes from the mouth of the Lord.*

Was Satan tempting Christ with bread for bread's sake, or was something else going on? From Christ's response to Satan, we learn that the curse of famine is not about the bread itself but about acknowledging the provider of the bread.

This was the same temptation Satan had previously used on Adam and Eve. They lived daily in great prosperity and rulership, with God, over the entire Earth, yet despite having everything, Satan focused their eyes on the one thing they couldn't have, something which was *good for food and pleasing to the eye,* and we all know what happened.

In forgetting the vastness of their provision from God and yearning for the one thing God said they couldn't have, they personally lost everything and brought the curse of famine down onto the heads of all mankind.

Christ was presented with the same *lust of the eyes* temptation but was not deceived. If Christ had chosen what was *good for food and pleasing to the eye,* he would, ironically, have come under the curse of famine as Adam did, but Christ, the second Adam, didn't fail!

This temptation of Christ shows that the curse of famine is not about bread or fruit but about acknowledging the Lordship of God and being thankful for his chosen provision.

PLAGUE – *Deut.28:58-59*

Plague is reflected in sickness and is a direct result of not revering the name of God, which includes the reputation that name commands. God promised that fearful plagues, harsh and prolonged disasters, and severe and lingering illnesses would affect families who did not honour his holy name. *The lust of the flesh* (1Jn.2:16) is easy to see in this curse.

> *Fear the Lord your God, serve him only and take oaths in his Name... Do not test the Lord your God as you did at Massah. (Deut.6:13-18)*

> *You made the Lord angry at Massah... I lay prostrate before the Lord these forty days and forty nights because the Lord had said he would destroy you. (Deut.9:22-25)*

At Massah, God became angry with his people when their actions showed they didn't trust him enough to believe his word and so obey his commands. This action of making God angry was called *putting God to the test.*

When the Israelites put God to the test, God became so angry with his people he wanted to destroy the whole nation. Moses knew the people had gone too far, and so he prostrated himself and prayed for forty days and forty nights that God's people would not be destroyed, and here in a second wilderness, we see Jesus doing the same thing for exactly the same reason.

In the wilderness, Satan tempted Christ to enter into the pride of personal ambition by asking him to prove he was the Son of God by throwing himself off the top of the temple without harm. Thankfully, Jesus wasn't fooled! He was not in the world to promote himself or his own reputation, and so he responded, *do not put the Lord your God to the test*.

When Satan previously used the *lust of the flesh* temptation on Adam and Eve, by saying, *God knows if you eat this fruit, your eyes will be open, and you will be like God, knowing good and evil,* they both succumbed and entered into the sin of personal ambition, choosing to serve themselves, rather than God. This sin affected Eve immediately through childbirth and committed all future generations to pain and suffering, which gradually grew until sickness and disease became commonplace. Christ, the second Adam, didn't fail!

If Jesus had given in to this temptation, he would have entered into the curse of plague and would not have been able to stop the effects of this curse on anyone. However, because he revered the reputation of his Father's name more than his own, God elevated Christ's name to a position higher than his own; so that now, in his glorious name, we are freed from the effects of all disease.

> *For those who revere my name, the sun of righteousness will rise with healing in its wings. (Malachi 4:2)*

SWORD – *Deut. 28:64*

Sword is reflected in sudden disaster and is a direct result of being uprooted from your home and reduced in number, for God promised that scattering, ruin and destruction would be the result of not loving God enough to worship him. *The pride of life* (1Jn.2:16) is easy to see in this curse.

This temptation of Christ was about worship. Satan took Christ to an extremely high position, showed him the splendour of the kingdoms of the world and offered them all to him if he would just worship him rather than God.

> *Jesus said to him, 'Away from me, Satan! For it is written, "Worship the Lord your God, and serve him only". Then the devil left him, and angels came and attended him.* (Matt.4:10-11)

This temptation was a very attractive offer, the same offer Satan presented to Adam and Eve in the Garden of Eden, the concept that they would not have to die. *Did God say you would die? Surely you won't die!*

Jesus came to the world to save everyone from the destruction and devastation of sin. Saving the world God's way would mean Jesus would, like Adam and Eve, suffer personal shame, pain, humiliation, separation from God and death, yet here was Satan appealing to *The pride of life,* offering a simple and effective, easy way out. Jesus would not have to die! He could save all the people of the world without having to go through any personal pain or suffering; all he had to do was switch his worship of God to worship of Satan.

If Christ had entered into idolatry to save his own life, he would have come under the curse of the sword and died anyway. Christ was not fooled! Adam failed this test, but Christ, the second Adam, didn't fail!

When Adam gave in to the temptation to *worship the creature rather than the creator (Rom.1:25)*, he brought death to the world, which included destruction, scattering, and broken families, and it started within his immediate family, with Cain killing Abel and then being banished from the community.

This temptation shows that the curse of death, which includes destruction, scattering, anxiety and a decrease in family numbers (sword), is directly related to choosing the easy way rather than God's way, therefore replacing worship of God with the idolatry of worship of self.

> *Death has been swallowed up in victory. Where, O death, is your victory? Where, O death, is your sting? The sting of death is sin, and the power of sin is the Law. (1 Cor.15:54-56)*

THREE CURSES OF THE CROSS

Jesus came to save the world from the sin of Adam, so three times, he stood his ground and quoted the Law of Moses until the devil left him. Our wonderful Saviour showed by his temptations in the wilderness that he had the power to overcome the sin that had destroyed mankind and was personally free from the curses of the Law; yet even though he remained sinless throughout his life, he still chose to take on the wrath of God for the sin of mankind.

It is precisely because Christ took responsibility for all the sins committed by mankind, from Adam to eternity, that he received the curse of the Law in his flesh. There was no sin in him that God could righteously punish. All the punishment he received was for other people's sins. When we look at what he endured while he was dying, we can see how each of the three curses was worked out in Christ's personal physical experience.

FAMINE - *Deut.28:47-57*

Because you did not serve the Lord your God with joy and gladness of heart, for the abundance of everything, <u>therefore you shall serve your enemies, whom the Lord will send against you in hunger, in thirst, in need of everything, and He will put a yoke of iron on your neck until He has destroyed you</u>.

Jesus knew what he was about to face; how brave he was to volunteer! The Scriptures said that under this curse, he would serve his enemies, and this is exactly what happened. In the Garden of Gethsemane, his freedom was taken from him, and from that time on, he was in the control of his enemies and forced to do their will.

The same Scriptures said he would be hungry, thirsty and in need of everything, which, again, is exactly what happened. He was given nothing to eat or drink but was finally offered vinegar when he said he was thirsty. His clothes were taken from him and divided by lots so that, at the time of his death, he was in need of everything and had nothing.

Most importantly, the Scriptures said God would put a yoke of iron on his neck until he was destroyed. The yoke, in those days, was a log tied onto the shoulders via outstretched arms and wrists; in Jesus' case, the yoke was attached with iron nails, and he remained under that iron yoke until his flesh was totally destroyed by death.

This curse foretold in detail the way Christ would suffer and die. In willingly submitting to it, Christ removed the curse of famine from God's children, his beloved Bride, and placed it onto himself. What love! *By this, we know love because he laid down his life for us. (1Jn.3:16)*

PLAGUE – *Deut. 28:58-61*

If you do not revere this glorious and awesome name, the Lord your God, the Lord will send fearful plagues on you...harsh and prolonged disasters, and severe and lingering illnesses... every kind of sickness and disaster not recorded in this Book of the Law, until you are destroyed (Deut.28:21-22). The Lord will plague you with diseases...The Lord will strike you with fever and inflammation (Deut.28:27-28). The Lord will afflict you with... festering sores and the itch, from which you cannot be cured...confusion of mind and blindness...

From the time he was arrested until the time he died, Christ was plagued with the severe and lingering effects of torture, the results of which covered his body with weeping wounds, festering sores and inflammation.

He was led *like a sheep to the slaughter* to his place of execution and was granted an assistant to help him carry his cross. This was not because the cross was heavy, though it was; rather, he was blinded by wounding and by the blood in his eyes. Contrary to popular belief, he would not have been able to see where he was going because of the crown of thorns. The purpose of the crown of thorns in torture was to pierce the eyes and render the victim blind. This was also part of the curse and the reason Jesus needed to be 'led'. Joshua refers to this ancient torture.

They will become whips for your back and thorns in your eyes until you perish from the good land, which the Lord your God has given you. (Josh.23.13)

These two elements of the curse are written again in Psalm 69:23, where it appears that the Lord is praying about those who have dealt harshly with him. *May their eyes be darkened so they cannot see and their backs be bent forever.*

Cruel to the extreme and prolonged over two long, agonising days, Christ's torture was filled with as much physical pain and suffering as any human could bear prior to death. Incredibly it was this very suffering which now brings about our healing, for *by his wounds we are healed (Isa.53:5).*

His wounds, which caused him to bleed to death, are the reason those who love him have been freed from the guilt and effects of dishonouring God's name by disobeying his word. This terrible curse covered the suffering, emptiness and death of Christ, which paid the price for the forgiveness, healing and eternal life required to save his cherished Bride.

SWORD – *Deut. 28:62-64*

You who were as numerous as the stars in the sky will be left but few in number because you did not obey the Lord your God. Just as it pleased the Lord to make you prosper and increase in number, so it will please him to ruin and destroy you...

Jesus had been popular. He had healed and fed thousands and been followed by tens of thousands, yet he was now all but alone. Around the cross, there were only a handful of people who openly loved him; three women, including his mother, and only one disciple. His brothers and sisters didn't come; Peter and the other close disciples, whom Jesus had called his friends, didn't come. The throngs didn't come. As the curse dictated, though he had been prosperous, he was left few in number and publicly ruined.

Another very visible proof of the curse of the sword was the final blow to his physical body; the stab of the sword itself (a lance is a form of sword) through his lungs to his heart, which proved to his antagonists that he was dead.

To the Jews of his day, the way Christ died would have been absolute, physical proof he was receiving the famine, plague and sword of God's righteous judgment for sin. Until God himself stepped in!

While Christ was dying, the sky was darkened for three hours, the Earth shook, and a tremendous earthquake split the curtain in the temple from top to bottom. These manifestations of the sword of God's judgment were given in such a way and with such precise timing, they showed the opposite of the curse of the sword. They revealed the authority and deity of the dying 'King of the Jews' as the holy Son of God. Astounding!

These judgments were given with such precise timing that they revealed the deity of the Christ as the holy Son of God.

What he endured over those hours, he endured deliberately. At any time, in any second, during his torture and right up to the moment of his death, he could have stopped the pain and suffering. Instead, he consciously decided to lay down his life, second by agonising second, because his love for God's children, his precious Bride, was so much greater than the physical pain of being cursed by God.

Now, because of the great love he has shown us, we who love him in return, and believe in his victory, will never have to face the pain of the curse of breaking God's Law. This is the Good News of the Gospel of Christ! The redeemed are free from the judgment of the Law!

ONE ETERNAL MESSAGE

From Adam through Moses and from Christ to the judgments of Revelation, the message of the Bible is consistent. It doesn't change! It repeats the same three-pronged message over and over again. The three temptations Adam faced were written about by Moses, experienced by Christ, and will usher in the end of the age. Adam failed! Christ succeeded! Christ is in you!

Though many soft-hearted Christians would like to believe the death and resurrection of Christ freed everyone in the world from the curse of the Law, that is simply not true. The Law of Moses is still in effect in the world, and Jesus said it would remain active until the last day of human life on this planet. Only the redeemed of Christ are free from the multiple judgments of God for the breaking of his Law. Everyone outside Christ is still under the judgment of the Law of God and subject to its curses.

The Good News we have to offer those suffering under the effects of tribulation is that breaking out of the curse of the Law and into the blessing of God is possible now because of the death and resurrection of Christ. There is no other solution except Christ! This is why the world needs the Gospel! Christ is the only antidote to judgment!

Captivated by wonder!

14

THREE CURSES OF REVELATION

Christ put an end to the Law so that there may be righteousness for everyone who believes. (Rom.10:4)

Now we come to the good part; what we can access and live in because of Calvary. The reality of living in righteousness is that there are no curses in righteousness. There is no 'right and wrong' and, therefore, no judgment. We can't 'break' righteousness the way we can break the Law of God, for righteousness is unbreakable. But what does that mean? How can anyone live in righteousness and not in Law? Is it possible to live above Law while we live on Earth? Can we live in both? What is the difference between Law and righteousness?

If Christ was willing to sacrifice his life to give his greatly loved Bride the freedom to live in righteousness rather than Law, then it stands to reason we should take a good look at what righteousness is and how to access its blessings. To do this, it may help to step back and take a broad look at the big picture. Seeing both the Law and righteousness from Heaven's point of view will bring them both into focus and help us to see how different they are from each other.

SEEING THE BIG PICTURE

The first significant difference we notice between the Law and righteousness is that the Law of God is visible, temporary and confined to this world, while righteousness is invisible, eternal and is the mesh that holds the entire invisible Kingdom of God in place:

- ♥ The Law of Moses can be seen and touched and has a beginning and an end, but

- ♥ Righteousness can't be seen or touched, has no beginning or end, and so will continue forever.

Like every other precious thing God has taught us about his invisible Kingdom, righteousness is invisible; we can't see it or any of its rules. What we *can* see is the Law of Moses, which was written by the hand of God in stone. The Law is temporary! Righteousness is not!

More than any other reason for its existence, the Law of Moses was given to mankind as a teacher to help us understand the power and authority of righteousness. There is no way our human brains could fathom any understanding of the invisible authority of righteousness without first seeing the worldly authority of the Law. Through the Law, we can now have a confident understanding of what righteousness is and why God requires us to be righteous. Simply put, the Law is an earthly parable that points to the greater reality of the way of the Kingdom, which is called righteousness.

JUST LIKE A CHRISTMAS TREE

A perfect analogy is a Christmas Tree. Just imagine the world itself is a round bauble hanging on a branch of a Christmas tree. Now imagine that the Law is also a sparkling ornament hanging on a different branch.

When we stand back, we can easily see that the whole tree is decorated with the things of this world. Up to the left, there is a spiral of time. Down to the right, there is an icicle of sin. Slightly off-centre is a fragile teardrop of flesh. Close to the top is a bell of judgment, and various eggs of human history are spaced precisely in the gaps. Imagine also that beneath the tree are packages in various colours, filled with all the temporary rewards of this world. What a pretty picture! The problem is it doesn't last.

What a pretty picture!

The problem is it doesn't last!

The world, the Law, sin, judgment, human history, and time are all temporal; we see them only for a moment, and then they are gone. They are like the baubles on a Christmas tree; they only shine for a time. The only reason for their existence is to remind us of a greater eternal truth. Therefore, the best way to keep the Law in focus is to remember that, like this world and everything in it, which has been created to reveal the invisible nature of God, the Law has also been created as a parable to reveal the invisible nature of righteousness.

Though righteousness is shown to us through the Law, righteousness is completely different to Law. It was designed to soar above, totally eclipse, and at the same time, automatically fulfil the Law of God. When we put the Law in its correct place, dangling for a time from one single branch of God's will, there is no more confusion; everything becomes crystal clear.

The freedom we have in Christ is that we no longer see 'the Law' as the great and mighty overlord it used to be; rather, we see the keeping of the Law as a necessary part of God's continuing lesson on righteousness.

LIVING IN LIBERTY

When we understand the enormous authority of righteousness, our focus is no longer on obeying the Law but on living to a higher standard than the Law can require. For example, the Law may command we not kill, but righteousness compels us to refrain from every sentiment which may lead to the desire to kill. This means that when we live above the greed, envy, malice, jealousy, anger, hatred and rage of man, we live so far above the desire to kill we actually have to step down from multiple positions of righteousness in order to break the Law which forbids killing. Living in righteousness makes breaking the Law a very difficult thing to do. Not impossible! Just difficult!

This is the freedom, or liberty, which Christ won for his redeemed. His victory has given us the ability to live so far above the Law that keeping it is just a side effect of a more powerful Kingdom lifestyle.

KNOWING GOD IS RIGHTEOUSNESS

Knowing God and what *he* would do in any given circumstance is what righteousness is all about. We have heard it said that when we live in righteousness, we automatically fulfil the requirements of the Law, so we have to ask, what is the number one requirement of the Law? It is this; that we show God we love and trust him. That is the whole purpose of the Law and why the Law was written.

Righteousness fulfils the requirements of the Law before any Law is even obeyed because the Law is only there to provide physical proof of our invisible love and trust. When love and trust already exist, proof of our love and trust flows through everything we do. In other words, we no longer live by Law but by knowledge of the nature of God.

Conversely, when love and trust of God do not exist, the Law is automatically broken because the purpose of the Law is to show we love and trust God. The word of God is again shown to be one hundred per cent true; *without faith, it is impossible to please God (Heb.11:6).*

CHRIST PUTS IT ALL TOGETHER

The clever amalgamation of the Law of Moses with the righteousness of Christ is stunningly brilliant and no more clearly explained than in the Book of Revelation. The Law, with all its curses, still applies to the world, for it is still the judgment of God for sin, but now we see, in Revelation, that the application of the judgment of the Law has changed to include the higher effect of righteousness on believers, as a direct result of the death and resurrection of the Lamb of God.

The three judgments of Revelation are spectacular in that they detail how God will now punish Satan and mankind, not only for the rejection of his Law but for the rejection of his Son and his powerful Spirit as well. They beautifully and wonderfully show how God, his Son, and his Spirit all work together as one. Furthermore, they reveal that, as his eternal Bride, his redeemed are, for the first time in the history of Heaven itself, partners with Christ and the Spirit of God in bringing these judgments to completion.

In other words, the Law of Moses hasn't changed, and mankind is still judged by the Law as it was written all those centuries ago. However, because of the death and resurrection of Christ, the application of the Law has changed. Revelation is the most distinctly individual book of the Bible because it was not possible for God to reveal how this would work until after the death and resurrection of Christ and the Spirit of God was sent to dwell within mankind at Pentecost.

The way God now judges the Bride of Christ according to righteousness, rather than according to the Law of Moses, is expressed by God in one single verse;

They overcame him by the Blood of the Lamb,
the word of their testimony and by loving Christ
more than their own lives. (Rev.12:11)

Though Satan may tempt us to break the Law of God, so we will forfeit our righteous position and be judged as lawbreakers, we actually overcome all judgment by repentance, testimony and showing our Saviour we love him. This simple and effective key is not only the source of our protection from judgment, but it also elevates us to the position of working alongside the one bringing the judgment. When all the hype is taken from the interpretations of the warnings of Revelation, we are able to see that God's ways are not only righteous, they are absolutely perfect!

SEVEN SEALS

The judgment of *The Seven Seals* is the judgment of the Blood of the Lamb. It is the Lamb of God who opens *The Seven Seals* of Judgment, and he could only open them because he was found worthy because of Calvary.

We overcome by the Blood of the Lamb because, through the Blood of Christ, we are 'sealed' by the Spirit of God with the 'mark' of salvation. *When you believed, you were marked in him with a seal, the promised Holy Spirit (Eph.1:13).* This seal, or mark, is not only our protection but our absolute and sure guarantee of Salvation, for the Blood of Christ first overcomes our sin, and then reconciles us with God, allowing us to enter into his presence. Once we are reconciled with God through repentance, we are 'marked' by the Spirit, as sheep of the Shepherd, and 'sealed' for protection from judgment.

The alternative is very sad. Those who do not honour God by accepting the sacrifice of his Son cannot enter into the presence of God because of their sin. Therefore they do not receive God's 'mark' of protection but continue to carry the mark of sin, which puts them in the camp of the goats. In that place, there is no escape from the wrath of God poured out through the judgment of *The Seven Seals.*

Tribulation is the outworking of the righteous judgment of God for sin, and the Great Tribulation, described in Revelation, begins when the Lamb opens *The Seven Seals.* When Christ opens *The Seven Seals,* the judgments read like an eternal 'who's who' of the sheep of the Shepherd, 'marked' for salvation, and of the scapegoats of Satan, 'marked' for destruction. It is a comprehensive list, and the seven individual seals reveal the following:

1. The First Horseman; The crowned Christ himself, who sets out to *place all the enemies of God under his feet.*

2. The Second Horseman; The Sword of Christ himself, who said, *I have not come to bring peace, but a sword.*

3. The Third Horseman; He who will bless and curse, Christ himself, who said, *Do not harm the oil or wine.*

4. The Fourth Horseman; The one in charge of life and death, Christ himself, who said, *I hold the keys of death and Hell.*

5. White Robes of Righteousness; Given to both the living and dead who endured persecution during tribulation.

6. Judgment falling on the unrighteous; just prior to the collecting of the full number of 'sealed' righteous.

7. Preceded by Silence in Heaven; *The Seventh Seal* opens, like a flower, to reveal *The Seven Trumpets* and *The Seven Golden Bowls* of God's final judgment.

The holy judgment revealed in *The Seven Seals* shows that our wonderful Christ is in complete control of everything in judgment, including death and Hell. It shows that his Bride lives on the Earth during judgment, and it also confirms that while she is covered by the Blood of the Lamb she is protected from the automatic and unstoppable outworking of the curses of the Law of God for sin. The judgment of *The Seven Seals* reveals the righteous as 'marked' by the Blood of Christ for protection from the judgment of the Law of Moses.

> *The judgment of the Seven Seals reveals those 'marked' by the Blood of the Lamb for protection!*

Sadly, it also shows that, out of hatred for Christ, some of Christ's loved ones will be slaughtered by Satan and his agents. This action is not the judgment of God; it is simply pure evil at work. This is why the four loyal horsemen of Christ ride out to bring sure and certain judgment against all evil and why Satan and his followers are judged so harshly.

SEVEN TRUMPETS

The judgment of *The Seven Trumpets* is the judgment of the Spirit of God. It's all about testimony, for it is the Spirit who works through the redeemed to produce testimony to the Salvation Christ won at Calvary.

We overcome by the word of our testimony because the judgment of *The Seven Trumpets* is the judgment of our testimony to Christ. In Rev.1:10, the Apostle John tells us that the voice of God sounds like a trumpet; *I heard a loud voice, like the sound of a trumpet, speaking behind me.* Later we see that all the plague, famine, and sword judgments of the Law come from the temple, which in Revelation is called the *Tabernacle of Testimony.*

After this, I looked, and I saw in Heaven the temple, that is, the Tabernacle of Testimony, and it was opened! (KJV Rev.15:5)

The Spirit of God does the work of Christ through us and then trumpets our testimonies of Christ's achievements across the Heavens. We overcome by the word of our testimony simply because the Spirit of God records our testimonies to be used during judgment.

This is how we rule and reign with Christ and how we share his throne. We don't do the actual judging; we merely provide testimony to the work of Christ and trust the Spirit of God to use it to glorify him. When the righteous judgments of *The Seven Trumpets* are poured out by angels onto the Earth, what we see is the effect of famine, plague and sword:

1. Hail and fire, mixed with blood, burns one-third of the trees and all the green grass.

2. A volcanic eruption turns the sea to blood and destroys a third of the ships and a third of all sea creatures.

3. Fire-filled rocks from the sky hit the Earth and poison one-third of the rivers and springs. Many people die.

4. A third of the sun, the moon and the stars are darkened, causing daylight hours to be shortened.

5. Smoke covers the Earth. Human locusts arise who infect those not 'sealed' with a sickness worse than death.

6. The Euphrates River area sees the death of one-third of mankind, and the two witnesses arise.

7. The beasts and the great harlot are recognised, the true Gospel is revealed, and those who reject Christ are harvested from the Earth.

Though it is easy to see famine, plague and sword at work in this judgment, the question we all need to ask is, 'Have we seen any of these things happening on the Earth?

- *Hail and fire mixed with blood* sounds a lot like war, and will *burn one-third of the trees and green grass*, so has this already happened? Are there any areas of the Earth that have not been burned at one time or another?

- *Massive volcanic activity will kill a third of the creatures of the sea and dim the sunlight.* This has happened many times in part but has not yet been total.

- *Flaming rocks will poison one-third of the rivers.* Chemical fallout from missiles, acid rain and runoff from factories and farms have been poisoning many rivers for a long time, so has this already happened?

- *'Smoke' will produce sickness that will affect one-third of mankind.* Chemical poisoning through various smoke substances like car emissions, cigarettes, and depleted uranium has already affected one-third of the Earth, so is this old news?

- Has *death in the Euphrates area* reached one-third of mankind yet? How many wars do we count?

Not one of these things is strange or unbelievable. Alongside modern-day disasters, only one could be termed cataclysmic, and that would be the darkening of a third of the sun, moon and stars and the shortening of daylight hours.

Then there are the two witnesses, who are also called two olive branches and lampstands. Who are they? Do they represent two people, or do they represent God's two faithful olive branches, Messianic Jews and Spirit-filled believers? Both of these groups arose in Jerusalem and were martyred there before spreading out from there around the world.

The last judgment of *The Seven Trumpets* includes the preaching of the true Gospel. What is the true Gospel? The Gospel of Repentance is the only true Gospel! This Gospel and the Testimony of Christ have been preached for over 2000 years, so this has definitely been fulfilled.

The judgments of The Seven Seals and The Seven Trumpets are almost completed!

Also, as part of the last judgment of *The Seven Trumpets*, Satan is exposed, along with his two beasts, his harlot and all the tactics they could possibly use in spiritual warfare against the Bride of Christ. Has this already happened? Yes! It has! The Book of Revelation is the proof! The Book of Revelation is the only book in the Bible that explains who Satan is and displays his tactics. Revelation was written nearly 2000 years ago and could only be written because the deceit of Satan was exposed in the victory of Christ at Calvary. So has this part of God's judgment been completed? Yes! Absolutely!

If we recognise that some aspects of the judgments of *The Seven Seals* and of the judgment of *The Seven Trumpets* may already be fulfilled, then surely it is time to realise that the rest of the judgment, the completion of the judgment of *The Seven Golden Bowls*, is close at hand.

SEVEN GOLDEN BOWLS

The judgment of *The Seven Golden Bowls* is the judgment of the Bride of Christ. That sounds shocking, but we shouldn't be shocked. Christ loves his Bride and has promised we will rule and reign with him, and now we see the fulfilment of that promise in exquisite detail, for this last judgment comes through the prayers of Christ's beloved.

The first judgment comes through the Blood of the Lamb; the second comes through the testimony of his achievements, and the third comes through our prayers; yet, though these three things are different from each other, we can understand how they can all happen together. Therefore, we can also understand how the three judgments of Revelation, though distinct from each other and written separately for clarity, can all happen simultaneously.

What this means, in reality, is that if we can see that the majority of the other two judgments are already complete, then we know this judgment also is almost complete.

So how do we know the judgment of *The Seven Golden Bowls* involves the prayers of the Bride of Christ? Once again, the answer is in Revelation, which teaches us that the heartfelt prayers of the saints are recorded and stored by God in golden bowls.

> *They were holding golden bowls full of incense, which are the prayers of the saints...then the angel took the censer, filled it with fire from the altar and hurled it onto the Earth. (Rev.8:3-5)*

When the angel takes fire from the altar of God and adds it to the bowl of prayer in his hands, it becomes one of *The Seven Golden Bowls* of God's wrath, which is hurled onto the Earth to begin the three judgments which commence at the opening of *The Seventh Seal*. Later we are told there is a total of seven of these golden bowls, which are hurled onto the Earth to finalise the righteous judgment of God.

> *Then I heard a loud voice...saying to the seven angels, 'Go pour out the seven bowls of God's wrath on the Earth'. (Rev.16:1)*

This is not new doctrine. This is old doctrine. It is the reason we are encouraged to bless our enemies, *for in doing this, you will heap burning coals on his head (Rom.12.20)*. That is exactly what is being described here. The prayers of the saints, when mixed with fire from God, become the burning coals of God's wrath poured out onto the heads of those who reject Christ. We don't do any judging, all we do is bless, and the resultant judging is done by Christ and his Spirit. Amazing! Christ has chosen not to complete his final judgments of the world without the heartfelt prayers of his loving Bride. What an enormous privilege!

> *Blessing our enemies has always brought 'burning coals' down on their heads.*

When these holy bowls of judgment are thrown down to the Earth by God's obedient angels, they are hurled onto:

1. The land, causing ugly, festering sores on the people who had received the mark of the beast.

2. The sea, until it turns red, and everything (not just a third) in the sea dies.

3. The rivers and springs, which turn to blood.

4. The sun, which scorches people with heat, and they curse God for the plagues but refuse to repent.

5. The first and second beast, and the woman who rides the beast, who are all plunged into darkness.

6. The Euphrates River area, which dries up in preparation for the battle of Armageddon (a battle which never actually happens according to Rev.20:9!)

7. The air, which is filled with hail mixed with fire. Then severe earthquakes bring about the end of the world.

The judgment of the *Seven Golden Bowls* shows the depth of Christ's love for his Bride. He becomes most vehement in his support of his beloved. The Blood of Christ begins the judgments; his testimony increases them, but it is the prayers of Christ's faithful Bride which bring about the final apocalypse! This is a true and mysterious wonder! How awesome to know our prayers are so vital and necessary to our loving God that he stores them in Golden Bowls and uses them to fill his temple with a pleasant aroma. How surprising that he then takes our prayers and converts them, by his Spirit, into the final cataclysmic judgments at the end of time.

This is not our work. We don't bring this judgment or even point the finger. This is the result of God, Christ and the Spirit working together, but here we see they choose to include the Bride as well, elevating our humble prayers to a position of awe-inspiring prominence.

This is what Christ meant when he said his saints would do 'greater' things, in his name, than he has done. It again shows how we are destined to 'rule and reign' with Christ and is a tiny glimpse into how we will judge the angels. How wonderful to be loved by our Saviour!

SPATTERED WITH JEWELS

These incredible judgments, harsh to the extreme for the enemies of God, glorious to witness for those protected by Christ's love, are nevertheless just the background used to showcase the spectacular jewels of Christ's sparkling achievements. Scattered throughout these judgments are cameo images; multi-faceted, precision-cut gemstones, which reflect the glory of Christ, the enormity of his victory at Calvary and his crushing defeat of Satan. Furthermore, each of these wonderful images shows how Christ has protected and will continue to protect his beautiful Bride.

In the next few chapters, we will take a closer look at some of these beautiful jewels. Starting with the image of the ten-horned beast, we will go on to explore the meanings of the second beast, the woman who rides the beast, the mark of Satan, the number 666, the final battle and the glorious future Christ has planned for his righteous Bride.

Though most of these images have been totally misrepresented and regarded with horror, they are not horrible. They are the testimony of the triumphant King of kings, Jesus Christ, and each one of them was written to highlight the brilliance of God's wisdom and give him the glory he deserves, which they give him in abundance!

Surprised by simplicity!

15

THE FIRST BEAST

And I saw a beast coming out of the sea. He had ten horns and seven heads, with ten crowns on his horns and on each head a blasphemous name. The beast I saw resembled a leopard but had feet like those of a bear and a mouth like that of a lion. (Rev.13:1-9)

Who's afraid of this big, bad beast of Revelation? Not God! Not Jesus! Not the Spirit! Neither will you be when you know what his image represents. This image is simply a parable, a sparkling jewel that glorifies Christ. It not only exposes the tactics of Satan's warfare but reveals how Christ has beaten him at every turn and teaches us how to join Christ in his victory and outwit Satan's schemes every single time.

There is nothing new in this image of Satan's ten-horned beast. Every description of him has already been written for us somewhere else in Scripture. He is not frightening. He is well and truly defeated. Nevertheless, there has been a lot of fear and outrageous speculation written about this gruesome image, despite the fact that neither fear nor speculation is necessary, for the word of God is very, very clear.

WHY ARE WE SHOWN THIS BEAST?

When we read the Scriptures, it becomes abundantly clear that the description of this beast is written as a progression of previous thought, for it begins with the expression, *and I saw...* When we trace the 'and' back to its original statement (below), we find the reason for the beast's existence.

> *The dragon went off to make war...on those who keep the Commandments of God and bear testimony to Jesus. And the dragon stood on the shore of the sea. And I saw a beast rising...* (Rev.12:17-13:1)

John was first told by God that the direction of Satan's warfare would be against *those who keep the Commandments of God and bear testimony to Jesus,* and then he was immediately given a visual picture of how that warfare would be specifically carried out. It is no mistake the beast has ten 'horns', for it is clearly stated that Satan's warfare is against those who keep the Commandments of God, and so the beast who rose out of the sea had ten horns because there are Ten Commandments for him to battle.

It is no mistake the beast has ten horns.

There are Ten Commandments!

In his warfare against those whom God loves, sin has always been Satan's greatest weapon, for it is the only thing in all creation that can separate us from God and, therefore, bring about spiritual death. *For apart from the Law, sin is dead (Rom.7:8).* Scripture tells us sin does not exist outside the Law of God, and that means there is no punishment for sin unless we break God's Law. In other words, if we don't break God's Law, we won't die.

As there is no sin outside God's Law, Satan must use what God has created, his holy Law, to lead us into sin and its consequential punishments, including death. Since he only has ten sin kingdoms, or principalities, to work with, these ten horns represent the only ten ways Satan can cause God's people to join him in his rebellion against God and so receive the ultimate punishment, from God, for unrepentant sin, which is death.

It is no mistake the beast has seven heads.

There are Seven Spirits of Christ!

It is also no mistake his ten horns rise out of seven heads, for there are seven horns of Christ revealed in Revelation. These horns give us a clue to the spiritual nature of the beast's horns, for the seven horns on the head of Christ are explained as representing the seven powerful Spirits of God sent out into the world, by Christ, after his resurrection.

> *Then I saw between the throne and the four living creatures and among the elders, a lamb standing as if it had been slaughtered, having seven horns and seven eyes, which are the seven spirits of God that have been sent out into all the Earth. (Rev.5:6)*

The ten horns of the beast rise out of seven heads full of blasphemous names because blasphemy is opposite to testimony. This shows that for believers, every temptation to sin rises out of this central core of satanic motive to see the name, or testimony, of Christ blasphemed.

The seven horns of Christ are spiritual horns. If the horns of Jesus are spiritual horns, then the horns of his copycat enemy will be spiritual as well.

OUR WEAPONS ARE SPIRITUAL

Millions of dollars have been made through books and movies which misinterpret Scripture and create fear when the purpose of these images is to destroy fear and show the awesome superiority of Christ over all the enemies of God. Christ's warfare is not against flesh and blood, and so neither is ours. His warfare has always been against principalities, rulers and powers in Heavenly places. Our warfare is our Lord's warfare; it is spiritual warfare. We overcome in exactly the same way he overcame.

> *They overcame him by the Blood of the Lamb*
> *and the word of their testimony, and they loved*
> *not their lives until death. (Rev.12:11)*

God has told us we will overcome Satan and his beasts through the Blood of the Lamb and the word of our testimony. When we understand that the beast is set up to promote sin against God and blasphemy against Christ, we can see why the only weapons we need are the Blood of the Lamb and our testimony to Christ's work.

THE WHOLE IMAGE IS A PARABLE

As the parable unfolds, we learn that the seven heads of the beast are also called mountains and kings.

> *The seven heads are also seven mountains on*
> *which the woman sits; the seven heads are also*
> *seven kings. (Rev.17:9)*

There has been a lot of speculation about where these literal mountains would be found and who the flesh and blood kings might be. That kind of speculation is useless because this picture is a parable that describes spiritual warfare.

Logically speaking, these mountains cannot refer to any mountains on this planet, for they are not set in *terra firma* but are mobile. The mountains are positioned on a lion-headed beast who is roaming around, moving and walking. Have you ever seen, anywhere on earth, mountains with legs - walking mountains, so to speak? But wait, doesn't this image sound familiar? I think it does! What Christ is describing here is a big, bad beast who has the loud mouth of a roaring lion, the swift body of a leopard and the razor-sharp claws of a bear. This beast is the roaring lion the Apostle Peter warned us about.

This big, bad beast is the roaring lion that the Apostle Peter warned us about!

Be alert and sober-minded, your enemy, the devil, roams around like a roaring lion looking for someone to devour. (1Pt.5:8)

Another clue this is not a description of things we will ever see with natural eyes is the woman who lounges on these mountains as they carry her to her final destination. The mind boggles! Where is the woman so big she would be able to sit on seven earthly mountains at the same time? She would have to be more than a giant, I think! This cannot be any more than a parable, and it is a parable, for it shows the relationship between Satan and the rebellious of the Earth, whom he has deceived and is leading to destruction.

THE LEOPARD, BEAR AND LION

The description of the beast as a leopard, lion and bear is also not a new description, and yes, it's another well-known parable. These three animals are figuratively described, throughout the Old Testament, as the disciplinary arm of God.

They describe the anger of God for the rebellion of man. This is not the anger of Satan; it is the anger of GOD for the rebellion of mankind. Just as God used the rainbow as a symbol of his unbreakable Covenant with his people, so these three animals are always used, by him, as the symbol of his discipline. In choosing to use these three animals as an analogy, God is revealing that he, himself, has given Satan permission to attack those who deliberately rebel against him.

> *I am the Lord your God. You shall acknowledge no God but me...(but) they became proud and forgot me...so, I will come upon them like a lion, like a leopard, I will lurk by the path, like a bear robbed of her cubs, I will attack and rip them open. (Hos.13:4-8)*

By placing the heads and horns of Satan on these animals, God is showing us Satan is riding on the back of his will! God has given the beast permission to attack his people, but within definite limits...*only when they become proud and forget me.* This is not a new understanding. It is well known that the *roaring lion* has permission from God to attack those who deliberately choose to revel in sin.

Just because God has given the ten-horned beast permission to attack those who rebel against Christ does not at all mean we are vulnerable to Satan's attack. Those who accidentally fall into sin while trying to overcome the old nature cannot be touched by the roaring lion because the grace of God protects us while we are trying to overcome. The confidence we have been given by Christ, who gave us this image, is that this ugly beast can only attack those who choose to turn their backs on repentance and the grace which comes with it and accept sin as a normal lifestyle.

CHRIST GAVE US THIS IMAGE

Far from being scary, this holy description of the ten-horned beast shows us Satan is way out of his depth. He is entirely controlled by the iron will of God, who has stated he can only attack those who become proud and forget him. He is bound in heavy chains by the Blood and testimony of Christ and can't touch anyone or anything without God's permission. The only things he is allowed to attack are the *Commandments of God and the Testimony of Jesus.* He has no authority in warfare to attack anything else. Though in recent years, his extremely limited power has been blown way out of proportion, Satan is only one of God's angels, and the limited intelligence of a mere angel can never possibly compete with the superior intellect of the creator of all existence.

> *The limited intelligence of a mere angel can never compete with the superior intellect of the creator of all existence!*

This encouraging image is placed by Christ in the middle of the three judgments to remind us and all of Heaven of his victory over Satan and how simple it is, because of Calvary, to stand with him and overcome the temptations of this beast and so remain free from judgment. The sure confidence we gain in looking at this precious jewel is the knowledge that, while ever we uphold the victory of Christ at Calvary, God's judgment won't come near us! This simple truth, and a little bit more, also applies to the second beast.

Armed and equipped!

16

THE SECOND BEAST

Then I saw another beast coming out of the Earth. He had two horns like a lamb, but he spoke like a dragon. He exercised all the authority of the first beast on his behalf and made the Earth and its inhabitants worship the first beast ... (Rev.13:11-18)

The second beast is no more frightening than the first, for Satan has set it up to deceive Christ's redeemed into following the first beast. It's just a little bit sneakier than the first beast! This second beast looks like a lamb, joins with the lambs, and pretends to be a lamb but *speaks like a dragon*.

It's all in the mouth! The horns on this beast have no purpose other than as a description of the way he looks. There are no crowns, no eyes, nothing to make them significant in any way. They are purely descriptive. The second beast will 'look' like a lamb. This beast is a spiritual beast and has been given the spiritual appearance of a 'lamb' so it can mix with the lambs without being easily detected. The common name for an imitation lamb is a *wolf in sheep's clothing,* and another name is *false prophet.*

LAMBS GATHER IN CHURCHES

The domain of the second beast is always in the church; it must be within the church because the domain of an imitation lamb can only be with true lambs. Doing good works and even miracles, imitation lambs or false prophets set themselves up alongside genuine lambs and become accepted as part of the flock of Christ. However, the real identity of these spiritual frauds is revealed when they open their mouths, for when they do, they *speak like a dragon.*

> *Watch out for false prophets. They come to you in sheep's clothing, but inwardly they are ferocious wolves. (Matt. 7:15-25)*

Jesus warned us to be aware that wolves, or false prophets, would disguise themselves as sheep. There would be no point in disguising themselves as sheep if they were going to remain with other wolves, for the whole point of a disguise is to deceive. False prophets pretend! It is foolish to believe false prophets do not exist within all churches or that they are somehow excluded from every gathering of believers. The exact opposite is true, for Christ warned us there would be many and that every one of us would face them.

> *Many false prophets will appear and deceive many people. (Matt.24:11) False Christs and false prophets will appear and perform great signs and miracles to deceive even the elect – if that were possible. (Matt.24:24)*

It is obvious from Christ's warning that many false prophets will be sent to deceive the elect. Christ was even more brutal in explaining this when he referred to wolves as 'vultures' who gather around a body. (Matt.24:28)

In the light of Christ's warning that many false prophets will gather with true believers in order to deceive us, it's wonderful to know he has provided us with one more vital clue to help us recognise and overcome their influence; he has told us how they will speak.

The second beast is far more subtle than the first beast. He is well-disguised and sneaky. The only way we can recognise him is by listening to what comes out of his mouth because the words of his mouth will not be the words of a holy lamb.

> *The second beast is quiet, sneaky and well disguised, but when he opens his mouth, he speaks like a dragon!*

The biggest advantage we have in this warfare against wolves in sheep's clothing is knowing there are only three ways believers can stumble, and because of that, false prophets can use only three types of deception against the Bride. Those three things are disobedience to the Commandments of God, blasphemy of the name of Christ and loving self and this world more than God and his Kingdom.

> *They overcame him by the Blood of the Lamb and the word of their testimony, and they loved not their lives until death. (Rev.12:11)*

THEY WATER DOWN OBEDIENCE

Those who *look like a lamb but speak like a dragon* make excuses for sin and misinterpret the Commandments so that they don't clash with their own social standards, annihilating the need for repentance and obliterating the opportunity for forgiveness by using phrases like, 'oh well, we must love the sinner more than we hate the sin'.

These ferocious wolves lead believers into the trap of accepting sin as a normal way of life, while they themselves appear to abound in good religious works which gain the praise of man. Though the excuses given sound good, the truth is we are supposed to overcome sin by the Blood of our obedient lamb, not accept sin as a normal way of life under the guise of loving the sinner. The whole purpose of the cross was to show that Christ overcame sin so we could now turn away from sin by the power of his Spirit, indwelling those who choose to live by faith in his great sacrifice.

THEY WATER DOWN TESTIMONY

False prophets boldly encourage self-glorifying testimonies of religious works, which avoid the testimony of Christ's work altogether. 'I used to be bad, but I changed, and now I am good – isn't that great?' 'I have been giving money to the missions for years, and now a village has water because of me!' In accepting false testimony, innocent lambs are deceived into forgetting what true testimony is all about. True testimony is always about what Christ has done.

Sadly, true testimony is hardly spoken in the Churches anymore, for these days, most people believe testimony is about them. It is not! It has never been about us! True testimony proclaims Christ's life, his death, his resurrection, his Spirit, his name, his Gospel, his Kingdom, his promises, his glory and his salvation. True testimony is never about what we have done. True testimony will always bear witness to *The Testimony* already given by Christ.

> *There is one God and one mediator between God and men, the man Christ Jesus, who gave himself as a ransom for all men, the testimony given in its proper time. (1Tim.2:5-6)*

THEY WATER DOWN FAITHFULNESS

In order to carry out his warfare successfully, this beast brings out his most powerful weapon. The greatest tool of deception this beast has in his arsenal is flattery. Through flattery, loyalty and faithfulness are undermined. This is the tool Satan used to deceive Adam and Eve in the Garden. He made out he was their friend while encouraging them to see God as not necessarily trustworthy. He sidled up to them, enveloped them with charm and pretended to be their wise and knowing counsellor, as he asked them, 'Did God really say..?' 'Oh, but surely, you won't really die..?' By manipulating the truth, he successfully deceived them into being disloyal to their loving God.

False prophets water down the need for repentance, remove the opportunity for testimony, and provoke disloyalty to Christ!

Those who *speak like a dragon* are masters at looking like a lamb, invariably appearing innocent of any wrongdoing because their flattery is done for all the right reasons, out of 'love' for the person and for the 'good' of the body. Have you ever felt flattered that you were taken into someone else's confidence? 'I just thought I'd better warn you about him.' 'Oh, did you notice the way she looked at them?'

The answer to every spiritual problem will always be found in the direct application of the Blood of the Lamb and the word of our testimony to Christ. There is never any need for gossip, malice, slander or flattery. They are the tools false prophets use to water down the need for repentance, remove the opportunity for testimony, and provoke disloyalty to Christ. Giving in to them will bring desolation to our faith.

THE GREATEST FALSE PROPHET

If there could be a king of all false prophets, it would surely be Judas. Judas is the greatest historical example of a false prophet, and his life and ways are the blueprints for all false prophets today. For example:

- ♥ Judas believed firmly in the existence of God.

- ♥ He believed the Torah (Bible) was the word of God.

- ♥ He believed in the physical existence of Jesus.

- ♥ He worked with Jesus and heard all his teaching.

- ♥ He talked with Jesus every day.

- ♥ He participated in miracles, signs and wonders.

- ♥ He ensured money was distributed to the poor.

Despite all of this, Judas was the greatest betrayer of Christ the world will ever see. Though he outwardly served Christ, he didn't love him. How important it is for true believers to learn to judge by fruit rather than by appearances.

ALL 'WOLVES' WILL DO THE SAME

There will never be a wolf who can do more damage to you than the damage done to Christ by this single disciple. His target was Christ himself, and the devastation he brought was total. While acting as a friend, Judas first misjudged Jesus' motives, then passed on his false assumptions as gossip, causing division even in Jesus' own small select group. His mistrust had been percolating for some time, and his grumbling influenced Jesus' natural brothers to lash out at him.

His target was Christ and the devastation he brought was total!

The Apostle John noticed all this and recorded it. He tells us that on one occasion, after Jesus had finished teaching his disciples about betrayal and telling them one of the twelve was a devil, a nasty scene of bickering and division erupted in their small group, which left Jesus isolated from his disciples and going to the Feast of Tabernacles alone.

Going To The Feast - *Paraphrased (Jn. 7:1-10)*

After Jesus had fed the masses with bread and walked across the water, the crowd met him and demanded more bread. When Jesus told them he himself was the *Bread of Life* which had come down from Heaven, they began to grumble, saying; *Is this not Jesus, the son of Joseph, whose father and mother we know?*

Jesus rebuked them for grumbling and explained to them why he was the *Bread of Life*. This teaching was hard for many to take, and so most of his disciples and other followers deserted him at that time, and the Pharisees became so angry with him that they wanted to kill him.

After many had left them, Jesus explained to his remaining followers that even some of them still did not believe his words and specifically stated that one of his twelve was not a believer. *Have I not chosen you, the Twelve? Yet one of you is a devil!*

Later, when the disciples and Jesus' natural brothers were alone with Jesus, a nasty argument broke out. It seems the stress of the day had taken its toll, and it was important to John these events be recorded in context. The attitudes of the ones who deserted him and the accusations of Jesus' brothers, who at that time were not believers, reflect the reasoning behind the later betrayal of Christ, by Judas, to the highest Jewish court of authority of the time, the Sanhedrin.

It seems apparent that Judas agreed with the dissenting followers and with Jesus' brothers, and also would have left the group, yet because his father Simon (possibly Simon the Zealot) was also one of the Twelve, he remained as part of the group, though grudgingly and with a heart full of discontent. (See KJVJn.6:17, Jn.13:2 and Jn.13:26, which reference Judas as *the son of Simon*.)

Jesus' brothers, because of their relationship with Jesus, were in the position of being able to express the discontent evident in the group in a way Judas was not. Jesus was their brother, and they loved him as a brother even though they did not believe in him. So, after a stressful day, Jesus' brothers brought the tension in the group to a head and spoke what Judas did not have the courage to say directly to Jesus' face; *You ought to leave here and go to Judea so that your disciples may see the miracles you do. No one who wants to become a public figure acts in secret. Since you are doing these things, show yourself to the world.* Ouch!

It is evident from these statements Jesus' brothers also misunderstood his motives. They spoke for the group as they urged him to promote himself as a public figure and use miracles to gain popularity with the people and so win his disciples back. Jesus replied; *The right time for me has not yet come; for you, any time is right. The world cannot hate you, but it hates me because I testify that what it does is evil.* Then the tension reached boiling point. Jesus' brothers and all his disciples, including the disgruntled Judas, left together to go to the Feast of Tabernacles, and Jesus stayed behind.

Grumbling had led to false accusations, which attacked loyalty to Christ and caused a physical division that left Christ alone. After his brothers and disciples had left for the Feast, Jesus also went, not publicly, but in secret.

Jesus spoke the truth, and the *wolves in sheep's clothing* in his small group caused grumbling, discontent, misjudged motives and spoken false witness against Jesus himself, which led to a division of loyalties, separation and eventual isolation. This is the blueprint for desolation and the aim of all false prophets!

> *This is the blueprint for desolation and the aim of all false prophets!*

Soon division wasn't enough for Judas. As his grumbling and discontent grew, he began to plan how to bring this teacher down a peg or two. His grumbling developed into full-blown malicious slander as he betrayed Christ to the religious authorities and then stood silently by while his 'friend' was mercilessly persecuted.

THE SAME EVERY TIME

This Judas brand of betrayal became the blueprint for all the division and persecution which would plague the early Christian church. Stephen, the first martyr, was also the victim of Christian 'disciples' who complained about him to the religious authorities and then stood silently by as he also was mercilessly stoned to death. The Apostle Paul was one of the religious who approved his death. (Acts 22:20)

The ugly persecution of the early Christian church began because Christian 'wolves' became jealous of Stephen and stirred up *good religious trouble* against him, which culminated in his death and began a bloodbath of widespread persecution against other innocent Christians (Acts 6:8-15). The second beast is always behind all persecution!

It's good to note here that though Paul was running with the wolves for a time, his subsequent salvation shows that those who are deceived by wolves can still be redeemed.

The purpose of the second beast is to *speak like a dragon,* and we know the dragon is Satan! Christ has shown us, through this jewel of revelation, that Satan intends to plant his pretend lambs alongside Christ's genuine lambs in order to lead us away from faithfulness to our God.

When flattery doesn't work, the last resort is persecution. The two major tools this beast uses are flattery and persecution. False prophets and *wolves in sheep's clothing* will always use flattery first, and if that doesn't have the desired effect, then persecution will always follow. We can see a further example of this pattern in the life of Jesus.

Jesus Rebukes Satan - Paraphrased (Mt.16:13-28)

Jesus had just asked his disciples, *Who do you say I am?* and Peter had responded that Jesus was the long-awaited Messiah of Israel. It had taken three years of constant witness for the disciples to finally 'get' who Jesus was. Jesus had been waiting for this moment because he couldn't go to the cross until his disciples knew who he was.

Now finally, because of Peter's revelation, Jesus was free to tell them that his time to die had come and to describe to them all that was awaiting him on his next visit to Jerusalem.

Peter was disturbed by Jesus' words and, without realising what he was doing, used flattery to try to turn Christ away from loyalty to the will of God. He took Jesus aside and began to rebuke him, saying; *Never, Lord! This will never happen to you!*

In response, Jesus said to Peter, *Get behind me, Satan! You are a stumbling block to me; you do not have in mind the things of God but the things of men.* After that, Jesus taught in great detail that anyone who wants to follow him must also take up his cross.

When Jesus spoke the truth, the devil used flattery to try to trip him up. *This will never happen to you!* was like saying, *You don't have to die!,* which was the same temptation Satan had offered Christ in the wilderness. Christ had already overcome this temptation, but now, here was Satan using Peter to tempt Christ again. He was way out of line, and Christ was not fooled! This is why Jesus rebuked Satan and not Peter. Satan was *speaking like a dragon* through Peter.

Flattery, through Peter, didn't deceive Jesus, so all Satan had left was persecution, which we know ultimately backfired on him, for Satan still doesn't know what hit him!

THE PATTERN DOESN'T CHANGE

The dragon, Satan himself, conjured up the first beast to encourage the world to break God's Commandments and blaspheme Christ. Then he conjured a second beast to trick loyal believers into sin and blasphemy without realising that's what they were doing. Sneaky! Sneaky! Sneaky!

The Good News is, the antidote to the second beast is exactly the same as the antidote to the first beast. We overcome by the Blood of the Lamb in repentance and forgiveness, and we overcome by the word of our testimony when we speak about Christ's victory at Calvary. In doing these two simple things, we overcome everything Satan can throw at us.

The final temptation of Satan is even more sneaky and is shown through the woman who rides the ten-horned beast! This 'mistress of Satan' is so personally deceived she actually believes she has control over this nasty beast, which she rides with great pride to her inevitable destruction.

Enlightened and ready!

17

THE SCARLET WOMAN

I saw a woman sitting on a scarlet beast...
dressed in purple and scarlet. She held a
golden cup in her hand filled with abominable
things...and was drunk with the blood of those
who bear testimony to Jesus... (Rev.17:3-6)

The famous scarlet harlot of Revelation, also known as Babylon, the Great Prostitute, has always been regarded as a bit of a mystery. Some have said she represents America, others believe she represents various nations of the Middle East, while others tell us she represents the apostate church, meaning those who say they are Christian but don't actually follow Christ. I couldn't come to terms with any of those views because, to me, they didn't make any sense.

I couldn't see how America could be responsible for all the sinful abominations done by all the other nations from the beginning of time. Neither could I see how that role could belong to any of the Christian churches, which have only been around for a less than 2000 years. Furthermore, I couldn't see how her influence could possibly be limited to the physical area of the Middle East.

As what I'd heard preached didn't make sense, I found myself looking in another direction to find the meaning of this God-given picture. Instead of speculation, I began to study the Book of Revelation, and surprise, surprise; I didn't need to go any farther afield because the description of this sin-saturated woman was right there, hidden in plain sight. With minimal study, I discovered the answers are not in world history or bizarre speculation but can be clearly seen in the Book of Revelation itself.

WHAT DOES REVELATION SAY?

In the chapter of Revelation that introduces and explains the existence of the woman who rides the beast, God has this to say about his enemies, that is, the first beast, the second beast and the great prostitute.

> *The waters you saw, where the prostitute sits, are peoples, multitudes, nations and languages...God put it into their hearts to accomplish his purpose by agreeing to give the beast their power to rule until God's words are fulfilled. (Rev.17:15-17)*

The two beasts and the scarlet woman are a team. The peoples, multitudes, nations and languages which make up the great whore, willingly agree to give over their power to the beast. They all work together but, and this is a big 'but'; they are totally under God's control at all times. They are on a leash! God himself put it into their hearts to do all they do! What they are doing is his purpose! Astounding, isn't it? These enemies of God are allowed to bark, but they are not allowed to bite! God has only given them the authority to go as far as his will and his word allow. Is this not something all Christians should be taught? I believe it is!

ALL SATAN'S TACTICS ARE EXPOSED

Revelation shows Satan can't think for himself. He can only react against the stated will of God. He can only make distorted copies of what God has created or tear down what God has created. He can't make anything new. This is why he and his assistants are 'anti' everything Christ does.

- The First Beast was set up to fight against the Ten Commandments and the name of Christ, which is why there are ten horns coming out of heads full of blasphemous names. He is totally anti-Christ!

- The Second Beast was set up to pervert the Gospel and deceive the elect with seven religious traps disguised as good works. He is totally anti-Spirit!

- The Great Prostitute, the greatest of all temptresses, was set up to seduce Christ's beloved with worldly distractions, which will keep her too busy to lovingly serve Christ. She is totally anti-Bride!

These images, provided to us by our intelligent Saviour, are precious treasures. Through them, it becomes easy to see the battle tactics of Satan and his agents. Each one reminds us of not only how Christ overcame Satan but how we, too, can easily overcome all the wiles of the devil and his agents simply by following Christ's example. Through these superb images, Christ teaches us that Satan, his beasts and his whore are 'anti' everything to do with God.

Since Satan's aim is to be the exact opposite of Christ or 'anti' Christ, it stands to reason we should look to Christ to see what Satan is fighting, and that's precisely what Revelation does for us. It takes us behind enemy lines and exposes Satan's battle tactics so Christ's beloved can confidently say; *we are not ignorant of his devices. (2Cor.2:11)*

ORIGINAL V COPYCAT

The following examples are just a few of Satan's battle tactics exposed by Christ in Revelation; there are many more. Revelation reveals over and over again that Satan cannot create. He can only copy, distort and mutilate that which God has already created. No other book of the Bible shows the nature of Satan so clearly. What you will see is a comparison between Christ, 'the original' and Satan, the 'copycat'.

- ♥ Original: Christ appears in Heaven with a glorious Name on his head and many crowns.

  Then I saw Heaven open, and there was a white horse. Its rider is called Faithful and True, and with justice, he judges and makes war...he wears many crowns on his head...His name is 'The Word of God' (Rev.19:11-16).

- ♥ Copy: Satan, attempting to copy Christ, has heads filled with blasphemous names and many crowns.

  Then I saw a beast coming up out of the sea. It had ten horns and seven heads; on each of its horns there was a crown, and on each of its heads there was a name that was insulting to God (Rev.13:1).

- ♥ Original: Christ is described as a Lamb - who had appeared to be fatally wounded yet lived.

  Then I saw a Lamb standing in the centre of the throne...the Lamb appeared to have been fatally wounded (Rev.5:6).

- ♥ Copy: Satan's second beast looks like a Lamb and insists all people worship the first beast, who was fatally wounded yet lived.

Then I saw another beast... It had two horns like a lamb's horns, and it spoke like a dragon. It forced the Earth to worship the first beast, whose wound had healed (Rev.13:11-12).

● Original: God gave his authority to Jesus.

Jesus said, 'All authority in Heaven and Earth has been given to me' (Matt.28:18).

● Copy: Satan gave his authority to the beast.

The dragon gave the beast his own power, his throne and his vast authority (Rev.13:2).

● Original: Jesus has a Bride dressed in gleaming white linen, her good deeds. She is called *Jerusalem the Holy City,* lovingly adorned with gold, jewels and pearls. Her husband delights in her and seeks to glorify her,

Come, and I will show you the Bride, the wife of the Lamb (Rev.21:9-21). He showed me Jerusalem, the Holy City, coming down out of Heaven from God and shining with the glory of God...(v19). The foundation stones of the city wall were adorned with all kinds of precious stones...(v21). The twelve gates were twelve pearls; each gate was made from a single pearl. Let us rejoice... for the time has come for the wedding of the Lamb...She has been given clean shining linen to wear (the linen is the good deeds of God's people). (Rev.19:7-9) Jerusalem...you will be called by a new name...you will be like a beautiful crown for the Lord...He will be like a husband to you... as a groom is delighted with his Bride, so your God will delight in you. (Is.62:1-5)

- Copy: Satan's 'Bride' is a whore, dressed in red and drunk on wickedness. She is called *Babylon the Great Prostitute* and the mother of all perversion. She is covered in ornaments of gold, jewels and pearls. Satan and the beast hate her and delight in destroying her.

Come, and I will show you how the famous prostitute is to be punished, that great city that is built near many rivers. (Rev.17:1-16). Then I saw a woman sitting on a red beast that had names insulting to God written all over it. The woman was dressed in purple and scarlet and covered with gold ornaments, precious stones and pearls (v3-4). On her forehead was written a name that has a secret meaning 'Great Babylon, the mother of all the prostitutes and perverts in the world' (v5). The ten horns you saw and the beast will hate the prostitute; they will take away everything she has and leave her naked; they will eat her flesh and destroy her with fire (v16).

Not only do we see how the two beasts are copycats, but we also see that the woman dressed in scarlet, who sits comfortably on the sin-saturated beast, happy to be carried about by him, is actually a drunken prostitute, hated by her master so much he exposes her shame, leaves her with nothing and ultimately destroys her completely. The hated, used, betrayed and shunned mistress of Satan is the exact opposite of the loved, cherished and protected Bride of Christ.

The hated mistress of Satan is the exact opposite of the cherished Bride of Christ!

The scarlet harlot may be the exact opposite of the Bride of Christ, but she has a job to do, and she does it very well. Satan's whore is not innocent; she is active in her rebellion against God. She is described as the *merchant of merchants*, a trader in luxuries, which she uses to buy and sell human souls. This is not the buying and selling of people, as in the slave trade; rather, this is the buying and selling of 'souls'.

> *Woe, O great city, O Babylon, city of power! In one hour, your doom has come! The merchants of the Earth will weep and mourn over her because no one buys their cargoes anymore... cargoes of the finest luxuries...and the bodies and souls of men. (Rev.18:10-13)*

HOW DOES SHE BUY AND SELL SOULS?

The 'Great Whore of Babylon' has always used luxuries to seduce the souls of mankind. Luxuries are things that are usually just a little bit out of our reach, things we can't have on a daily basis. Adam and Eve were seduced by something they couldn't have at all, let alone on a daily basis, something they could see, for it was right in front of them, but something that was well and truly out of their reach. Giving in to the *lust of the eyes (1Jn.2:16)* destroyed them. Nothing has changed!

She sells the illusion of satisfaction!

It is still through the desire for things we don't yet have, things which are just a little out of our reach, that all the sin, evil and abominations of the earth come. For it is the illusion of the satisfaction that comes with the possession of luxuries or achievements which tempts every person to sell their eternal birthright for immediate earthly gain.

'Love of money' is the root of all evil, for it is via the love of money that everyone on Earth is tempted to *worship and serve the creature rather than the creator (Rom.1:25)* and so find themselves lured away from salvation before they even know their souls have been purchased.

MONEY IS NOT THE PROBLEM

Money itself is not evil. Buying and selling necessities is essential to existence. It is not the love of money that is the problem. Rather, it is love for the pride of ownership and the power over other people that money, luxuries and position can buy that is the root of all evil. Those who belong to Satan will use money and possessions to vaunt themselves over others and subtly gain power over other people's lives. They will corrupt the innocent with bribes or use positions and possessions to control people. They will use the power of money to *buy and sell human souls.*

> *He (the beast) forced everyone, small and great, rich and poor, free and slave, to receive a mark on his right hand or forehead so that no one could buy or sell unless he had the mark, which is the name of the beast or the number of his name. (Rev.13:16-17)*

As we have seen, the whore of Satan is made up of people of all nations and languages who have chosen to use the various aspects of sin and blasphemy to their advantage. As part of Satan's team, the whore is submitted to the purpose of the beast, and it is her role to use the things of this world to buy and sell human souls. Whether small or great, rich or poor, free or slave, those people who use the 'power' of ownership to bend the will of another person to theirs are displaying the character or mark of the beast and his scarlet rider.

This vile trading of human souls can't be done by those marked with the nature of God! The buying and selling of human souls can only be done by those who are marked with the nature of Satan. In fact, those who are marked with the nature of Satan will not be able to resist the seduction of the whore. The love of luxury, desire for power and use of even small amounts of money as a tool of control will seduce everyone who is not protected by the Spirit of God.

FALSE PROPHETS BUY AND SELL SOULS

The church is not immune from false prophets, or from this evil behaviour, for even in the churches, this vile trading of souls can be seen coming from the hearts of those marked with the nature of Satan. For example, false prophets will always claim ownership of their 'sheep' and complain that others may try to 'steal' them. True prophets, however, know all sheep belong to Christ and that no one has the power to steal them out of his hand. (Jn.10:28)

Those who have the Spirit of God flowing through them will not even consider using position as a means of control!

False prophets will claim a 'degree' has given them the right to minister and preach the Gospel, while true prophets know their authority comes from Christ, not a college. False prophets will boast about 'their ministry' and what 'their ministry' has achieved, while true prophets will boast in their weaknesses, knowing that only the ministry of the Spirit can bring glory to Christ. Those who have the Spirit of God flowing through them will not even consider counting God's people as possessions or using money, awards, degrees or positions to coerce, seduce, bribe, control or 'lord' it over others.

193

LUXURIES ARE NOT THE PROBLEM

Just as Satan set up the first and second beasts to distort the works of God and Christ in order to deceive the elect, so Satan's mistress also attempts to distort the Bride's understanding of her royal position and lead her, by default, back under the control of the first beast. It is the clear aim of the Great Whore to seduce the Bride of Christ into seeking her own pleasure above Christ's so that she will become weak and fall into the trap of blasphemy and then into outright sin. Her weapon of choice is 'love of money', and she is powerfully successful because this 'love' is hidden behind the 'goodness' of the things which are used to seduce. Most things used for moral corruption are not evil in themselves; they are good, acceptable and necessary for living. However, it's the way they are used once they are attained that corrupts the owners or those who desire to own.

'Love of money' is hidden behind the 'goodness' of the things used to seduce.

It's perfectly acceptable to lead a 'flock' of people in order to bless them; it is entirely unacceptable to claim those people as possessions or trophies. It's perfectly acceptable to gain a degree in order to show what has been learned; it is totally unacceptable to use that degree to make oneself superior to the Spirit of God in others.

It has always been perfectly acceptable to share luxuries in order to bless, but totally unacceptable to use those same luxuries as a tool of control or corruption. The best example we have of exactly the same luxuries being used in two different ways, one for blessing and the other for corruption, is shown in the Old Testament. There are two women in Proverbs; one is called Wisdom, and the other is called Folly.

Wisdom And Folly - Paraphrased (Prov.9)

Wisdom builds her house with seven pillars, prepares her meat and mixes her wine. She sets her table in preparation and sends out her maidens to call from the highest point of the city; *Let all who are simple come in here.* She says to those who are not wise, *Come, eat my food and drink the wine I have mixed. Leave your simple ways, walk in the way of understanding, and you will live.*

Folly sits at the door of her house, which is also at the highest point of the city but has no pillars, and since she has no maidens, she calls out herself to those who pass by; *Let all who are simple come in here. She says to those who are not wise, Stolen water is sweet, and food eaten in secret is delicious.* But those who go into her do not know the dead are there.

Wisdom and Folly both open their homes to the simple. Both call out from the high places of the city, and both offer food and drink to their prospective guests. But while the food and drink offered by Wisdom produce life, the food and drink offered by Folly produce death. Wisdom offers food and drink in order to bless, but Folly uses food and drink as a means of seduction to corruption. This Scripture teaches that possessions and luxuries are good when they are used for blessing but clearly warns that what is good can be used as an ugly tool of seduction to bring corruption to the 'foolish'.

EVERY COIN HAS TWO SIDES

Love of money may be the root of all evil but money itself is not evil; a coin is just a piece of metal. Every coin has two sides, and every purchase can either be used to promote life or death, for each coin also has added spiritual value when it is used for either blessing or corruption.

Jesus saw rich men dropping their gifts into the temple treasury, and he also saw a poor widow dropping in two little copper coins. He said, 'I tell you that this poor widow put in more than all the others. For the others offered their gifts from what they had to spare of their riches; but she, poor as she is, gave all she had to live on'. (Lk.21:2-4)

According to Old Testament Law, the part of the tithe not used as a sacrifice for sin was given to the Levites for their provision. However, it was not given to them for their personal financial upkeep but also needed to be shared with the foreigners, orphans and widows who lived among them; that is, everyone who was not able to own their own 'portion' in Israel and so could not produce an income through their private land. (Deut.14:22-29)

This poor widow was not required by the Law to tithe at all, and in fact, as a widow, she received income from the tithe, and so it was literally a proportion of the tithe that kept her alive. There were no regular Government handouts or superannuation schemes; this widow relied solely on the tithe to keep her, and so her financial trust was firmly centred in God. Despite her lean financial circumstances, this poor widow loved God so much that she was prepared to express her love by generously giving back to God what he had given her! What faith! No wonder Jesus' heart melted when he saw what she did! Those two little copper coins may have had only limited purchasing value, but when they were used as a blessing, their spiritual value became enormous.

What faith!

No wonder Jesus' heart melted when he saw what she did!

Jesus later used the parable of *The Shrewd Manager* to show money is not a problem in itself, that it's only the corrupt use of money that is evil. Like *Wisdom and Folly*, Christ taught that, though money can be used corruptly to gain worldly acceptance, it can also be used as a blessing to gain Heavenly acceptance and favour.

The Shrewd Manager - Paraphrased (Lk.16:1-15)

Jesus told the story of a scheming and dishonest manager who was faced with the sack because he had been filling orders without collecting payment for the goods he had sold, and his boss had just asked him why he had not called the company's long-term debtors to account. When this corrupt manager realised his job was on the line and he was about to become unemployed, he decided to get smart and call in the debtors to redeem as much money as he could in the hope that he could save his job.

Even though he suspected he had already lost his job, this shrewd manager understood the power of deal-making, 'You scratch my back, and I'll scratch yours', and made deals with all the remaining debtors. By giving each of them a favourable discount, he gained a quick return for his employer, but more importantly, he gained the notice of rich and powerful men, men he could later call on if he still found himself out of work. This unscrupulous manager used the 'hidden' power of money to provide for himself a vast security base for his pending unemployment.

Jesus explained that, just as the shrewd, worldly manager had used the 'hidden' value of money to open doors for his earthly future, so God's children could equally use the 'hidden' value of money as a blessing to open doors to our eternal future and concluded by saying, *You cannot serve two masters, you cannot serve both God and money.*

197

SATAN PROMOTES HIDDEN VALUE

The Great Whore of Babylon has widely promoted the corrupt use of the hidden value of money and possessions by encouraging everyone in the world to judge everything we do and everything we own by its hidden worldly 'value'. Whether worldly value is seen through awards, recognition, scholarship, positions, fine homes, clothes, jewels or other luxuries, we are all taught from an early age to judge every worldly thing according to the hidden value which can be used by us as we live in this world.

Furthermore, we are falsely led to believe we will gain a sense of self-worth and satisfied fulfilment on the successful attainment of every earthly goal. However, when we travel down this road, we also find that once a particular goal is achieved, the dream of fulfilment disappears like a mist and a new dream is needed to produce the promised satisfaction. Time after time, we see it is 'value' that is the dream, and its promised satisfaction is no more than a vapid illusion.

All temptation to corruption comes through the vague and shifting value of the power of possession.

The mistress of Satan has been specifically set up to promote the illusion of the 'hidden' value of luxuries and achievements, and the greatest illusion she has spread across the Earth is the promise of power and fulfilment through the value of possession. This is what the 'love of money' is about; the power and control which luxuries and achievements can bring. All temptation to corruption comes through the vague and shifting value of the power of possession. But the value of possession is a complete fantasy. Value itself is an illusion!

The power of possession always promises the elusive attainment of happiness and self-worth, of unlimited freedom and total satisfaction; however, just like the fable of the pot of gold at the end of the rainbow, those who chase the pot find the rainbow keeps moving and, at the end of the day, the rainbow and its promised pot are nowhere to be found.

Everyone on Earth is born without possessions, and we all die without possessions. Spending a lifetime chasing self-fulfilment and happiness through possessions will eventually prove to be a complete waste of time. Does this mean we are not to achieve at all? Does it mean we should give up all ambition? No, it does not! Our wonderful Saviour has given us an alternative. We can choose to use the 'hidden' value of our worldly possessions and achievements righteously to store up treasure in Heaven.

We can choose to use the hidden value of possessions to store up treasure in Heaven!

Empowered and authorised!

18

COME OUT AND BE SEPARATE

*Come out of her, my people, so that you will not
share in her sins so that you will not receive
any of her plagues. (Rev.18:4)*

Ambition and achievement are not our enemies. The Apostle
Paul used everything in his experiential arsenal as tools to
assist him in promoting the Gospel (1Cor.9:19-23). His goal was
the Kingdom of God, and so he used every credential, every
achievement and every experience as just another stepping
stone of praise and glory to God.

      Achievements and riches are not evil. It's the assumed
value of achievements and riches and the power over people
that value can command, which is evil. By choosing to accept
everything we do and everything we own as a blessing from
the hand of God, we worship God. Instead of being seduced by
the value of worldly possession, worldly possession becomes
a gift we can use as a powerful expression of gratitude to God
for the life and talents he has given us. In fact, the greatest
temptation Satan can offer the Bride is now our greatest
opportunity to bless the heart of our heroic Lord.

JESUS IS OUR BEST EXAMPLE

In the wilderness, Satan tried to tempt Jesus with bread. Did Jesus refrain from eating bread for the rest of his earthly life? We know he didn't! The worldly value of the temptation was small, but the victory gained by Christ in rejecting it was enormous. *God turns everything to good,* and so we see that since the Last Supper, bread has become the universal symbol of the Body of Christ throughout the Earth. The very thing Satan used in his temptation of Christ has become one of the greatest blessings amongst God's people worldwide.

This shows us that every material thing which can be used by Satan and his mistress to tempt God's children can, in turn, be converted into great blessing for both God and mankind, which means that every goal and every achievement, no matter how small, can become a great blessing. Bread itself is very commonplace, but there is nothing commonplace about the hidden value of Communion!

POSSESSION IS UNAVOIDABLE

Just because Satan wants to use worldly possession as a temptation to evil does not at all mean that we should try to avoid worldly possessions. It is impossible to maintain life without food or drink or health or a home to live in; therefore, it is impossible to live without worldly possessions, yet Satan's mistress uses every possession to tempt us to worship and serve ourselves more than God.

Our Lord's experience in the wilderness shows us Satan will use hunger, thirst, poverty, or disease, as well as power, riches and luxury, as catalysts for temptation. Just as we cannot avoid living in the world, we cannot prevent temptations from coming. However, we can respond to all of them in the same way Christ did.

LOVING GOD MORE THAN SELF

We overcome the first two beasts by living under the Blood of the Lamb and actively upholding the testimony of Christ; however, we overcome the seductions of the mistress of Satan by loving our Saviour more than our own lives in this world. How do we do this? Again, our beloved shows us how; he has left nothing to chance.

Christ continually made his Father the centre of his attention by taking his own desires out of the picture. He did this throughout his life, up to and including the moment of his death. While Jesus was hanging on the cross, he said, *Father forgive them; they don't know what they are doing.* There were no 'me's' or 'I's' in this prayer; it was totally unselfish because Jesus' eyes were focused on God and on others, and not on himself. Christ didn't say, 'God help *me* forgive them for what they have done to *me*'. He was not looking for personal satisfaction; his dying words showed his perfect love for God and his perfect love for others.

If our focus is on loving God and sharing his love with others, we can run that marathon and win for his glory and not for our glory; we can climb that corporate ladder for his glory and not for our glory; we can use all our talents and personal ambitions unselfishly for his glory rather than for personal glory. When our goal is the Kingdom of Heaven, and we emulate the love and life of Christ, our entire lives become a *living sacrifice of worship (Rom.12:1).* The resultant blessings of living daily in worship will bring more satisfied fulfilment than the world continually promises but can never actually produce.

More fulfilment than the world promises but can never actually produce!

203

WHAT DOES GOD CALL VALUABLE?

As the agent of Satan, the whore of Babylon has done her best to deceive everyone on Earth into worshipping themselves through the pursuit of things this world calls valuable. But God has ensured that the satisfaction of true fulfilment can never be found in selfish ambition, for eternal life can only be discovered in knowing God and appreciating the things God calls valuable.

So what does God call valuable? Simply put, the most valuable things to God are the things he did not create himself! We all know God has given us everything; this Earth and all that is in it, our lives, our families, our circumstances, our provision, our health, our security, our gifts and talents, our faith and love, and even our hopes and dreams; all these things have been freely given to us by God. So what is left that he hasn't given us? What can we give him? There are several things we can give him that he has not created; our love, our praise, our gratitude, our appreciation and our thanks. These are the things God regards as highly valuable. They are his greatest treasures simply because he didn't create them.

They are his greatest treasures simply because he didn't create them!

Dad's Paddock - *(A Story Of Appreciation)*

Taking off his wide-brimmed Akubra, Kelly wiped the sweat from his brow and headed for the dappled shade of his favourite tree. The ancient ghost gum stood like a sentry on top of a slight rise, and from the shelter of its wide branches, Kelly could enjoy a panoramic view of his home and the thirty acres of paddock which surrounded it.

It was February, and the scorching heat of the Australian sun was at its peak. Kelly had spent the morning with his father mustering sheep on their 3000-acre property, and it was time for lunch. While he waited for his father to return the dogs to their kennels and reward them for a good day's work, he took a few minutes to escape the airless persistence of the suffocating heat. Stretching himself out on the rough ground and tossing his battered old hat under his head as a pillow, his eyes naturally looked upwards.

At first, he saw patches of brilliant blue sky peeping through a dark silhouette of gum leaves. Slowly, idly, his gaze wandered down through the twisted, spindly branches of the ancient tree before coming to rest on the frayed end of an old weather-worn rope, still clinging hopefully to a sturdy limb. A slow smile spread across Kelly's face as he remembered the day his father made him his first rope swing and the many happy hours the swing had given him.

The sudden relaxation was soothing, and closing his eyes, Kelly began to drowse. As pleasant childhood memories tumbled one after another through his mind, Kelly realised his happiest memories all had one thing in common, they all revolved around this gently undulating paddock - home paddock - Dad's paddock.

This was the paddock where tents were pitched or caravans sited under shady trees when the family came to stay, where Christmas party games were played, and countless hours of family cricket were interspersed with water fights to keep everyone cool. This was the paddock where Kelly gained the skill of push-bike riding, even though his father set up obstacles to make riding difficult, and where, as a reward for overcoming the obstacles, his father had presented him with his first motorbike.

His smile grew to a grin as he remembered the pride in his ten-year-old heart when his father first asked him to jump on his motorbike and help him muster a mob of sheep; that day, he was eight feet tall.

This was the paddock where he saw his first snake, caught his first possum, taught his dog to ride a skateboard, witnessed the miracle of birth and broke his arm trying to conquer the highest tree, where days were long and happy and evenings were filled with the pleasant aroma of his mother's cooking and the satisfaction of being content.

It was in this paddock that Kelly began to realise how his father thought and the process of reasoning which guided his actions, for this was the paddock where sick or injured animals came to be nursed back to health, where the condition of new stock was assessed, and problems in individual sheep noted before being moved into suitable paddocks, and where old bulls and horses were brought for their final spell.

It was in this paddock that Kelly discovered his father's kindness as he watched him spend days and nights patiently encouraging a cow whose calf had died to adopt an orphaned calf, and he remembered the quiet satisfaction on his father's face when, eventually, the two of them become inseparable.

This special paddock was the place where Kelly had learned to drive everything from billy-carts to tractors, unclog water lines, mend fences, fix broken pumps and think things through before expending any energy on action. It was in this paddock his father had quietly taught him all the skills he would need to take him through the rest of his life.

The familiar torque of the old, red trail bike hailed his father's return. Shaking himself out of his reverie, Kelly picked up his dusty hat and, ignoring the dirt, slapped it back on his head. In a few short moments, he had begun to see his father in a new light, and a wave of gratitude flooded his senses. Never again would he take his father for granted, and never again would he be able to look at this paddock as just another patch of ground.

This particular paddock held the countless stepping-stones of his life. Life, his father had gently encouraged him to embrace and enjoy. Life, he could now pass on to his own children in this paddock - home paddock - Dad's paddock.

GOD'S PADDOCK

The entire Earth belongs to our Father, and there is nowhere we can go on this Earth that God has not already been. God created us and brought us into his world. He loves every individual, and he gently encourages each of us to learn from him everything we need to know to take us through the rest of our lives. Everywhere we go, there are reminders of his presence, and everything we experience is just a stepping stone of his teaching. Every day we have the opportunity to work with him, learn from him, appreciate what he has taught us, and pass what he has taught us on to others. It is in working with him that we begin to know how he thinks and why he does the things he does, and in understanding his attitudes, we begin to appreciate his loving nature.

A word aptly spoken is like apples of gold in settings of silver. (Prov.25:11)

God cannot demand our love or gratitude, and he cannot force us to worship him, but our words of appreciation are as valuable to him as gold, silver and rare jewels simply because he did not create them. They are a gift crafted by his children for his pleasure, and therefore they are the perfect expression of our love for him.

Sincere appreciation is not something people can touch, purchase or possess, so therefore, gratitude is not regarded as valuable on Earth, but every word, thought, or prayer of appreciation is valuable to God, and its priceless value is only assessed in Heaven where it is esteemed by our loving father, and estimated, by him, to be as precious as the finest jewels and as perfect as the purest, most refined gold. When we offer him our appreciation, he not only accepts our simple, little gifts of love with a delighted smile but rewards us by treating them with honour, putting them on display in the most prominent position in his house. How wonderful to know our appreciation of his work is treasured by our Heavenly Father and regarded as more valuable than gold. Who would not want to give him the praise, appreciation, gratitude and thanks he deserves?

> *Where your treasure is, there will your heart be also!*
>
> *(Matt.6:21)*

THE BRIDE'S DOWRY

In ancient times a groom always presented the Father of the Bride with a substantial gift. It was called a dowry and consisted of gold, jewels and sometimes acts of service to the family of the Bride. Without this dowry being paid to the Father, there would be no marriage. Christ paid the price for his Bride and has given her the means to present her Father with gold and jewels beyond compare, and it is because he has paid the price and given many gifts that the marriage can now go ahead. Those who love Christ, and have come out from the empty ways of the Whore of Babylon, will have their hearts and minds set on the promise of their 'happy ever after' future with him, and everything they do, no matter how insignificant, will be dedicated to the one they love.

Unlike Christ's beautiful Bride, those whose souls have been seduced by Satan's hated mistress will have their eyes on themselves and their personal needs and wants in this world. They will have no praise for the creator of the universe, no gratitude for the sacrifice of his Son, nor any appreciation for the many spiritual gifts he has provided for the redeemed. They will enter into his presence, on judgment day, without a groom and without a dowry.

The difference between Christ's cherished and majestic Bride and Satan's empty-handed pretender is massive and exceedingly easy for all the angels of Heaven to see. A worthy Bride comes with a dowry!

No longer fooled!

19

TESTING THE SPIRITS

Dear friends, do not believe every spirit but test the spirits to see whether they are from God. (1Jn.4:1-6) Test yourselves. Do you not realise that Christ is in you – unless, of course, you fail the test? And I trust that you will discover that we have not failed the test. (2Cor.13:5-6)

Our great hero has easily overcome Satan and his two beasts on our behalf, but Satan's wicked queen is the one we have to overcome. She is the one we have to avoid. She is full of deceit, and her temptations are poison. She uses all the schemes of the two beasts in her attempts to destroy the Bride. She disguises herself, speaking through many different people in various ways, both inside and outside the church. Can we see this in play in the world today? Yes! Clearly!

The Apostle John taught us to test the spirits of the people who are influencing us to see if they are from God, and it's not hard to test the spirits of people when we know that the first beast encourages sin, the second beast attacks testimony, and the wicked queen promotes selfish ambition.

BODY – SOUL – SPIRIT

The first beast is super simple to recognise and overcome because his temptations are all about obvious sin and blasphemy. They are the temptations of the physical realm; they affect our bodies. Overcoming the first beast is simply a matter of choice. If we choose to obey God's Commandments and testify to the comprehensive work of Christ, the Holy Spirit will rush to our assistance and ensure we overcome all obstacles every time.

The second beast is a little more difficult to recognise and overcome, for this is about resisting the temptation to enter into other people's choices, that is, the flatteries or persecutions other people bring to us in an attempt to blur our spiritual boundaries. They are temptations that affect our minds and will and, therefore, our decision-making. They affect our souls! Overcoming the second beast is about overcoming other people's sins and other people's blasphemies that, if we are not careful, can trip us up and weaken our spiritual resolve before we realise we are entering into Satan's trap. To overcome, all we need to do is listen to the words being spoken, for those who speak like a dragon will always encourage the watering down of uncompromising loyalty to Christ.

We are not ignorant of Satan's devices!

The wicked queen is the most difficult of all to recognise and overcome. Her job is to wrap all the sin, blasphemy and deceptions of the two beasts into a pretty package that can be presented person to person as a reasonable, logical and sane reason to ignore obedience to Christ. This temptation is the deadliest of all as it aims at the very heart of our belief. It is set up to bring total spiritual devastation to our faith.

Her sneaky temptations are programmed to affect our spirit and, specifically, our ability to hear the Spirit of God speaking to us. All we need to do to overcome her evil devices is recognise who she is when she speaks because she too will always *speak like a dragon* encouraging, with reason and logic, the soundness of the world's point of view.

The good news is *we are not ignorant of Satan's devices (2Cor.2:11),* and the Apostle John, who told us about these beasts and the whore who rides them in his Book of Revelation, also taught his own disciples how to recognise those who *speak like a dragon,* including wolves and false prophets, in any gathering of believers.

HE DEVISED A SIMPLE TEST

John's test involves the words which come from a person's mouth, words that reveal the heart of the person speaking, the fruit of their own lips. It reflects Jesus' teaching that we will know them by their 'fruit'.

> *From the fruit of his mouth, a man's heart is filled, and with the harvest of his lips, he is satisfied. The tongue has the power of life and death, and those who love it will eat its fruit. (Prov.18:20-21)*

This test does not involve miracles, signs, wonders, numbers converted, size of churches, education, clothes, houses, cars, appearances or any other works or deeds, as none of these things is 'fruit'. All through Scripture, 'fruit' has always meant *the words of the mouth,* which reflect the things we love the most. John's test is the same test God used on Adam and Eve in the Garden of Eden, and it is as effective now as it was then.

213

God asked Adam and Eve to speak their choice, and when they did, the fruit of their lips revealed their hearts. What he found was they were more interested in their own lives, that is, in gaining knowledge of the things of this world, than in knowing him. John's test is exactly the same.

The Apostle John was a brilliant teacher. He was able to take all the teaching of the Old Testament about fruit and all the teaching of Christ about *knowing them by their fruit* and condense it into one simple 'how to do it' teaching, a teaching so simple it could be understood by a child. The problem is this truth is not practised or even taught in most churches, yet it should be taught and practised in all.

> *Dear friends, do not believe every spirit, but test the spirits to see whether they are from God... for many false prophets have gone out into the world... they are from the world and therefore speak from the viewpoint of the world, and the world listens to them. We are from God, and whoever knows God listens to us. (1Jn.4:1-6)*

False prophets and false teachers in the Body of Christ never reveal the character of God and his Kingdom through their words. They don't teach about the beauty of the nature of God, as Christ did, they can't see parables in ordinary day-to-day activities, and they never show how the nature of God can be seen in absolutely every single thing he has created on this planet. Instead, they speak of worldly things and give every spiritual truth a worldview application.

You will have heard them; instead of talking about Christ's victory and God's nature, they speak on behalf of the wicked queen and Satan's beasts as they describe how people can use the things of God for their own advantage.

For example, there are some who try to give spiritual concepts a worldly application as they describe how the principles of the Bible can be used to make money or can make the user successful in the world's eyes. Not understanding the beauty of the Kingdom of God, they turn things upside down and try to explain every spiritual thing through their own limited worldview. This kind of teaching brings confusion to those who love Christ. When false prophets try to give the spiritual concepts of Revelation a worldly application, the same thing happens; they bring confusion to the Bride of Christ.

False teaching brings confusion to those who love Christ!

No believer needs to be confused or deceived by false teachers. As the Apostle John says, This is how we recognise *the Spirit of Truth and the spirit of falsehood*. If you really want to understand the Book of Revelation, test the interpretations you hear by using John's test. Ask yourself: 'Is this interpretation revealing the nature of God and Christ, or is it promoting a worldview?' If it's promoting a worldview, it's not from God. It's the same with all teaching coming from every book and pulpit; if it is not giving glory to God and his Kingdom, it is not being given by the Spirit of God.

> *Whoever speaks on their own does so to gain personal glory, but he who seeks the glory of the one who sent him is a man of truth; there is nothing false about him. (Jn.7:18)*

Truth, according to Jesus' own words, is proven by the words of a person's mouth, and he assured us those who promote the glory of God and Christ rather than themselves or the things of this world could never be regarded as false.

215

FRUIT IS THE KEY

The fruit of the Spirit is love, joy, peace, patience, kindness, meekness, faithfulness, gentleness, and self-control. (Gal.5:22-23)

Jesus also tells us we can tell genuine Christians from false just by looking at the fruit they display, but what does that mean? There are a lot of people who are not Christian who are very, very nice, but their niceness does not display the fruit of the Spirit, or does it? How do we tell the difference between the fruit of the natural man, which is shown in appearances, and the fruit of the Spirit of God, which is shown in righteousness? This is not as easy as it may seem.

Most of the teaching on the fruit of the Spirit which I have heard revolves around the following points, not one of which describes righteousness:

- ❤ that we should show love, joy, and peace on our faces at all times, even in grief;

- ❤ that judging others by the emotions they display is judging them by their fruit;

- ❤ that our obvious business/financial/church or family success or failure is our fruit;

- ❤ that judging others by their popularity or reputation is judging them by their fruit;

- ❤ that the behaviour of children is the fruit of parental righteousness or sin;

- ❤ that the size and quality of the congregation are the minister's fruit;

- ❤ that sickness and disease are the direct results, the fruit, of the sick person's sin.

WHOSE FRUIT IS IT?

What I have learned about the fruit of God's Spirit is that it is not about people and, therefore, not about our feelings or our worldly appearances; it is not about us at all! The nine fruits of righteousness have very little to do with how we feel or how our actions or circumstances may appear to those around us, and neither are they something we can control. We can't bring any one of the righteous fruits of the Spirit into existence, and neither can we 'make them better'. These wonderful fruits do not depend on us for their existence at all. They are, as stated, the fruit of the Spirit of God. They are God's fruit! They are offered to us, already perfect, as a gift,

We can't grow these fruit. They are already fully grown and perfect. They are God's fruit!

yet sadly the teaching that comes through many pulpits about the precious fruit *of the Spirit* bears almost no resemblance to the truth about the fruit of the Spirit of God shown through the righteousness of Christ. Why is this? Why are we not told this fruit is God's fruit?

FALSE TEACHERS LIE ABOUT FRUIT

False teachers in the Body of Christ do not want anyone to be able to discern true fruit from false fruit simply because their own fruit would be found to be false. It seems a little obvious when said so bluntly, but it is nevertheless true.

False teachers live according to the ideals promoted by the wicked queen. They promote worldly values and worldly appearances and, very convincingly, teach God's people to judge by worldly standards, presenting false teaching about God's fruit in a very pretty and believable package.

They teach that the fruit of the Spirit is all about us, that we can 'grow' feelings of love and patience etc., that we should learn the discipline of self-control and should do these things with a joyful smile on our face at all times. What an insult to righteousness! Feelings that produce the appearance of mushy love, giggly joy, negotiated peace, martyr patience, doormat meekness, timid gentleness, arms-length kindness, count-to-ten self-control and dutiful faithfulness are the most common examples of what has been called 'fruit'.

These may be the fruit of the human heart, but they are not the fruit of God's mighty Spirit at all. The best way to see the fruit of righteousness at work in a person's life is to look at the life of Jesus. Do you see any of these commonly accepted attributes in the life of Christ? I can't say that I do.

He didn't gush with gooey words, laugh all day, spend his time trying to stop arguments, patiently sigh over things he couldn't change, speak in soft tones, avoid disputes, take deep cleansing breaths to control his anger and put his duty to his family above all else. That's not Jesus at all, yet that is exactly what seems to be expected of believers. The reality is that if Jesus had lived that way, he wouldn't have gone to the cross, no one would now be saved, and no one would be following him. Since these are not his fruit, we need to ask...

WHAT FRUIT DID CHRIST DISPLAY?

Jesus spent his whole life on this earth, pleasing God. The fruit he displayed was not about his own personal feelings ever; it was always about what he did and said to please his father. This is the key to understanding how these fruits are supposed to be seen in us. Christ's life motto was *not my will but yours*. If we love our Lord, we will do as he did and display the fruit he displayed in the way he displayed it.

218

This means that the fruit we reveal will show our love for God, our joy in God, our peace with God, our patience with God, our gentleness and kindness toward God, and our faith in God through a mind consciously set on God. Does this sound like Jesus? This is his fruit!

The life of Christ was filled to the brim with the fruit of God's righteousness, but this fruit made him so socially unacceptable to those who judge by human standards of acceptability they wanted to kill him.

There is a misconception amongst Christians that if we are super nice to people, they will miraculously 'see' Christ in us and turn to God for Salvation. What a hideous deception! It didn't work out that way for Jesus, and he was perfect; it didn't work out that way for his disciples either, so why would it work out that way for you and me? It must always be remembered that we cannot measure the fruit of love by man's mushy idea of love. God's love took Christ to the cross! Therefore, to understand the fruit of the Spirit the way God intends us to understand it, we must look at his fruit from Christ's perspective and not from the world's, for instance;

God's idea of love is not mushy; it took Christ to the Cross!

Love is the Fruit of Sacrifice

The love Christ taught involved laying down self and taking up sacrifice. He was not known for being a lovable person; rather, his life showed that *love your neighbour* is not about being a nice person but about sharing the good news of the Kingdom of God in word and deed, even if it means those around you will hate you or want to kill you. When Jesus gave up his need for a good personal reputation, the fruit of his sacrifice enabled his Father's love for the world to be seen.

Joy is the Fruit of Obedience

The deep abiding joy which enabled Christ to endure the cross did not manifest itself in the worldly understanding of joy, that is, through happiness, laughter or even a smile. Jesus did not giggle his way through his death! The fruit of joy that enabled him to endure the cross was shown in his determined obedience, even while he was in excruciating pain. The joy set before him was not frivolous personal joy but was the exceeding joy his Father would have in seeing salvation come to the whole world. That joy, *the joy of the Lord,* was Jesus' strength. When Jesus obeyed his Father, the fruit of his obedience brought joy to God.

Peace is the Fruit of Repentance

Christ's peace with God was shown in the way they worked together. He saw his Father working and worked with him. They were united and in harmony, with no sin to block their relationship. That's peace with God! That's the peace Christ has given us; not peace as the world understands peace, but the *peace of reconciliation* with our Heavenly Father. When Jesus turned away from temptation in the wilderness, the fruit of his rejection of sin was peace with God.

Patience is the Fruit of Trust

On the night he was arrested, Christ lay prostrate before God in prayer. He prayed with every ounce of his being that God would let this cup of hardship pass him by, yet despite his desperate situation and the passion of his pleas, *God did not answer his prayer*. Instead of becoming frustrated that his prayer wasn't being answered, Christ submitted his will to his father's will, trusting his wisdom completely. He swapped any temptation to impatience for absolute trust, which brought the fruit of patience toward God.

Gentleness is the Fruit of Mercy

Jesus showed the fruit of gentleness in his treatment of the temple soldier who came to arrest him. Peter acted with worldly justice as he tried to physically protect his Messiah from arrest, cutting off a soldier's ear in the fray. In response, Christ showed Godly justice, not by defending himself but by gently healing the wounded ear. In doing justice to his arresting officer, Jesus showed he was united with God in the gentleness of his mercy. When Jesus showed compassion for suffering, his mercy revealed the gentleness of God.

Meekness is the Fruit of Praise

Meekness is not a personality trait and has nothing to do with being quiet, easily imposed upon, or submissive. Meekness is an action. It is similar to prayer in that it is the action of privately acknowledging that the work being done through us is God's work. The worldly description of meekness could never be applied to the man who cast out demons, commanded the wind and caused arguments wherever he went, yet the Godly description of meekness was evident in absolutely everything Christ did. He did everything in consultation with his Father, working when he saw him working and praising him for his achievements. When Jesus showed he valued the work of his Father more than his own work, the fruit of his praise was meekness towards God.

Kindness is the Fruit of Honour

When Christ tore the temple apart, it was a manifestation of his kindness towards God; his Father was being dishonoured, and Jesus' loving heart couldn't stand it. Jesus never once grieved his Father or his Spirit, nor did he participate in anything that did. When Jesus acted in honour, the fruit of his honour was kindness towards God.

Self-control is the Fruit of Courage

Self-control is not about physical fitness, correct diet or religious discipline. Neither is it about our ability to control our emotions and desires. It's about the courage to take sides. It is specifically about putting on the armour of God and standing strong in the light though we live in a dark world. *Since we belong to the day, let us be self-controlled, putting on faith and love like a breastplate. (1Thes.5:8-10)* It's about having the self-controlled courage of a soldier going into battle. He may not feel brave as he faces the enemy, but he stands his ground anyway, no matter what the cost will be to him personally. That's self-control! When Jesus 'stood up for what was right', the fruit of his courage was self-control.

Faithfulness is the Fruit of Unity

Just as a Bride is faithful to her husband, so Christ was faithful to God and his Spirit. They were totally united; one will, one name, one purpose. Everything Christ did showed his unity with his Father and with his Spirit. He gave God and his Spirit credit for everything. He called them his 'witnesses'. He was dedicated to them from the inside out, and because his heart was focused on doing their will, he spoke about them constantly, revealing the complexity of their personalities and telling of their sweeping achievements. When Jesus threw his whole heart and soul into working as 'part of the team', the fruit of his unity with God was faithfulness.

A VERY NARROW ROAD

This simple glimpse of the way God's fruit was displayed in Jesus' words and actions shows us Christ was saturated in the fruit of the Spirit of God. No false prophet can live this way because this way does not make anyone popular. It's not an easy road, and it can't be faked.

It doesn't matter how much a false prophet may want to deceive the elect; the reality is those who display the fruit of the Spirit of God will easily recognise the pretenders in the church who promote false fruit and shun or even persecute those who do not live by their false standards. Their persecution will never have the power to prevent those who love Christ from displaying the fruit of the Spirit of God themselves and recognising true fruit in others.

The reality is that giving up the desire for personal recognition, living in an unshakable joy and peace which is not shown on the face, promoting Christ's name instead of our own, trusting God even when it seems our prayers are not heard, refusing to lash out at those who hate us, praying for everyone God brings across our path, and standing up for righteousness no matter what the personal cost, is the true work of the Spirit of God in all those who love Christ. This is HIS fruit! This is how HE lived! This is not the way that false prophets and false teachers live!

Living his way is the very reason Christ sent us his Spirit, so that we could also do the work he did and display the same fruit he displayed, being his genuine followers, in *Spirit and in Truth.*

Christ warned us to watch out for false prophets and told us we would *know them by their fruit.* The Apostle John encouraged every believer to test the Spirits of those who say they belong to Christ, for he said, *do not believe every spirit, but test the spirits to see whether they are from God (1Jn.4:1).* The Apostle Paul further encouraged everyone to test themselves, *Examine yourselves to see if you are in the faith; test yourselves,* and also asked everyone to test him and his teaching (2Cor.13:5-6), not testing for testing sake, but so we would be free from any wrongdoing.

APPLY THE FRUIT TEST

It seems from all the encouragement in Scripture that testing the fruit of the Spirit was extremely important to Jesus and to the first disciples, and therefore it should not be unreasonable to suggest it should be important to every believer today. It's not difficult to learn how to *test the spirits,* and it can easily become automatic and casually applied to every conversation.

This test never fails, and it can't be faked, for true knowledge of God always has a consequence; it speaks life! This test is completely inoffensive. It is so gentle it is undetectable to the one who is being tested. Applying it places us in the position of being *wise as a serpent but innocent as a dove* (Mt.10:16). All we need to do is listen to the words coming out of other people's mouths, for their words will reveal their heart attitudes. If they love the world, they will speak from the viewpoint of the world. If they love God, they will speak about Christ, the nature of our Father and his Spirit, and unfold the beauty and wonder of his Kingdom.

> *This test never fails, and it can't be faked!*

TOTAL PROTECTION FROM DECEPTION

If we apply this test to all the teaching we hear from pulpits, we will always recognise the false doctrine of the beast. If we apply this test to all those who want to influence the way we think, we will never be deceived by the beastly rhetoric used by *wolves in sheep's clothing.* If we apply this test to every conversation, we will never fall into the wicked queen's trap of living according to worldly appearances rather than wholesome Kingdom truth.

A POWERFUL SECRET WEAPON

Christ has provided his greatly loved Bride with the most powerful of weapons. A secret weapon so well hidden it can't even be detected by the enemy when it is being used. His secret weapon, his word test, is completely invisible to the enemy and leaves no evidence it has been used. How awesome is that? How amazing! Only God could devise such a perfect and painless weapon!

The most amazing thing about this seemingly simple and inoffensive weapon is that it is so incredibly powerful God himself will use it to judge the living and the dead when we all stand before his judgment seat at the end of time. How important it is for all God's children to understand how we will be judged when we stand in final judgment before the Great White Throne of God.

Delighted by truth!

20

JUDGMENT BY FRUIT

Do people pick grapes from thornbushes or figs from thistles? Likewise, every tree that does not bear good fruit is cut down and thrown into the fire. Thus, by their fruit, you will recognise them. (Matt.7:16-20)

At the end of days, after the world as we know it has disappeared, all the dead who have ever lived will gather around the Great White Throne in Heaven, where it will be decided who will live forever and who will enter into the final and eternal second death (Rev.21:7-8). How this judgment is made is really important, for Scripture says at that time a plea will go out from many, *Lord, didn't I do all these things in your name?* And the answer will come back, *Depart from me you worker of evil, I never knew you (Matt.7:21-23).*

Have you ever thought about this judgment and wondered why it is so harsh? I've thought about this a lot, and on consideration, I don't think it's harsh at all. The explanation for that judgment is found in 'fruit', and the determining test, given by God, will be the same as the invisible test we are encouraged to use on ourselves and on others.

227

HOW DOES GOD TEST US?

At the final judgment, *books will be opened...and the dead will be judged according to what they have done (Rev.20:12)*. Understandably, people will want to say, 'But didn't I do this for you? Didn't I do that for you?' The problem is that those questions will prove to God that the people asking them have no fruit. How so? God is not looking for our good works but for works of the Spirit which glorify his Son. If we offer up to him the worldly fruit of our own efforts, we actually show him we don't value the death of his Son enough to promote *his* righteousness instead of our own.

If the fruit we offer God is the fruit of our own efforts, we insult him!

It is understandable that God would reject those who offer him the fruit of their own efforts, for their questions insult him like a slap in the face. Not a wise thing to do to God on judgment day! The self-glorifying works of personal achievement offered ignore the costly death and enormous victory of Christ and show God that his Son's righteous works are irrelevant to them. They show they do not understand that righteous fruit is the only fruit a righteous God can accept.

> *Each one should test his own actions. Then he can take pride in himself without comparing himself to somebody else. (Gal.6:4)*

Testing our own actions prior to the day of judgment means looking at ourselves to see what the Spirit of God has done through us to promote the righteousness of Christ. This is easy to do once we realise the fruit of God's Spirit is like the fruit we find in nature, which is always attached to something else, like a vine or branch.

As we have seen, natural fruit is a perfect example of the way spiritual fruit works. In the same way, natural fruit grows from a branch, so spiritual fruit does not just appear out of nowhere; it always comes from a powerful spiritual action of righteousness. When we test our action of righteousness, the fruit of the Spirit, which is attached, becomes easy to see. These fruit of the Spirit and the works of righteousness they spring from, I believe, are the works God will judge us for as we stand before his Great White Throne. The following list is just a quick refresher;

- Love is the fruit of Sacrifice.
  (Give up your own way, and you will show love)

- Joy is the fruit of Obedience.
  (Do as you are asked, and you will bring joy)

- Peace is the fruit of Repentance.
  (Seek forgiveness, and you will make peace)

- Patience is the fruit of Trust.
  (Look at 'the big picture', and you will find patience)

- Kindness is the fruit of Honour.
  (Give respect, and you will show kindness)

- Meekness is the fruit of Praise.
  (Value the work of God, and you will show meekness)

- Gentleness is the fruit of Mercy.
  (Have compassion for suffering, and you will show gentleness)

- Self-control is the fruit of Courage.
  (Stand up for what is right, and you will show self-control)

- Faithfulness is the fruit of Unity.
  (Work with God, and you will show faithfulness)

TAKE THE 'TEST' CHALLENGE

If you have not tested yourself before, now is as good a time as any to give yourself a quick spiritual check-up.

- Is your love for God and others built on laying down your personal wants and needs? Or is it built around warm fuzzy feelings of mutual acceptance?

- Is your joy in God a deep abiding emotion that remains all day despite changing circumstances? Or does it come from intermittent spurts of happiness?

- Do you have peace with God because there is no sin barrier between yourself and God? Or do you feel peace because your circumstances are okay at the moment?

- Do you patiently trust God even though he has not answered your latest prayer? Or do you feel patient because you are able to 'get along' with difficult people?

- Is a quiet and gentle spirit an automatic response to God in times of injustice? Or is gentleness what you show only to those who are weaker than you?

- Does your kindness towards God show itself in defending his honour? Or do you feign kindness by being nice to those who blaspheme him or take his name in vain?

- Do you have the courage to 'stand up' for the Kingdom of God in your everyday living? Or is self-control about what you have eaten today?

- Does your meekness show strength of purpose and willingness to move when God moves? Or do you believe meekness is about being small and insignificant?

- Can you truly call yourself faithful to God and his Spirit as Christ was to them? Or is faithfulness dismissed as loyalty to your friends and family?

The sure reality is; when we live in repentance, people will see our peace; when we live in honour, people will notice our kindness; when we live in trust, people will recognise our patience; when we *abide in the vine,* the fruit will take care of itself. Test it out! Look for the results!

THE KEY TO DISCIPLESHIP

Branches don't choose the type of fruit they grow; they only exist to support the chosen fruit until it is harvested. We are branches that have been grafted into an existing vine, and the chosen fruit we must bear is the fruit of the Spirit of God.

Jesus said that any branch which does not bear fruit would be cut off and thrown into the fire. In short, if we want to abide in his vine, we must bear his fruit. Placing any effort at all in trying to grow our own fruit will end up bringing us eternal shame and regret.

> *I am the vine; you are the branches. If you remain in me and I in you, you will bear much fruit. If anyone does not remain in me, he is like a branch that withers; such branches are picked up, thrown into the fire and burned. It is to my Father's glory that you bear much fruit; this is how you show yourselves to be my disciples. (John 15:5-8)*

Most people know that believers are supposed to be able to recognise a false prophet by the fruit they display, but how many know, as the Scripture above shows, that bearing the right fruit is the mark of a disciple? Have you ever wondered how to *go in my name and make disciples?* This is it! Making disciples is also all about fruit! Displaying the right fruit makes us his disciples, and teaching the right fruit makes others his disciples!

FALSE PROPHETS CAN'T DO IT!

As we become familiar with the flow of God's fruit through our lives, we will then easily recognise the fruit of his Spirit as it flows through others. As a consequence, we will begin to recognise the lack of fruit in those who say they believe in Christ but are pretenders, lying about whom they really are in order to deceive the elect.

Satan and his followers, *who speak like a dragon,* can't understand the simplicity and power of Honour, Unity, Repentance, Obedience, Praise, Mercy, Trust, Courage or Sacrifice. They can't live in these Godly character traits and so can't manifest their fruits, which is why their false fruit becomes easy for those who live in the Spirit to recognise.

THE ABOMINATION IS EASY TO SEE

Christ told us we would know false prophets by their fruit. When we look at true fruit, the fake fruit of the *abomination that causes desolation* becomes easy to see; for desolation also is always about fruit. Desolation is a fruit! Desolation is the fruit of fear. Fear prevents us from living in the Spirit, that is, from laying down our lives, being obedient, living in repentance, trusting God, showing mercy, defending his honour, remaining faithful to him and standing against the darkness created by Satan. In short, fear desolates our walk with Christ. Perfect love, however, casts out

Desolation is a fruit!

It is the fruit of fear!

fear, and perfect love is seen in fruit simply because the fruit of the Spirit is perfect! When we display the fruit of Christ's perfect relationship with his Father, Satan's fruit of desolation cannot find a place to lodge. It is totally overcome!

BAD FRUIT ALWAYS TASTES BITTER

The false works of false prophets and the false teachings they promote are easy to recognise, for they are always about self-centred and worldly appearances; they are never Christ-centred.

Christ's fruit is always about God, Christ, his Spirit and his Kingdom and eating it will always lead to life. False fruit is always about 'me' and this world, and eating it will always lead to death.

On the day of final judgment, everyone will be required to account for their words and deeds. This is the day when the fruit we have chosen will be revealed for all to see.

On that day, false prophets and false teachers will say to God, 'Didn't I do this in your name? Didn't I do that in your name?' Their self-centred fruit will be rejected.

Meanwhile, those who love their Saviour and carry true fruit will say to God, 'Thank you for what you have done for me. Thank you for what you have done through me for others.' Their fruit will be accepted with gratitude; *well done, good and faithful servant!*

Ultimately, all of Heaven will see the huge difference between the fruit being offered to God by those who *speak like a dragon* and by those who *speak like a Lamb*.

No longer deceived!

21

THE RAPTURE THEORY

Everyone who looks to the Son and believes in
him shall have eternal life, and I will raise him
up at the last day. (Jn.6:40)

Now you will have an opportunity to use John's test for
yourself. We have just been through most of the Book of
Revelation; the Royal announcement in chapter one, the
protection and promises given to the Bride in chapters two
and three, the throne room in chapter four, the crowning of
our hero in chapter five, the opening of the first six seals in
chapters six and seven, and the breathtaking opening of the
Seventh Seal in chapter eight. Then we ventured on through
the famine, plague and sword of the three judgments of the
Seventh Seal in chapters eight to sixteen and looked at the
two beasts, placed strategically by God in the middle of those
judgments, before arriving at the exposure and destruction of
the Great Whore of Babylon in chapters seventeen to twenty.

Considering there are only twenty-two chapters in
Revelation, and the last two are about the Bride, it has to be
asked, 'Where do we find the Rapture, One-World Government
and Antichrist world leader theories in this beautiful book?

There is so much confusion concerning the end-times; most of the ideas presented contradict one another and conveniently change as world events change. I spent years simply trying to avoid the subject and was not interested in how it would all work out, for I was happy just knowing I belonged to Christ and my future was in his hands.

Then I began teaching Scripture to children in State schools, and the children began asking questions about the end-times. Many had heard nasty rumours and were afraid of what might happen to them. It struck me as amazing that children as young as eleven were seeking answers to major subjects like being 'left behind' or the prophecies of Nostradamus while adults in the churches, like myself, didn't want to talk about the end-times. These children needed answers, and now, so did I, but what I found stunned me!

I started looking for confirmation in Scripture of Satan's 'mark of death' and the 'political Antichrist' leader who will rule over kings in a 'One-World Government', but instead, what I found horrified me! I discovered that popular theology and its many claims about gruesome, Satan-controlled, end-time chaos is a total fantasy. It's not referred to anywhere in the Book of Revelation, and worse, proof that such terrible things can never possibly happen abounds in Revelation! With the Rapture theory, I found so much evidence in Scripture to prove it cannot ever take place that I wondered how this false teaching could have taken hold of believers' minds and hearts in the way it has. There is so much Scriptural evidence to the contrary that I needed to write it all down, and you are about to read some of what I found.

I found that the popular end-time theology is nothing more than fantasy!

WHAT IS THE RAPTURE THEORY?

In general, the Rapture Theory proposes that sometime in the near future, there will begin a great time of Tribulation throughout the world. This time of chaos will supposedly be overseen by a Satan-in-the-flesh, anti-Christ, political leader who will rule the whole world through his One-World Government system. Under this Antichrist government, so the theory goes, all the prophetic destruction described in the Book of Revelation will be played out on the Earth with devastating consequences for all mankind.

What a horrible story! How can anyone think this glorifies Christ?

The power of the Antichrist will be so great (this is so blasphemous I don't even like writing it) even the Spirit of God will turn his back on the world, leaving the Earth's inhabitants to go through what can only be described as 'Hell-on-Earth'. Meanwhile (this also is also part of that hideous blasphemy), just prior to the beginning of 'Hell-on-Earth', Jesus will come down from Heaven, and his precious Bride will be 'taken up' in a glorious 'rapture' so that she will not have to endure the terror Satan is about to unleash on the Godless inhabitants of the world. What a horrible story! How can anyone think this glorifies Christ?

This is so far from glorifying Christ; it does the exact opposite. It betrays him! Those who have believed the lie that Christ is coming to help them escape from Satan's fury have, in reality, shown they believe Satan is more powerful than God and has the power to put Christ and his Bride to flight! How can anyone believe, even for a minute, that Satan has crushed Christ to the point where he now has to take his Bride and run? What horrible blasphemy! What a cruel betrayal of our mighty and victorious King!

237

But it doesn't end there. Within this terrible tale of betrayal, there are all kinds of mini-theories. Some believe all Christians will be raptured, and others believe some will be taken while others remain to face Satan's wrath. Arguments abound, and confusion reigns. How ugly! Meanwhile, there is the enormous problem of not one but two returns of Christ and two end-time resurrections. It doesn't matter a jot whether one of the resurrections is called a rapture, for (to misquote Shakespeare) a resurrection by any other name is still a resurrection.

> *Nowhere in Scripture are there two end-time resurrections!*

JESUS WILL ONLY RETURN ONCE

The first end-time return and resurrection, or rapture, (they say) will be to gather believers only, while the final return and resurrection will be to gather everyone else for judgment. The problem is, no matter how many doctrines and theories there may be on the Rapture Theory, all of the doctrines and theories I have heard fail to recognise one simple fact; Scripture clearly teaches Jesus will only return once. Nowhere does it say there will be two end-time resurrections or that Jesus will return twice. On this matter, Scripture is very, very clear.

Over and over again, Jesus teaches he will return *on the last day.* He does not say, nor do any of the disciples, that he will return before the last day to collect a select few, but only *on the last day*, which will be the last day of mankind's earthly existence, simply because there is no day beyond the last day. Jesus has stated this truth clearly, and many other Scriptures support his promise. The question we all have to answer is, 'Do we believe him?'

And this is the will of him who sent me, that I shall lose none of all that he has given me, but raise them up at the last day. (Jn.6:39)

For my Father's will is that everyone who looks to the Son and believes in him shall have eternal life, and I will raise him up at the last day. (Jn.6:40)

No one can come to me unless the Father who sent me draws him, and I will raise him up at the last day. (Jn.6:44)

If Jesus has said, over and over again, that he will raise us up on the last day, then surely we need to believe he knows what he is talking about and means what he says. There is no room in his teaching for people to continue to live on the Earth after the last day.

The Apostle John, who wrote the Book of Revelation, warned us to test the spirits of those who teach us to see if they speak the truth of the Kingdom of God or speak *from the viewpoint of the world (1Jn.4:4-6)*. So, let's do as he suggests and apply his test, keeping in mind that;

- ♥ If an interpretation promotes a worldview, it will be looking at how the world is affected by every event and circumstance.

- ♥ If an interpretation promotes a Kingdom view, it will be looking at how God, Christ and the Holy Spirit are glorified in every event and circumstance.

To understand how the test works in reality, let's do a quick review of the New Jerusalem theory, which you will quickly see fails John's test. It's a strange argument that shows what happens when people take the Book of Revelation literally rather than figuratively.

APPLYING THE TEST

Some people teach that before the return of Christ, God will bring a physical city, the New Jerusalem, out of the sky over the current city of Jerusalem and somehow fit within it all the Christians who have lived and died since Jesus' time. They believe that from there, Jesus will take political control of this world, and all Christians will be his high officials, 'lording it' over everyone else. This is a worldview, for the emphasis is this planet.

This theory sounds very similar to the theory about the Messiah, which abounded in Jesus' day. At that time, the Jews were looking for a Messiah who would take back Jerusalem from the Romans and exercise political control. They thought Jesus could be this Messiah, for they, too, were looking for a worldly manifestation of a spiritual promise. Jesus told them, *my Kingdom is not of this world,* and his words are still true today.

Jesus' disciples also started out with a worldview!

Since Christ's Kingdom consists of *righteousness, peace and joy in the Spirit (Rom.14:17),* it is clear his teaching does not encourage a worldview but rather knowledge of the nature of his Father. Nevertheless, Jesus' disciples also started out with a worldview and thought the New Jerusalem would be a physical structure. When Jesus told his disciples the old temple would be torn down and he would build them a new spiritual temple in just three days, they assumed he was talking about bricks and mortar. He wasn't! He was talking about an indestructible spiritual temple, the New Jerusalem. It wasn't until after he died and was raised on the third day that they understood his teaching. *Then they believed the Scripture and the words that Jesus had spoken (Jn.2:24).*

Jesus showed, by his death and resurrection, that the old temple was merely a shadow, or parable, of an eternal, invisible reality. A short time after he ascended into Heaven, the Spirit came down from Heaven and entered the new and indestructible temple which Christ had created for his Father, a dwelling not made by human hands. In his new temple, after centuries of being separated from mankind because of sin, God was able to dwell with mankind 'as one'. The New Jerusalem had arrived!

> *Do you not know that your body is a temple of the Holy Spirit who is in you, whom you have received from God? (1Cor.6:19)*

This is why believers are now given the description of being a holy temple. We are all part of the New Jerusalem that has come down from Heaven, and Jesus is already ruling and reigning, by his Spirit, through this temple, his Bride, on this Earth. This is the Kingdom view because the love of God, the sacrifice of Christ and the indwelling of the Spirit dominates the viewpoint.

The two viewpoints are worlds apart, and the conclusions reached, and taught, are total opposites to each other. The worldview of the New Jerusalem promotes a physical structure that can be recognised as a building, and its purpose is the political control of this world. The Kingdom view of the New Jerusalem promotes a spiritual home within the hearts of the righteous, which our Father has been longing for since the fall of mankind. Two clearly opposing views!

The two viewpoints are worlds apart and their conclusions are total opposites!

241

NOW TO TEST THE RAPTURE THEORY

It's not difficult to test what we are being taught because everyone who loves God and his Kingdom will speak from the same viewpoint as Christ; that is, they will show how everything that happens reflects the nature of God. In contrast, those who love this world will speak about the world and how those who live in it will be personally affected by the things which happen to people in this world.

I am about to show through Scripture that the Rapture Theory is a worldview. It not only opposes what the Bible actually teaches but fails John's test because it eliminates the profound love of God and the nature of his Kingdom. The Rapture Theory is a false teaching!

The false Rapture Theory is based on two suppositions, both of which are impossible according to Scripture:

- That people will be able to escape via 'rapture' before Tribulation begins.
- That those 'left behind' will go through great and terrible Tribulation.

We have already seen that the Great Tribulation has been in operation since Pentecost when the Apostle Peter announced the last days had begun. If we believe what Scripture says, then we are not waiting for the last days to begin, as the false Rapture Theory proclaims, but have been living in the last days for close to 2000 years.

- The Rapture Theory teaches God's Spirit will *leave* when the last days begin.
- Scripture teaches God's Spirit *came* when the last days began at Pentecost.
- Which do you think is true?

We have also seen that Jesus will only return once, and we know that when he returns, no one will be 'left behind' simply because there can be no existence on this planet after the *last day*, as it will be the last day of human existence on this Earth.

The truth is not shrouded, confused or mysterious. It is easy to see!

The only concept within this false 'rapture' theory which comes close to being true is that the Great Tribulation would be sandwiched between two resurrections. This happens to be true. However, it is the corrupt interpretation of the two resurrections which has deceived the elect.

Generally speaking, the Rapture Theory implies there will be a 'rapture' followed by a time of Tribulation, followed by a final resurrection. The timing of these events is shrouded in confusion and mystery, yet the truth is not shrouded, confused or mysterious. It is easy to see!

So what is the truth? Scripture shows there are indeed two mighty resurrections with a time of Great Tribulation sandwiched between them, but, and this is a big 'but', the Rapture Theory, like most false teachings, totally ignores the resurrection of Christ. Christ's own resurrection was the first of those two resurrections; our resurrection, on the last day, is the second. There are no other resurrections written about or alluded to anywhere in the New Testament.

Scripture shows, without doubt, the first multi-person resurrection in history was the resurrection of Christ himself, closely followed by the beginning of the last days tribulation, which began at Pentecost. It also shows that when the Great Tribulation of the last days ceases, the end will be closely followed by Christ's return *on the last day.*

THE SIGN OF THE MESSIAH

A long-held and still current Jewish belief, *the thirteenth principle,* states that during the Messianic age, the righteous will be raised from the dead in bodily form. There have always been disputes about who would be raised; the righteous in the Holy Land, the righteous everywhere, or everyone ever born, whether righteous or not.

> *Multitudes who sleep in the dust of the Earth will awake: some to everlasting life, others to shame and everlasting contempt. (Dan.12:2)*

Paul had many disputes with the Jews of his day, some of whom believed in the resurrection of the dead, while others did not, and this shows that active belief in the resurrection of the Jewish Patriarchs was commonly understood and expected in Jesus' time.

> *I have the same hope in God as these men that there will be a resurrection of both the righteous and the wicked. (Acts24:15)*

Why is it important to know this? Jesus, as the Messiah of Israel, completely fulfilled this prophetic expectation during his days on the Earth, for when he died and was raised, he was not alone!

CHRIST'S RESURRECTION

Pentecost was the beginning of the last days. Prior to that, there was only one multi-person resurrection recorded in Scripture, and that was the resurrection of Christ himself. This is where it gets interesting! What is not usually taught is that when God raised Christ from the dead, he was not the only one raised! At the time of his death, the tombs of all the patriarchs opened, and when Christ rose from the dead, so did they.

*The tombs broke open, and the bodies of many
holy people who had died were raised to life.
They came out of the tombs, and after Jesus'
resurrection, they went into the Holy City and
appeared to many people. (Matt.27:52-53)*

In the forty days after his resurrection, until his
ascension, Jesus appeared to many believers in bodily form,
and so did the resurrected patriarchs. What an amazing sight!
Can you imagine what it would have been like for the Jews
living in Jerusalem to see Moses and Elijah, Jeremiah and
Esther, Joseph and David? There were so many - but what
happened to them? These multitudes of Jewish patriarchs
could not return to a normal life on Earth, and neither could
they arrive in Heaven before Jesus. So, where did they go?

A GREAT CLOUD OF WITNESSES

*After Jesus said this, he was taken up before
their very eyes, and a cloud hid him from their
sight. (Acts1:9)*

This army of patriarchs made up the *great cloud of
witnesses* who went with Christ to glory when he ascended
into Heaven. Calling groups of people 'clouds' was common,
for we see the great Jewish patriarchs described this way by
the Apostle Paul; *therefore, since we are surrounded by such
a great cloud of witnesses...(Heb.12.1)*. According to Acts,
Jesus will return on the last day the same way he left, which
means this same *great cloud of witnesses*, who went with him
to glory, will come with him when he returns.

*This same Jesus, who has been taken from you
into Heaven, will come back in the same way
as you have seen him go. (Acts1:11)*

Does this resurrection sound like the Rapture? Yes, it does, but it's not! This is the resurrection of Christ; the only multiple resurrection event that occurred prior to the beginning of the last days, which started at Pentecost. The Rapture Theory is nothing more than a twisted corruption of the most precious and triumphant gift of Christ to the world, his own mighty resurrection from the dead, which included the resurrection of the patriarchs, vital proof to Israel that he was indeed the promised Messiah.

> *Resurrection of the Jewish patriarchs was vital proof that Jesus was the promised Messiah.*

COMMON KNOWLEDGE

This multi-person resurrection was common knowledge, for the first disciples had to rebuke some believers for telling others that since the Messiah had come, and therefore the promised resurrection of the righteous dead had already occurred, there was no point in continuing to believe.

> *They have left the path of truth, claiming that the resurrection of the dead has already occurred; in this way, they have turned some people away from the faith. (2Tim.2:18)*

In response to this misunderstanding, the Apostles taught that those who held this view had *left the path of truth* and were leading others away from understanding the salvation of Christ, and it's the same with the Rapture Theory today. Those who teach it have *left the path of truth* and are leading people away from understanding the power and prophetic fulfilment of Christ's resurrection, which, in itself, proves he was, and is, the long-awaited Messiah of Israel.

THE DAYS OF NOAH

Supporters of the Rapture Theory also use the story of Noah to try and prove Christians will be 'taken' while the ungodly are destroyed. I am about to show you that interpretation is not only impossibly inaccurate but is the exact opposite of what is written in Scripture. It is incredible to me the Rapture Theory can be believed at all!

It's true Jesus said the end of days would be like the days of Noah, but the 'left behind' interpretation is completely false. In the days of Noah, it was the wicked who were swept away by the floodwaters, not the righteous. In other words, it was the wicked who were 'taken', and it was the righteous who were 'left behind'. There was no one left on Earth after this judgment except Noah and his family. Eight righteous people were left behind to tell future generations about the salvation of their God. How does the story of Noah prove the Rapture Theory? It doesn't; it shows the exact opposite.

In this account, the 'wicked' were taken and the righteous were 'left behind'.

A COMMON THEME

The same pattern can be seen in the story of Lot and his family, who witnessed the destruction of the ungodly in Sodom and Gomorrah. Once again, the wicked were annihilated, 'taken', and the righteous were 'left behind' to tell of the judgment of the Lord to future generations.

The parable of the Wheat and Tares teaches the same thing; that the tares will be harvested 'taken' first and destroyed by fire while the wheat will be 'left behind' and harvested last. The word of God does not contradict itself.

Jesus carefully explained the parable of the Wheat and Tares, stating that, at the end of time, the wicked tares would be 'taken' to destruction while the righteous wheat would be 'left behind' to shine with glory in the Kingdom of God.

As the weeds are pulled up and burned in the fire, so will it be at the end of the age. The Son of Man will send out his angels, and they will weed out of his Kingdom everything that causes sin and all who do evil. They will throw them into the fiery furnace, where there will be weeping and gnashing of teeth. Then the righteous will shine like the sun in the Kingdom of their Father. (Matt.13:35-43)

In each of these Scriptures, and there are more, the wicked are 'taken' and destroyed while the righteous are 'left behind' to witness the righteous judgment of God. The Rapture Theory teaches the exact opposite of these Scriptures. It totally ignores the fact that all sinners will be harvested (taken) from the Earth and thrown into the winepress of the Lord's fury prior to the last resurrection. It totally ignores the role of the (left behind) righteous to be his witnesses to the end, the last people alive and ready to join him in the sky.

THE GREAT WINEPRESS

As Jesus is coming to gather the elect, he commands his angel to *put in the sickle for the time is right.*

The angel swung his sickle on the Earth, gathered its grapes and threw them into the great winepress of God's wrath. They were trampled in the winepress outside the city, and blood flowed out of the press. (Rev.14:17-20)

248

After the trampling of *the grapes of wrath*, the elect will be taken up from the Earth to join with Christ in the clouds. This will include both the elect who are living at the time of Christ's return and those who have died prior to his coming. In other words, the wicked will be 'taken' first, and the righteous will be 'left behind' just long enough to witness the destruction of the wicked and the raising of the dead in Christ before they themselves rise to meet Christ in the clouds.

> *For the Lord will come down from Heaven with a loud command, with the voice of the archangel and with the trumpet call of God, and the dead in Christ will rise first. After that, we who are still alive and are left will be caught up... (1Thes.4:16-18)*

The Rapture Theory teaches the exact opposite of this truth, proclaiming that the righteous leave so that the wicked can live in a kind of Hell-on-Earth long after the righteous are gone. What an impossible doctrine!

What an impossible doctrine!

The distortion of Christ's resurrection has consequences. If we can't understand the glory of Christ's resurrection, how can we understand our own? Like Christ's resurrection, our resurrection is not an escape; it is a result. It is the ultimate sign of Christ to the principalities and powers that their reign of sin is over.

Just as Jesus could not be raised from death to life until sin was destroyed, neither will we be raised until all sin is destroyed. We are not greater than our Lord. If the precious Son of God needed to go through tribulation before his resurrection, then so, surely, will we.

BAPTISED INTO CHRIST

Modern-day Rapture theorists are terrifying believers with stories of post-Rapture 'beheadings' because of the strictly literal interpretation of one tiny section of Revelation, which is not read in context with the rest of the testimony of Christ in Revelation, and definitely not in context with the rest of the word of God, or the message of the Gospels.

> *Those who had been beheaded...and had not received the mark of the beast...came to life and reigned with Christ a thousand years. The rest of the dead did not come to life until the thousand years were ended. This is the first resurrection. Blessed and holy are those who share in the first resurrection, the second death has no hold over them, but they will be priests of God and of Christ and will reign with him a thousand years. (Rev.20:4-6)*

The above refers to those who have died in Christ without the mark of Satan and who would, therefore, not be subject to the second death. It tells us that all who have died without the mark of Satan will be a kingdom of priests and will be part of the first resurrection.

It also tells us that the rest of the dead will not rise in the first resurrection but will rise after the thousand years have ended. All these things supposedly support belief in a 'rapture' of just a few believers from one generation in history. Really? What an arrogant assumption! And how incorrect!

If this is taken literally, only a dead person can be raptured and specifically only those who have been beheaded can rule and reign with Christ. The rest of us will not be 'raptured' and will not reign with Christ. This is NOT what Scripture teaches - at all!

When we look at Scripture, particularly the Gospels, we see that the *first resurrection* actually happened 2000 years ago! The resurrection of Christ was the *first resurrection.* When he arrived in Heaven, he was crowned King of kings and given the Scroll of Judgment to open for one reason, *With your Blood, you purchased a kingdom of priests for your God, and they will reign on the Earth (Rev.5:9-10).* It was because Christ purchased a kingdom of priests with his Blood that he received the title *King of kings and Lord of lords.* We are the kings he is King over and the lords he is Lord over. This is not something that is going to happen for a small group of people in the future.

> *It is because he purchased a kingdom of priests for his God that he received the title King of kings and Lord of lords.*

Since Christ was raised from the dead, in *the first resurrection,* every person who has been baptised into Christ has been baptised into *his* death and *his* (first) resurrection, made priests and kings and asked to rule and reign with him on this Earth. Those who are baptised into Christ are no longer marked for death because of their sin but have entered into eternal life and therefore are no longer subject to the second death. This is elementary, foundational doctrine, and yet it seems false teachers have been able to deceive the elect because the elect have not been taught basic doctrine.

> *Don't you know that all of us who were baptised into Christ Jesus were baptised into his death? (v3) If we have been united with him in a death like his, we will certainly also be united with him in a resurrection like his. (v6) Since Christ was raised from the dead, he cannot die again. (Rom 6:-10)*

Secondly, the Apostle Peter explained the end-time concepts to believers of his day, telling them they must view what they were being told in context with everything previously revealed through Christ and the prophets. He encouraged them to keep in mind that scoffers will come and question the established word of God, presenting their own evil desires instead of the truth revealed by Christ, and he went on to explain that the term 'day' or 'thousand years' does not mean a literal period of time, as we count time in this world but rather denotes an unknown spectrum of time.

With the Lord, a day is like a thousand years, and a thousand years is like a day. (2.Pt.3:8) But the day of the Lord will come like a thief, the Heavens will disappear with a roar, the elements will be destroyed by fire, and the Earth and everything in it will be laid bare. (2Pt.3:10)

One thing is abundantly clear from Peter's teaching; no one will be able to live through *the day of the Lord*. When Jesus returns, it will be the end of this world. What Peter describes is so devastating that no life can be sustained. One minute everyone will be alive, and then Christ will return *like a thief*, and no life will exist on Earth from that moment. There is absolutely no room in Scripture for anyone to remain alive on the Earth after the return of Christ.

WHERE DID THE LIE BEGIN?

The Rapture Theory was unheard of in any Christian writings before the 19th Century. It has been attributed to a Scottish teenager named Margaret MacDonald, but there is no such theory in her writing. Rather, she warned that the anti-Christ spirit would be seen in those who held a wrong understanding of Christ and would, therefore, promote an illegitimate gospel, ironically, like the Rapture Theory itself!

No longer deceived!

How amazing that she should be blamed for introducing the Rapture Theory when that kind of corrupt theology was exactly what she was warning about. The following are excerpts of Margaret MacDonald's prophecy as published in *The Restoration of Apostles and Prophets in the Catholic Apostolic Church (1861)*.

I frequently said that night, and often since, now shall the awful sight of a false Christ be seen on this Earth, and nothing but the living Christ in us can detect this awful attempt of the enemy to deceive - he will have a counterpart for every part of God's truth, and an imitation for every work of the Spirit.

I saw the error to be that men think that it will be something seen by the natural eye but 'tis spiritual discernment that is needed, the eye of God in his people.

The trial of the church is from antichrist. It is by being filled with the Spirit that we shall be kept. Oh, be filled with the Spirit - have the light of God in you, that you may detect Satan - be full of eyes within - be clay in the hands of the potter - submit to be filled, filled with God. This will build the temple.

What hindered the real life of God from being received by his people was their turning from Jesus, who is the way to the Father. They were not entering in by the door. They were bypassing the cross, through which every drop of the Spirit of God flows to us. All power that comes not through the Blood of Christ is not of God.

Somehow this wonderfully accurate and Spirit-inspired understanding of the spirit of anti-Christ, which would tempt true believers with false teaching, became warped by preachers who simply wanted to create a new and popular theology, and so the futurist movement began.

DOWNWARD INTO DECEPTION

The futurist movement promoted the view that Revelation should be interpreted in the light of future events; therefore, overcoming tribulation became part of our future instead of part of our personal daily walk. Over time, the concept of a future time of 'Tribulation' became more and more horrible until finally, someone decided it was so horrible it must be the work of Satan rather than God's holy judgment, and the horror stories grew.

Preaching on 'hell-fire and brimstone' had become unpopular, so it was deftly replaced by this more believable theory about a living Hell-on-Earth. It is interesting to notice that in churches that promote the Rapture Theory, there is usually no teaching on Hell. After all, what could scare people more than the horrible fate awaiting those 'left behind'? The Rapture Theory is now more terrifying than anything that has ever been taught about Hell.

The Rapture Theory is now more terrifying than anything that has ever been taught about Hell.

As the blasphemous horror stories grew, there arose the even more blasphemous 'political Antichrist World Leader' theory, followed closely by the 'One-World Government' theory. Strangely no one knows how these false doctrines entered the teaching of the church or who introduced them. It seems they were, and still are, promoted and accepted out of fear and ignorance!

CONSTANTLY CHANGING

From the days of the first disciples, literal interpretations of spiritual end-time events have always led people astray. They change as world events change, and every generation has a new interpretation, but one thing remains the same, they still *deceive the elect* and lead people astray, yet the truth does not change. The Kingdom of God is *not of this world*, and the victory of Christ over Satan is *not of this world*. Revelation has been written to glorify Christ for his victory over Satan, sin and death and reveal the amount of protection afforded to his treasured Bride as the righteous judgment of God is poured out on all those who fight against Christ and God's eternal Kingdom. This precious, eternal message is never going to change, and those who believe it will never be deceived by the lies of false prophets.

TOTAL PROTECTION FOR THE BRIDE

What we are about to see in the next chapter is the amount of protection afforded to the Bride of Christ during the outpouring of the judgments of Revelation. Not only does the Bride remain until the end, but God commands that she be protected while the tribulation caused by his righteous judgments is poured out around her.

After that, we will take a closer look at some common literalistic theories, like the One-World Government theory, the Antichrist World Leader theory, plus the Abomination and Armageddon, and finish by finding out why the 'mark' of God is so much more powerful than the 'mark' of Satan.

Clothed in assurance!

22

WHO CAN AVOID THE CHAOS?

They were told not to harm the grass of the Earth or any plant or tree, but only those people who did not have the seal of God on their foreheads. (Rev.9:4)

The irresistible Book of Revelation is so encouraging for believers; it shows that during the time known as Great Tribulation, God orders his angels to protect those who carry the seal of his Son. How can any believer fear tribulation when they know they are under the protection of God, Christ, the Spirit and all the angels of Heaven? If anyone on Earth can avoid the chaos of tribulation, it is Christ's precious Bride!

The above Scripture again shows the Rapture Theory is a total myth. God's obedient angels bring the destruction, and God orders them not to harm the redeemed as they pour his judgments out on the rest of humanity. If believers were 'raptured' and out of harm's way, there would be no need for God to order this protection; likewise, if 'left behind' believers were going to be beheaded *en masse* God would also have no need to order this protection.

Contrary to Rapture theology, Christians will not escape the tribulation of God's judgment in any generation right up until the last day. However, the way we go through the fallout will show we are different to non-believers.

NOAH IS A PERFECT EXAMPLE

Noah suffered loss, destruction, inconvenience, discomfort, upheaval and a complete change of lifestyle but it did not destroy him!

The story of Noah reflects how the tribulation of the last days will play out for believers. Noah did not escape the distress of the flood, but lived through it, suffered because of it, and witnessed the destruction around him. It inconvenienced him and changed his lifestyle, yet, it did not destroy him. The rain fell on him, and he got wet, but he was not 'swept away'. He witnessed everything God did, but he was not subject to it. He was completely protected because of his faith in God.

In the same way, even though the elect will go through the full outworking of the judgments of tribulation, our role is entirely different to those who don't know Christ. Like Noah, we will experience loss, destruction, inconvenience, and maybe even a severe change in lifestyle, but it will not destroy us. The best way to explain this is by looking at an almost identical example from the Old Testament.

THE OLD SHADOWS THE NEW

In so many ways, the things which happened in the Old Testament predicted the things which would happen in the New Testament. The release of God's people from Egypt into the Promised Land is one of them. We all know the story…

The Promised Land was waiting, but God's people were trapped in slavery in a land controlled by those who had no respect for God or his people. God warned Pharaoh he would send judgments upon Egypt if he did not let his people go. Pharaoh defied God and refused to listen to Moses.

God then told his people to cover their houses with the blood of a sacrificed lamb so that his judgments would not affect them and also warned Pharaoh that judgment was about to happen. Again, Pharaoh defied God.

Consequently, judgment fell on everyone in Egypt not covered with the blood of a lamb until finally, after ten extremely harsh plagues, the Israelites were recognised by Pharaoh as God's people and were freed from slavery and allowed to leave Egypt. For us, there are three very important lessons to be learned from this event:

The judgment of God on Egypt reflects the final judgment of God on the world!

1. The children of Israel were not taken out of the land until after the judgment of Egypt was completed. They lived through the terrors, yet the terrors did not touch them. It's the same with tribulation; Christ's cherished Bride will witness God's judgment happening around, but it will not fall on us.

2. The purpose of the ten judgments on Pharaoh was to get him to recognise that these were God's people and not his. God constantly told Pharaoh, *Let my people go.* In finally letting them go, Pharaoh acknowledged the Israelites were God's people and not his. Likewise, when tribulation is over, the sons of God, also known as the Bride of Christ, will be revealed. (Rom.8:19)

3. The only thing that protected them was the blood of a lamb. In the same way, the only thing that will protect Christ's beloved from God's final judgment will be the Blood of the Lamb poured out for our Salvation.

Surely it is easy to see the correlation? These judgments were not intended for God's people. They fell on Egypt because of the rebellion of Pharaoh. The Israelites were not in rebellion, and so the judgments did not fall on them. Though God's precious children lived through the outpouring of God's judgments on Egypt, they remained protected; for the whole purpose of the judgments was to bring redemption to Israel. What God's people witnessed were incredible miracles on their behalf. In the account of the ten plagues, God's purpose is clearly recorded:

- When the plague of flies was pronounced on Egypt, God told Pharaoh there would be no flies where his people lived; *I will make a distinction between my people and your people (Ex.8:21-23).*

- When God sent a plague to kill all the livestock in Egypt, he promised the plague would not affect the livestock that belonged to his people (Ex.9:1-9).

- When the trees and crops of the Egyptians were destroyed by hail, God's people had no damage to their crops or food (Ex.9:22-26).

- When God plunged Egypt into darkness, the Israelites still lived in light. *No one could see anyone else or move about for three days, yet all the Israelites had light in the places where they lived (Ex.10:21-24).*

- Before the last plague killed only the firstborn sons of Egypt, God told Pharaoh, *Then you will know that God makes a distinction between Egypt and Israel (Ex.11:7).*

Furthermore, God told his people that he performed these signs *that you may tell your children and grandchildren... and may know that I am the Lord (Ex.10:2).*

God's ways haven't changed. He loves his people, and his last day's judgments will only fall on those who despise him and rebel against his commands. The redeemed of Christ will witness all that happens throughout the last day's judgments, so we can glorify our Saviour and tell others all he has done for us. This is what it means to be his witness! He would like us to witness what he is doing for us and praise him for both his judgments and his salvation.

This is what it means to be his witnesses, he would like us to witness what he is doing!

Before God's final judgments of the Earth and its inhabitants (tribulation) begin, Christ will not whisk his people away in some kind of mystical escape. If that was his plan, then we have all 'missed the boat' or been 'left behind' because the last days started at Pentecost. No! Instead, Christ intends that we live through the stress of this Great Tribulation in the same way the Israelites did when faced with their tribulation, with our eyes fixed firmly on our promised land.

Our promised land is the return of Christ, the revealing of the children of God in a glorious resurrection, the splendid and joyous marriage of the Bride to our victorious groom, and our entry, with Christ, into an eternal, entirely sin-free, new Heaven and new Earth.

Why is it so hard to believe that Christ loves us in the same way a young groom loves his beautiful, young Bride and doesn't want to see us hurt? Why is it so hard to believe in his costly and hard-won salvation?

COMPLETELY PROTECTED

It's interesting, in the story of the flight from Egypt, that Pharaoh tried one last time to re-capture and enslave God's people. He gathered the majority of his army together, and as they chased the Israelites through the Red Sea, they were totally destroyed by God. Meanwhile, Moses and the Israelites watched this destruction from the safety of a secure hilltop position. What an amazing analogy of the end-time Armageddon/Grapes of Wrath scenario!

THE BATTLE OF ARMAGEDDON

In Revelation, the final battle, the famous Battle of Armageddon, never happens. Instead, just like the escape from Egypt, the armies of all the kings and nations of the Earth gather to attack God's people, but in the nick of time, God intervenes to harvest sinners in a sea of blood, *the wine-press of God's fury*, a Red Sea (Rev.16:16-20). Meanwhile, as this is happening, the people who belong to Christ, his pure and spotless Bride, will stand in safety and look to the sky for Christ's return, entry into their new promised land, and a 'happy ever after' future.

According to Revelation, the Battle of Armageddon never happens.

How simple and uncomplicated it is to look to Scripture for the answers to the big questions. Scripture tells us:

- ♥ Jesus stated many times that he would only return once again, on the last day, which is exactly that, the last day of human life on this planet.

- ♥ Great Tribulation is the time sandwiched between two resurrections; the resurrection of Christ and the resurrection of believers on the last day.

- According to Jesus, tribulation, or stress, cannot be avoided by anyone on the planet; it daily affects both believers and non-believers alike.

- God has ordered sure and definite protection during tribulation for all sealed into the Salvation of his Son.

- Tribulation is not in the future, for the first thing the Apostle Peter did on the day of Pentecost was proclaim loudly that the predicted 'last days' had just begun.

Either we believe the word of God, or we don't, and no amount of 'interpretation' can change the simple fact that 'rapture' is merely another name for 'resurrection'.

The truth is crystal clear. Nowhere in Scripture is there a third resurrection between the raising of Christ and the raising of believers on the last day. It simply does not exist!

No longer gullible!

23

THE ONE-WORLD LEADER

I warn everyone who hears the words of the prophecy of this book: if anyone adds anything to them, God will add to him the plagues described in this book. And if anyone takes words away from this book of prophecy, God will take away from him his share in the Tree of Life and in the Holy City. (Rev.22:18-19)

I don't know of anyone, believer or non-believer, who has not wondered what will happen at the end of the world, and like many Christians, I've been forced to consider the concept of a single world leader who will create a One-World Government and bring a violent time of chaos before the world comes to an end. We have all certainly been made aware of the concept, even if we are unsure of what we personally believe. As a result, we watch world politics to see if we can predict who this one-world leader might be or if he will rise in our lifetime, and what type of government he will encourage.

On top of that, in Christian circles, we hear many conflicting stories about an Antichrist world ruler that are so detailed it makes them easy to believe.

Many books have been written espousing the evil of the end times, and some have been made into movies. Hollywood has added its own brand of horror in varying ways over the years, leaving true believers with a whole lot of overkill. The problem I had with all these accounts, both inside and outside the churches, was that they all contradicted each other. I couldn't find any theories which agreed, and the time frames presented were as flexible as rubber, but the worst thing about all the so-called end-time predictions was that none of them gave any glory to Jesus, and this bothered me – a lot!

Most of the predictions, like the Hollywood accounts, were easily seen as wild fantasies, the stuff of nightmares, yet the scenarios presented were supposedly based on Scripture. They

Scary stuff! Unless you actually read Revelation!

would quote verses of Revelation which talk about omens, like 666, vividly picturing what the Antichrist might be like as a child or how someone would behave if they were controlled by 'the beast'. Scary stuff! Unless you actually read the Book of Revelation!

The theories written about and believed in Christian circles were just as outrageous. They alluded to chaos and destruction and presented a cocktail of fear, which they claimed was also based on the prophecies of Revelation. Though some of these unfounded beliefs are still popular, predictions about a One-World Government or a single Antichrist world ruler can't possibly be attributed to Revelation simply because they don't exist anywhere in the Book of Revelation.

I can understand how those who reject Christ would not want to admit that he will be their final judge or that all the terrifying judgments of Revelation come from his hand. Terror is appropriate for those who face God's wrath for sin but not for those under Christ's protection!

When I read the Book of Revelation, with Christ as my sovereign victor, terror loses its power, and fear loses its mystique. That's not a particularly good outcome for those who want to sell lots of books, make scary movies or rule the world, but it's a wonderful outcome for believers.

NO MORE SCARY MYTHS

Before we begin to explore what Scripture actually says about recognising the 'Antichrist', there are a few other factors to consider, such as where the references to the anti-Christ are found in Scripture, the context in which they are written, and what God says the anti-Christ spirit will look like; for God tells us exactly what appearance the anti-Christ will have, and it is not at all what you may have been led to believe, in fact, God's description may surprise you.

Myths and legends can only hold power if the truth remains hidden. Once the truth is known, fantasies die. That big scary Antichrist you've heard about is nothing more than a fantasy! He is a pure fabrication! His political One-World Government is also a myth, but to break the power of both those deceptions, I need to show you what Revelation actually says, so let's begin.

BEWARE FALSE PROPHETS

There are several warnings in the Bible about false prophets, and we are always lovingly encouraged to flee from such men or women and their teaching. However, the warning you have just read is completely different and much more severe. It brings the strongest of warnings to every single person who hears the words of the Book of Revelation. It emphatically states that not one single person is allowed to add to or take from this word; therefore, it makes you and I individually responsible for any false teaching we accept.

That warning was written by the Apostle John in the strongest possible terms and is an outright command. If you or I disobey that command, it will cost us our Salvation. Don't believe the false teachers who say we can't lose our Salvation; this Scripture tells us we can lose it and will definitely lose it if we add to or take away from the prophecy given to us by Christ himself. Now that is a very, very strong warning! You and I have no excuse; we must not listen to those who add to or take anything away from the words of Christ's personal testimony. Why is it so strong? It's strong because this testimony is no ordinary testimony. It's not the testimony of a mere man; it's the Royal Testimony of the Son of the Most High God himself, personally dictated to his servant John for the benefit of his beloved future Bride. A Royal Testimony is not something anyone should ever alter without appropriate permission.

A Royal Testimony is not something anyone should alter without permission!

It is important to understand the strength of this warning, for it is only by ignoring it and 'adding' things to or 'taking' things from the Book of Revelation that the false notion of an Antichrist world leader can be accepted at all. Now that is a terrifying thought!

WHAT FALSE TEACHERS DO

Over the years, I have noticed that the first thing any false teacher will do is water down the power of this warning. Most will say this warning applies to the whole Bible and not just to Revelation; this is so they can 'add' things from other parts of the Bible to Revelation. Not a good idea! People may be fooled, but God is not, and God will hold them to account. They will not escape the effects of John's warning.

John's warning does not apply to the whole Bible. At the time he wrote Revelation, there was no other New Testament book in existence. He didn't mention the Torah, which was the Old Testament, so it was not included in his warning. When he referred to *this book of prophecy*, he made it clear he was talking about the Testimony of Jesus contained in the Book of Revelation. Three times in the warning, he said *this book* and the three punishments for ignoring his warning can still only be found in Revelation. *The plagues described in this book and the Tree of Life and the Holy City, which are described in this book,* are not found together in any other book of the Bible or Torah.

> *John did not warn us about adding to the Bible in general, his warning was for 'this book', the one he had just written!*

While this particular word of warning is taken as intended, people cannot be easily deceived. However, watering down, or bringing confusion to the word, is merely the first step in the process of deception. The next step is 'adding' to Revelation concepts which completely change the meaning and purpose of the victorious Testimony of Christ.

COMMON PRACTICE

It is common practice for false teachers to take Scriptures from other parts of the Bible and claim they are also part of this end-time prophecy. They are not! For example, the testimony of Daniel is often used to replace the Testimony of Christ, but Daniel is not Christ, and their testimonies are completely different. What does Daniel have to do with overcoming sin and Satan? We are warned directly by God not to listen to prophets who 'steal' words from each other and claim they are speaking for God.

I am against the prophets who steal from one another words supposedly from me...I am against those who prophesy false dreams, declares the Lord. They tell them and lead my people astray with their reckless lies, yet I did not send or appoint them. (Jer.23:29-32)

Everything written in Revelation can be and should be explained through the life of Christ and supported by Scriptures in other parts of the Bible. However, and this is a big 'however', randomly taking ideas from other parts of the Bible and 'adding' them to the Testimony of Christ in order to change the meaning and purpose of his powerful testimony is absolutely forbidden.

A PRIME EXAMPLE

To see whether or not you have been deceived by the lies of false prophets, ask yourself this simple question. 'What is Revelation about?' If your first thought revolves around an Antichrist person rather than Christ himself, then you, dear friend, have been deceived. If your mind immediately begins to swirl with vague concepts of a Rapture, an Antichrist political leader and a One-World Government rather than the beauty of the victory of the sacrifice of Christ and his unshakable Salvation, then you have listened to false teaching.

The scariest thing about each of those three beliefs is that not one of them can be found in the Book of Revelation. According to Revelation, they do not exist, which means they have all been added. Very, very scary! There is no getting around the truth of the above statements; the Rapture, a single, political Antichrist figure, and his last days One-World Government, are not referred to anywhere in the Book of Revelation at all. Quite the opposite, in fact!

Proof of the opposite of each of these three false teachings can easily be found in the Book of Revelation, and that, in itself, shows how thoroughly immoral and deceptive these teachings, and those who teach them, are.

> *There were also false prophets among the people, just as there will be false teachers among you...In their greed, these false teachers will exploit you with stories they have made up. Their condemnation has long been hanging over them, and their destruction has not been sleeping. (2Pet.2:1-3)*

The worst thing is, these three teachings exalt Satan at the expense of Christ. In order to 'add' them, we have to 'take away' the victory of Christ at Calvary, what he and his disciples taught, what God has said continually through his word, what the Holy Spirit has spoken through God's prophets and, most importantly, what the Book of Revelation, itself, says about the return of Christ, his victory over all the enemies of God, including Satan, and the sovereign government of the great King of Kings. Now that's a lot to take out, but that's what has to be removed in order to add these three false teachings to the Book of Revelation.

THE UNFORGIVABLE SIN

Have you ever wanted to know what the unforgivable sin is? This is it! This is what blasphemy against the Spirit is all about. God's word is superior to everything else in creation, and God's word is always brought to us by the Spirit of God. Anyone who removes God's word, given by the Spirit, adds to it, tampers with it, changes it, or replaces it, is blaspheming the Spirit, for they are saying, 'The Spirit of God got it wrong!' This sin is unforgivable and cancels Salvation.

271

Anyone who speaks a word against the Holy Spirit will not be forgiven, either in this life or in the age to come...I tell you that men will have to account on the day of judgment for every careless word they have spoken. For by your words, you will be acquitted, and by your words, you will be condemned. (Matt.12:31-37)

Those in leadership positions who know the word of God and yet choose to ignore the word of God in order to advance popular theology are already under the condemnation of God for their part in the deadly deception of God's people.

Therefore, dear friends, since you already know this, be on your guard so that you may not be carried away by the error of lawless men and fall from your secure position. (2Pt.3:17)

There is no such thing as 'once saved, always saved'. The truth is, we can not only *fall from our secure position*, as the previous Scripture tells us, but we can have our names *blotted out of the Book of Life* by Christ himself (Rev.3:5) and also have the *plagues described in this book* added to us. It is, indeed, a deadly thing to add to the Testimony of Christ!

THE SCARIEST DECEPTION

For me, the scariest and most heart-breaking of all deceptions is that a whole generation of young people worldwide has been lied to about the 'end-times' and deceived into believing fantasies that have been made up and added to God's word. This has been done in such a convincing manner, through books and movies, that many of those young ones are now in danger of losing their Salvation just because they believe the lie and pass it on as truth, without ever knowing they are participating in the ultimate deception.

These (false prophets) mouth empty, boastful words, and by appealing to the lustful desires of sinful nature, they entice people who are just escaping from those who live in error. They promise them freedom while they themselves are slaves of depravity (2Pt.2:17-20)

There are so many false prophets, teaching lies through so many books and from so many pulpits. Where are the true teachers of the word who will proclaim the truth about the glorious testimony of Christ no matter what the cost? *Who is on the Lord's side?* (2Kgs.9:32) (Ex.32:26). Who will stand with Christ and throw down these false teachings?

Young people, just escaping from the world, are the targets of wolves preaching from many Christian pulpits. Instead of becoming a powerful army of true believers who are willing to lay down their lives for Christ, these youth are being led down a deceptive road away from the salvation of Christ. When they need to be taught true discipleship so that they are equipped to go into the world to preach the Gospel, heal the sick, raise the dead and cast out demons, they are instead offered a gospel of freedom from responsibility. They are told life is a party; Sunday is a music fest, and when things get tough, God will zap them out of this world so that the Antichrist, and his One-World Government, can take the world to Hell while they 'party on' in Heaven. The eternal condemnation of these false teachers is just!

Who will stand with Christ and tear down these false teachings?

I want people to know the truth, but to teach the truth, I needed to ask a few hard questions, so I asked, 'Could there really be a One-World Government on the Earth just prior to the return of Christ?'

273

A RESOUNDING 'NO'

Reading Revelation showed me that concept is utterly impossible. I discovered that Revelation describes the end of days in plain language, for at the time of the end, just before God destroys the wicked, three evil spirits are sent out to gather all the kings of the Earth to Armageddon.

> *They go out to the kings of the whole world to gather them for the battle on the great day of God Almighty... Then they gathered the kings together in a place that in Hebrew is called Armageddon. (Rev.16:12-21)*

The point I am making is that for the final showdown outlined in the above Scripture, 'kings' is plural. This means that immediately before the end of the world, there is more than one king and, therefore, more than one nation. So, if Scripture says there are multiple kings and nations, then logic alone screams there cannot be a One-World Government in place at that time. If God's word says multiple kings will gather, and people say there will only be one Antichrist leader, whom should we believe? Well, for me, the answer was obvious. Next question!

WHY THREE EVIL SPIRITS?

Now I had to look at the problem of the three evil spirits themselves, which had to be 'sent out' to deceive the multiple kings into gathering at Armageddon.

> *Then I saw three evil spirits...they are the spirits of demons performing miraculous signs, and they go out to the kings of the whole world to gather them for the battle on the great day of God Almighty. (Rev.16:13-14)*

Why three? Surely if there were only one leader, there would only need to be one evil spirit sent out rather than three evil spirits? Hmm, logical, but not strong enough. So, I did what I had been trained all my life to do with every problem; I turned it around and looked at it from another angle. When I did, I saw how utterly ridiculous is the whole Antichrist, One-World Government scenario. Let me show you what I mean.

Let's turn everything around and pretend, for argument's sake, that there will be a One-World Government and a human Antichrist will rule it. Now a reasonable person would assume that Satan would be in charge of the Antichrist and all the evil spirits in his kingdom. Right? So, why would Satan need to send three evil spirits to deceive his Antichrist into taking the nations to Armageddon? If there were, in fact, a One-World Government controlled by Satan's Antichrist, wouldn't he simply tell the nations what to do?

> *There is no 'end-time' One-World Government anywhere in Scripture!*

Why would demons need to be sent to deceive the nations? End-time theology makes no sense because it's simply not true. According to Scripture, there is no 'end-time' Antichrist world leader, and there is no 'end-time' One-World Government!

ONE RULER OVER ALL KINGS

There is only one world ruler named in Revelation, and it is not Satan! Nor is it anyone who belongs to him or works for him! I don't understand how those who say they have read the Book of Revelation and who push the false theory of an Antichrist world ruler can miss the most definitive statement about the identity of the ruler over the kings of the Earth, stated plainly in the first chapter of Revelation. The ruler is pointed out and named, and his name is Jesus Christ.

> *Grace and peace to you from…Jesus Christ the*
> *faithful witness, the firstborn from the dead, and*
> *the ruler of the kings of the Earth. (Rev.1:5)*

Surely that is clear enough? Revelation teaches over and over again that Jesus Christ is already *King of kings, Lord of lords* and *ruler over all the kings of the Earth*. Meanwhile, despite what Scripture says, *wolves in sheep's clothing* insist Satan's Antichrist is going to suddenly appear in human form and become *ruler over all the kings of the Earth*. So which should we believe; the word of God or ever-changing popular end-time theories? Revelation makes it abundantly clear, over and over again, that Jesus Christ is ruling and reigning over this world and will continue to reign *forever and ever*.

> *The kingdom of the world has become the*
> *Kingdom of our Lord and of his Messiah, and*
> *he will reign forever and ever. (Rev.11:15)*

How can those who say they love Christ deny his Lordship? How can any of us say with one breath that Jesus is King of kings and ruler of the nations, and then in the next breath stand in Satan's camp, opposite to Christ (anti-Christ), and agree with Satan that he, through a single Antichrist figure, will rule over the nations in an end-time One-World Government? This belief is as diametrically opposed to the teaching of Revelation as teaching can get. It is an abomination!

THE NEW WORLD ORDER

I can't move on from this subject without addressing the glaringly obvious. World events are currently pointing to the development of a 'New World Order' or 'Great Reset!'; a One-World Government ruling through a worldwide socialist dictatorship, with the rich elites of the world pulling the strings. Surely this is what Revelation predicted? Well no! Absolutely not!

This deliberately introduced, Satan-glorifying 'end-time doctrine' points to a long-term political strategy that involves deceiving Christians into believing a lie. False prophets in the churches have twisted Scripture to produce the 'Antichrist and his One-World Government' propaganda, which fits the socialist agenda. It is not spiritual. It is a political strategy! Fooling Christians into believing that this lie comes from Scripture with the blessing of God is one of the greatest deceptions in history.

WE ARE POWERFUL!

Christians number nearly one-third of the world's population. We have the numbers and power to stop this New World Order before it starts. They know this! Hence the lies!

It is easier to deceive us than to fight us. Can they win? No! If Christians believe that a Satan-led One-World Government is God's prophecied will, we will not stand against it and the moral decay it promotes. On the other hand, if we know it's a lie, we can stand up like the mighty army we are for our God and for the democratic way of life Christianity supports.

A DEADLY DECEPTION

Can you see yet, how 'adding' to the Book of Revelation can be so deadly it can cost us our Salvation? Can you see how it can also cost us our worldly freedom? Can you see why Christ commands us to tear down false teaching in the church?

Throw out this 'added' Antichrist-led One-World Government theory, for it is a diabolic lie. This deadly doctrine was designed to weaken the church and bring mockery to the Lordship of our victorious Saviour. When you know the truth, it will not only set you free; it will keep you free.

Immersed in confidence!

24

IS THERE AN ANTICHRIST?

This is the spirit of antichrist, which you have heard is coming and even now is already in the world. (1Jn.4:3)

Once I had seen that the concept of a single human Antichrist-led One-World Government before the return of Christ was not supported by Scripture in any way, I was ready to ask the next question, 'Will there be an antichrist in any other form?' My short answer had to be 'yes', for the above Scripture confirms it to be true. However, I found that the *antichrist* of Scripture bears no resemblance to the Antichrist portrayed in the Satan-glorifying, though popular, end-time theology.

What Scripture shows us is that it is impossible for any single Antichrist person to appear on the Earth in human flesh. The word of God reveals there is not, and never will be, a 'Satan in the flesh' Antichrist person living on the Earth. For, while Satan may be inherently anti-Christ, three powerful witnesses show very plainly that he will never appear on Earth as a person. Those witnesses are the Revelation of Christ itself, the writer of Christ's testimony, the Apostle John, and the authority behind Revelation, the Spirit of God.

It is what these three mighty witnesses deliberately leave out of Revelation which proves that a physical, human Antichrist cannot possibly exist.

THE FIRST PROOF

There is no Antichrist person named, or even mentioned, in the Book of Revelation! That is a somewhat important and significant point, one would think! A reasonable person would assume that if a world leader of such significance was going to be as important as some would like him to be, God himself would have added him to the Book of Revelation, but he didn't; a political Antichrist figure is just not there! There is no such person even alluded to in Revelation. The word *antichrist* cannot be found at all! In fact, I discovered that there is only a total of four references in the entire Bible which use the term *antichrist*; none of them refers to a single person, and none of them is in the Book of Revelation.

> *There is no Antichrist person named, or even mentioned, in Revelation!*

This would surprise most people because the concept of an Antichrist world leader has been so widely accepted most people would assume there is a basis for that belief written in the Book of Revelation. There is not! It is a completely 'made-up' fantasy. This Antichrist person has been 'added' to the Book of Revelation.

THE SECOND PROOF

The Apostle John wrote the Book of Revelation, and he is also the only Apostle to mention the word 'antichrist'. The word itself is so insignificant in Scripture that it's only recorded a total of four times.

Of all the teachers in Christendom, the Apostle John understood the meaning of *antichrist*. He warned believers of its existence, yet he did not include any reference to an Antichrist world leader when he wrote the Book of Revelation. Why was that? Why did he leave it out? The answer is in his teaching. When he refers to the *antichrist,* the Apostle John refers to a spirit, an attitude, or a belief system in any individual that is against Christ and who is, therefore, anti-Christ.

> *The word 'antichrist' is so insignificant in Scripture it is only written a total of four times!*

> *Dear children, this is the last hour, and as you have heard that the antichrist is coming, even now, many antichrists have come... (1Jn.2:18)*

> *Who is the liar? It is the man who denies that Jesus is the Christ; such a man is the antichrist... (1Jn.2:22)*

> *Do not believe every spirit but test the spirits... every spirit that does not acknowledge Jesus is not from God. This is the spirit of the antichrist, which you heard is coming and even now is already in the world. (1Jn.4:1-6)*

> *Many deceivers, who do not acknowledge Jesus Christ as coming in the flesh, have gone out into the world. Any such person is the deceiver and the antichrist. (2Jn.1:7)*

These are the only four Scriptures in the entire Bible that mention the word *antichrist*. There are no others! How can anyone possibly build a futuristic, world-dominating, human Antichrist theory from these four Scriptures?

According to the Apostle John, 'antichrist' is just a term for people who don't believe in Christ. In fact, according to John's words, there are many anti-Christ's because there are many who do not believe in Christ. In the light of his understanding of the multitudes of anti-Christ's in the world, there would have been certainly no point trying to name them all in the Book of Revelation. That would have been an impossible task, for there were many unbelievers, anti-Christ's, in the Apostle John's generation as there are many unbelievers, anti-Christ's, in every generation.

John wrote Revelation, and John warned about the *antichrist* spirit. It would have been easy for him to add a single Satan in the flesh, Antichrist, world leader figure to his Book of Revelation if that was his understanding, but he didn't! It is clear this was never the Apostle John's understanding of the word *antichrist*.

If the writer of Revelation did not see fit to 'add' a single Antichrist world leader figure to his book of testimony to Christ, then neither should we. Rather we should learn from his teaching the true meaning of the word *antichrist* and begin using the term the correct way.

THE THIRD PROOF

God does not include a single Antichrist human person in his final judgment! This is another somewhat important point. If a single Antichrist world leader existed, then he would inevitably need to be punished for his rebellion against God, would he not? However, Revelation does not record any punishment for a single human Antichrist world leader.

The Book of Revelation exists to show how our King has triumphed and put all the enemies of God under his feet, yet a single Antichrist figure is not mentioned.

Revelation details who God's enemies are and how they will be punished. When these punishments are completed, there is no sin or evil left in God's creation, and the salvation of the saints is fully accomplished. Following is a list of all those whom God punishes. This list is complete:

1. Satan (the dragon)

2. Demons (fallen angels)

3. The ten-horned beast (sin and blasphemy)

4. The two-horned beast ('many' wolves/false sheep)

5. Satan's mistress (all those outside the Bride of Christ)

6. The Earth (contaminated with evil)

7. Death and Hell (the last enemy to be destroyed)

There are only seven enemies of God mentioned in Revelation. There is nothing else mentioned that either needs to be punished or can be punished. When these things are destroyed, God says, *It is done!* (Rev.21:6). I couldn't find a human 'Antichrist' world ruler in this list!

If there were going to be a single human as destructive to God's world and his people as the Antichrist figure is supposed to be, God would need to punish him for his evil. The fact that there is no mention of any punishment for a human Antichrist world ruler in Revelation or anywhere else in Scripture means there is no human Antichrist to punish. He doesn't exist and never will exist! Satan will never be allowed to appear on the earth in the flesh as a human being as Christ did. He was eternally defeated at Calvary and can now only work through his agents.

> *There is no human Antichrist person for God to punish!*
>
> *He doesn't exist!*

THE REAL ANTICHRIST IS A 'SPIRIT'

It has been widely assumed that an Antichrist political leader will gather the nations to fight God's people at Armageddon. Again, that is not what Revelation says...

> *Then I saw three evil spirits that looked like frogs; they came out of the mouth of the dragon, out of the mouth of the beast and out of the mouth of the false prophet. (Rev.16:13)*

Please notice that the evil spirits sent out to gather the kings are multiple. They are not one Antichrist human, but are definitely 'spirits'. They come out of the mouths of the dragon and his two beasts. Their job is to deceive all the kings and nations of the Earth and lead them to Armageddon. And they succeed! This is God's description; these are his words. God also gave physical imagery to these three spirits when he said they would *look like frog*s. Do kings listen to frogs? Apparently, they do!

Do kings listen to frogs? Apparently they do!

We know they do because the woman who is carried on the back of Satan's ten-horned beast to her destruction is symbolic of the great city that seduces all the kings of the Earth and deceives them into giving their authority to Satan. *God has put it into their hearts to hand over their royal authority (to the beast) until God's words are fulfilled (Rev.17:17-18).*

This is exactly what God did to the Egyptians; he hardened their already rebellious hearts so they would not obey the warnings of Moses, which ultimately brought about the plagues, miracles and final redemption of the Israelites. *I have hardened the hearts of his officials so that I may perform these signs of mine among them (Ex.10.1).*

284

Here again, we see that God hardens the hearts of those who already love the ways of the beast, sin and blasphemy so that his prophetic words will be fulfilled. A further reference to the previous plagues of Egypt is seen in the description of the three deceiving spirits; that these demons will *look like frogs* is simply a reference to the frog plague God sent on Egypt, for John was describing end-time plagues. These frogs, like the frogs of the previous plagues, would cover the whole world and touch the life of every person not protected by the Blood of God's Holy Lamb.

> *I will plague your whole country with frogs. They will come up into your palace and your bedroom and onto your bed, into the houses of your officials and on your people, and into your ovens and kneading troughs. The frogs will go up on you and your people and all your officials. (Ex.8:2-4)*

Nothing bound by the limits of a human body could possibly be that thorough. These three demonic beings are not earthly nations or kings, and they are not a single person. They are supernatural powers and enforcers of spiritual wickedness. Evil spirits! This is why we are told *our warfare is not against flesh and blood but against spiritual powers.* If the word of God is true, and our warfare is spiritual warfare, then we must conclude that our enemy is spiritual. We overcome these frogs the same way we overcome everything else, by repentance, testimony and faithfulness. They do not overcome us!

Our warfare is not against flesh and blood, but against spiritual powers of wickedness in high places!

(Eph.6:12)

285

Through these Scriptures, we learn that the end-time deception of many kings and nations comes from multiple spirits, not from one single Antichrist person. I believe this is why the Apostle John placed so much emphasis on teaching believers to test the spirits of all people. The *antichrist* is spirit! His role, generation after generation, is to deceive both the world and the elect, and he will be seen in 'many'.

IT IS NOT COMPLICATED

Christians don't have to be deceived by the lies of false prophets; the truth is in the word of God, and the truth about the last days is specifically in Revelation itself. The wonderful Book of Revelation is not complicated, but it has been made complicated by *wolves in sheep's clothing*, who have infiltrated the body and bombarded the Bride with lie after conflicting lie in order to get us to lose faith in the might and saving love of our beloved King.

The simple truth and beauty of the message of Revelation is that it's not about world politics or wars and rumours of wars. It's not about nations or world leaders. It's not about money markets or even the buying and selling of human souls. Revelation is about how Christ has saved us from all those things!

This is the truth about the Book of Revelation in a nutshell. Our Saviour has triumphed! Revelation is his 'how to' manual, which teaches us how we can join him in his success and reveals the promised blessings waiting for those who overcome in the same way he overcame. It is a personal word of encouragement and promise from Christ to his eternal partner, and though written in the language of parables, there is no image on any page which gives Satan glory, let alone victory. It's time to put Satan back where he belongs, under the feet of Christ!

There is no Rapture

The Rapture Theory is not found in Revelation, for there are only two multiple resurrections named in Scripture. The first is the resurrection of Christ, and the last is the *hope of our salvation* when all believers will be raised together on the last day. Sandwiched between them is the Great Tribulation of the last days, which we know began on the day of Pentecost.

There is no One-World Government

The One-World Government Theory is a false doctrine with no basis in Scripture. It was introduced to the church to smooth the way for a dystopian socialist New World Order. The purpose of such a regime is to destroy the power and influence of Christianity worldwide. Yet, Revelation shows that Armageddon only happens because Christians are so strong and mighty in number that all the nations of the world politically join together in order to try to 'wipe us out' and, despite their best efforts, they fail to destroy us!

There is no single human Antichrist

The notion of a single human Antichrist is totally absurd, for there is no such person mentioned anywhere in Scripture. The deceiving spirits of Revelation *look like frogs,* and John made it very clear that the word 'antichrist' simply means anyone who does not belong to Christ.

But that's not all

There is one more false teaching which needs to be destroyed before this whole Satan-glorifying blasphemy can be removed from the Book of Revelation. That teaching is a misinterpretation of Daniel's *Abomination that causes desolation*. It is another deadly 'addition'!

Educated and approved!

25

THE ABOMINATION

He will set up the abomination that causes desolation. With flattery, he will corrupt those who have violated the Covenant, but the people who know their God will firmly resist him. (Dn.11:30-35)

Part of the false doctrine of the human Antichrist teaching is the theory that the Antichrist will set itself up in the new temple of God in the current city of Jerusalem and use its power to destroy worship. Many false teachers encourage believers to look to the rebuilding of the original temple in Jerusalem to gauge the time of the appearance of the Antichrist. What a foul deception! How subtly these liars have deceived Christ's beloved into 'looking for the appearing of Satan' instead of 'looking for the appearing of Christ'!

As with all the other blasphemous end-time fantasies, this theory also removes Christ from the story. It's true that Scripture said 'an abomination' would set itself up in the Temple of Jerusalem, for this was prophesied by Daniel in the Old Testament. True! True! True! The problem is that prophecy was fulfilled nearly 2000 years ago!

The *abomination that causes desolation* is not something that will make its appearance in the vague and distant future. It has already made its appearance and has been around for a long, long time.

WHAT IS THE ABOMINATION?

The appearance of the abomination was fully manifested in Jerusalem nearly 2000 years ago, in Jesus' day, which is why Jesus advised his disciples to flee when they saw the abomination appear. Did his disciples see the abomination that causes desolation? Yes, they did! Did they flee? Yes, they did! So what did they see?

The orders for the death of Christ came from the highest authority within God's own Temple in Jerusalem. Further, it was only because the Holy Land was ruled by Rome that Christ could fulfil Scripture by dying on a cross, for crucifixion was a torture invented by the Romans.

These two separate but combined circumstances completely fulfilled the prophecy of Daniel in Jesus' time, for it was the abomination ruling in God's Temple in Jerusalem, under Roman authority, that put Christ himself to death.

There will never be, now or in the future, any greater abomination than the killing of the creator of all things. When Judas, working with the abomination to destroy the only true worship the world had ever seen, betrayed Christ and handed him over to be destroyed, the disciples did exactly what Jesus said they should do when they saw the abomination at work; they ran. But they only ran once!

The prophecy also said *the people who know their God will firmly resist him,* so because the Apostles' knew their God, they were able to recognise and firmly resist the abomination from that time on.

The only disciple who didn't 'flee' when the abomination appeared in the temple was John. He didn't bow to the abomination for a minute. He firmly resisted! He showed he was not afraid of the abomination, right from the start, by being the only disciple at the Cross to witness Christ's actual death, and because he was there, he was granted the high privilege of caring for Jesus' mother until the end of her life. This turned out to be his protection from violent persecution to death, which was suffered by all the other disciples.

JOHN SAW THE ABOMINATION

I believe this is why John understood the *antichrist* and was able to warn his disciples about the *spirit of antichrist,* teaching them how to test the spirits in order to tell the difference between those who know their God and pretenders who, like Judas, are prepared to *violate the Covenant* and trample true worship under their feet. What John witnessed and understood was that *the abomination that causes desolation* and *the spirit of antichrist* are one and the same! At the time Daniel received his prophecy, he was not able to give a name to the abomination he saw in his vision, so he

The 'abomination' and the 'spirit of antichrist' are the same thing!

only referred to it as the *abomination that causes desolation.* In contrast, John was able to give the abomination a name, for he saw firsthand that the abomination was set up to destroy Christ and was, therefore, totally anti-Christ.

In their time, the first disciples not only firmly resisted the abomination themselves, but they taught their disciples how to discern *the antichrist spirit* so they, too, could firmly resist him and the desolation the abomination promotes.

Since then, lies have brought terrible confusion to the Body of Christ. By not understanding the truth of the word of God, many believers have been left vulnerable to evil people who claim to be doing the will of God when they are, in reality, violating the Covenant and trampling it under their feet.

We don't have to look far for examples. For, from the time of Christ, *the abomination that causes desolation* or *spirit of antichrist* has been very active, particularly through the churches. Why through the churches? This is because the abomination likes to position itself in the holy place so that it can use flattery to deceive the elect. Generation after generation, his tactics and targets remain the same.

The original abomination still set's itself up in God's holy place to deceive the elect!

God's people are the New Jerusalem, the new and Holy City which has come down from God. We are *living stones* in his temple and the *dwelling place of his Spirit*. However, since the death of Christ, the abomination has been positioning his agents of flattery in God's new holy place within believers by placing his deceivers in positions of influence over us so they can, if possible, lead astray even the elect.

> *With flattery, he (the abomination) will corrupt those who have violated the Covenant, but the people who know their God will firmly resist him. (Dn.11:30-35)*

Acting like serpents while proclaiming their innocence of any wrongdoing, many deceivers have done unspeakable things in the name of Christ, supposedly for the 'greater good' of the people they have pretended to serve. When we look at church history, it becomes easy to see that the abomination has been brutally active from the beginning!

A BRUTAL HISTORY

We only have to look at church history to see that the practice of desolation, in all its forms, has always been an abomination. Let's do a quick historical overview;

- Judas (Christian) betrayed Christ to the Pharisees, who subsequently ordered his death;

- The violent (Christian) betrayals began the bloodbath of persecutions faced by the first believers;

- Constantine's (Christian) army ruthlessly hunted down and killed true believers who would not conform to Constantine's newly formed 'Christianity';

- Crusaders (Christians) massacred anyone who opposed them;

- Witch hunters (Christians) tortured, tore apart and burned at the stake;

- Missionaries (Christians) brutalised countless natives into submission;

- Modern religious leaders (Christians) still slaughtering by slander believers who don't conform to their particular creeds.

AN UNHOLY GOSPEL

The Apostle John gave true believers the perfect way to avoid entering into the abominations of false prophets, like the above, when he taught us how to *test the spirits* of people to see if they belong to God. If we do as John taught and take to heart what has been written into God's word by him, we will never be deceived by the lies of false prophets in the churches or become victims of *the antichrist spirit*, whose purpose is to desolate the testimony of Christ.

293

As we have seen from church history, many who say they believe are, in reality, deceivers who desire to bring desolation. Many times they succeed in deceiving the elect simply because the elect are not vigilant in *testing* what they are told. So what do we do when we see them at work?

There are many who set themselves up as leaders over God's people and yet bring desolation rather than harvests of righteousness. They are everywhere! Though they say they are speaking from a spiritual 'holy' place in the name of Christ, they are merely deceiving the elect. Contrary to being *wise as a serpent but innocent as a dove*, false prophets pretend innocence while they plan deception and revel in treachery. *Speaking like a dragon*, they call righteous works evil, 'speaking in tongues is of the devil', and promote evil works as nasty but necessary, 'you have to be cruel to be kind'.

> *Many leaders in the Body of Christ bring desolation rather than harvests of righteousness.*

There are so many preachers and teachers in the Body of Christ who never reveal the character of God and his Kingdom through their teaching. What comes out of their mouths is their obsession with the way things work in this world. They don't preach or teach about the beauty of the nature of God as Christ did; instead, they speak of worldly things and give every spiritual truth a worldview application. Not understanding the truth and beauty of the Cross of Christ, their words reveal their particular limited worldview, and they even discard the word of God when it clashes with their opinions. Those who openly disagree with them are publicly shunned, while those who disagree but remain silent do so because they believe they are not allowed to judge.

ARE WE ALLOWED TO JUDGE?

The words, *Judge not, lest you be judged* (Mt.7:1-2) have been used widely by false prophets and false teachers in the churches to shut down criticism and stop the righteous from objecting to their evil deeds. This false teaching is an abomination, and it has brought widespread desolation to the righteous in the Body, who can see evil being done but are forced to remain silent and watch as the evil destroys people. This is not God's will, and it is the opposite of what is written in his word and was taught by Christ, for Christ commanded us to judge with righteous judgment.

> *Stop judging by mere appearances and make a right judgment (Jn.7:24).*

No one can avoid judging; it is impossible to *not judge*. God created mankind to judge, and our brains are set up to continually judge everything. Every area of our life is affected by the way we judge a thing, situation or person, and our actions reflect our judgment. Each of our five senses has been set up for automatic judgment; is it hard or soft, sweet or sour, dark or light, fragrant or musty, loud or quiet? And our responses reflect our judgment. Every time we interact with another human being, we automatically judge their mood; are they violent, gentle, compassionate, vulnerable, happy, sad, dangerous or joyful? It's the same with sin. Before every murder, the judgment is made that the victim doesn't deserve to live; before every theft, the judgment is made that the owner doesn't deserve to own; before every lie, the judgment is made that the person being lied to doesn't deserve the truth.

No one can avoid judging. It is impossible to not judge at all; we must judge!

295

Judging is essential to life. Every thought is a judgment which is calculated and assessed automatically because the process of thinking is a process of judgment. Every waking moment of every day, we judge, and every time we judge, we have the opportunity to judge with righteous judgment. God has done this! Our ability to judge and make moral choices is what separates humans from animals. It's the reason we were given 'dominion' because 'ruling and reigning' is based on our ability to judge any given situation.

Every action that comes through our bodies is dependent on the way we judge our circumstances, motives, lives and situations. We can't stop thinking and choosing, and therefore we can't stop judging. You are judging now! Since Christ has commanded us to judge righteously, it is vital that we come to terms with our God-given judgment.

THE BLESSINGS OF JUDGMENT

I have found that the difference between righteous and unrighteous judgment, though very rarely explained, is massive! The vastness of the authority believers have been given to judge with righteous judgment is staggering, and the results are always breathtaking.

We have all heard that when the true Gospel is preached, believers will live in forgiveness, heal the sick, raise the dead, cast out demons, drink poison without being affected, speak in tongues of men and angels, turn water to wine and stones to bread, walk on water, command the wind and move mountains, yet every one of these actions begins by making a righteous judgment. None of them can happen, not even forgiveness, unless we judge they need to be done, for even forgiveness demands we judge that someone has done wrong and needs forgiveness. These are all 'judgment calls'!

On a less spectacular scale, there are the judgment calls we make regarding feeding the hungry, assisting the homeless, clothing the poor, aiding the feeble and visiting the lonely. All of these are righteous judgments that bring glory to God and blessing to the humble and helpless, and they are the real and practical, hands-on expression of *love God and love your neighbour as yourself.* In Scripture, blessing people is regarded as *true religion* (Js.1:27) and yet not one thing can be done unless we first judge.

The truth is we cannot obey our Saviour or enter into any of his blessings unless we judge! Without judging, there is no 'ruling and reigning' with Christ in this life or the next.

THE DESOLATION OF HOLINESS

Do you recognise the abomination yet? Can you see *the spirit of antichrist* at work in the Body of Christ? If you can, then it's time to make a judgment call. Don't be afraid to judge with righteous judgment. There is no place more holy than Christ's testimony of his victory over the enemies of God, which he has placed under his feet. Revelation is his holy and royal proclamation, the written record of his triumph. Yet, within his testimony, three powerfully wicked teachings have set themselves up to get us to take our eyes off Christ and place them onto Satan instead. Are we going to allow these false teachings to replace the awe which belongs to our mighty God and King with fear of a mere angel?

Isn't it time for those who love Christ to judge what we are being taught, tear down the lies, uphold the glory of our Saviour and proclaim the truth? This three-pronged false 'antichrist' teaching comes directly from the 'spirit of antichrist'. It is itself as anti-Christ as the antichrist spirit gets!

Free from fear!

26
SATAN'S MARK

He (the beast) also forced everyone, small and
great, rich and poor, free and slave, to receive
a mark on his right hand or on his forehead
so that no one could buy or sell unless he had
the mark, which is the name of the beast or the
number of his name. (Rev.13:16-17)

Another great lie that God's people have the authority to put
to death is the false teaching about the mark of Satan. So much
has been assumed about this mark and the forms it could take;
Hollywood has inflamed the imagination with movie after
movie and conjured up all kinds of scary scenarios. Though
most don't trust the Hollywood interpretations, they still
implant a nagging suggestion of possibility.

Doomsday prophets in our pulpits outstrip Hollywood
in the imagination area by terrifying people with outrageous
claims of Satanic power, warning believers that banks,
computers and technology itself could produce in people that
terrible mark, 666. Though many of these so-called 'warnings'
have fallen to the ground, there are always new prophets with
new warnings about the terrifying effects of the mark of Satan.

From the pope's mitre to bank cards and implanted microchips and from massive computers to global vaccinations and artificial intelligence, the form the dreaded mark could take continues to change, and every change fires the imaginations of those who don't actually read the Scriptures, yet Scripture is very clear about what a 'mark' is and how it is received.

TWO MARKS – LIFE OR DEATH

The mark of God and the mark of Satan are both applied the same way!

It may surprise many to know there are two types of 'marks' written in Scripture, one is the *mark of God,* and the other is the mark of the beast, which is the *mark of Satan.* Both marks, one for life and one for death, have been around since the dawn of time, and their meanings have not changed. These two marks are consistently applied the same way throughout Scripture and by the same person. So, to understand one, we need to look at both.

They were told not to harm the grass of the Earth or any plant or tree, but only those people who did not have the seal of God on their foreheads. (Rev.9:4)

Much has been assumed about the mark of Satan, and most of what has been written and taught is the product of wild imagination. In contrast, Scripture clearly defines the mark of Satan and the mark of God, which are almost identical. No imagination is needed. Sadly, even though there are many references to the mark, or seal, of God throughout Scripture, this truth is not widely taught. Therefore, many Christians seem unaware there is a mark of God, what it looks like, how it is received, or its purpose once received.

The good news for all believers is that, even though they may be unaware of what *the mark of God* is, what it's used for, or how it's received, they still personally carry the *mark of God* because his mark is placed upon every believer as soon as they are 'born again' by the Spirit of God. Now that's just good news! God's word shows that:

- God has already marked those who are his,

- Satan can never remove the *mark of God*, and

- Those who are marked with the *mark of God* cannot also be marked with the *mark of Satan*.

Now isn't that important information? That information should be proclaimed in every church! The truth is; when believers receive the *mark of God*, we are held within the grace, peace and protection of the mighty God of all gods, and there is absolutely no one with the power to snatch us out of his hand. That includes Satan! How great and powerful is the *mark of God*! If we desire anything on this Earth, let us desire to be marked with the *mark of God*, which gives us protection from all the judgments of God written about in Revelation.

SO WHAT IS THE MARK OF GOD?

There are various references to the *mark of God* throughout the Old and New Testaments, and they give a clear indication of what the mark is and how it is received. So let's look at the Old Testament first. In the Old Testament, God himself orders the marks on the foreheads and hands of his loyal people. This *mark of God* is figuratively on the forehead and hand because it is an invisible mark.

God's mark on the foreheads and hands of his people is an invisible mark!

Through the following Old Testament Scriptures, we see that honouring God by keeping his Commandments was regarded by him as the equivalent to being marked on the hand and on the forehead. The *mark of God* seen in the Old Testament is clearly an invisible spiritual mark given to those who revere and uphold God's Commandments.

> *This observance will be a reminder, like something tied on your hand or on your forehead; it will remind you to continue to recite and study the Word. (Ex.13:9)*

> *Fix these words of mine in your hearts and minds; tie them as symbols on your hands and bind them on your foreheads. (Deut.11:18-21)*

> *Keep these words that I am commanding you today in your heart... bind them as a sign on your hand, fix them as an emblem on your forehead and write them on the doorposts of your house and on your gates. (Deut.6:4-9)*

From these Scriptures, we learn that the forehead and the hand symbolise what people believe and what they do about what they believe. So when we read that Satan will cause people to be marked on their forehead or hand, the *mark* referred to will show, as God's mark shows, what the person believes and what they do about their belief.

THE MARK OF DEATH

The threat of death is not new or unusual. From the beginning of time, the sin of Adam and Eve marked all of God's creation with the penalty of death. The *mark of Satan* only highlights the established fact that everyone whose thoughts and deeds show they have turned their backs on God will be automatically marked for death.

There is nothing new here. Death is a normal result of sin. It is salvation from the effects of sin that is remarkable! Throughout the Bible, because of the sin of Adam and Eve, the only ones who could be saved from the mark of death were those who received *the mark of God*. In Ezekiel, we find that those who saw the horror of sin and groaned over its existence were noted and marked for protection from God's wrath.

> *Death is the normal result of sin.*
>
> *It is salvation from the effect of sin that is remarkable!*

> *'Go through Jerusalem, and put a mark on the foreheads of those who sigh and groan over all the abominations that are committed in it'. To the others, he said in my hearing, 'Pass through the city after him and kill... but touch no one who has the mark, and begin at my sanctuary'. (Eze.9:4-6)*

We see a similar story in Revelation when God sends out his angels to destroy the Earth. Once again, he orders protection for those *marked with the seal of the living God*.

> *I saw another angel ascending from the rising of the sun, having the seal of the living God, and he called with a loud voice... 'Do not damage the Earth or the sea or the trees, until we have marked the servants of our God with a seal on their foreheads'. (Rev.7:2-3)*

This is what our salvation is about. It's what salvation has always been about and why, through the Blood of Christ, we have been offered salvation. Salvation means freedom from the righteous judgment of God for sin.

THE MARK OF LIFE

The greatest story of *the mark of God* and the protection from death his mark affords is seen in the escape of the people of Israel from Egypt, or Passover. This account is commonly regarded as a symbol that points to Christ, who is our escape from the slavery of sin, our spiritual Passover. What is not commonly taught, though, is that according to the Scriptures we have just read, there will be a future Passover:

- ♥ During the first Passover, God's people received physical salvation through the physically seen mark of the blood of a sacrificial lamb.

- ♥ During the second Passover, God's people received invisible salvation through the physically seen blood of the sacrificed Lamb of God.

- ♥ During the final Passover, the invisible mark of the Blood of the Lamb, also called *the seal of the living God*, will be the only recognised salvation.

Throughout God's final judgments, only those who display *the mark of God* will be saved from the full fury of God's righteous wrath.

WHO DOES THE MARKING?

End-time fear teachers would like us to believe Satan will issue the mark of death, but that's not what Scripture shows, and when we ask the big question, 'Who does the actual marking, Satan or God?', the answer explains why believers never have to fear *the mark of Satan*. Ever!

> *Then the Lord called to the man dressed in linen who had the writing kit at his side and said to him, 'Go...and put a mark on the foreheads of those who grieve...(over sin)'. (Eze.9:3-4)*

Nowhere in Scripture does it say Satan has the power to order a 'mark' on anyone. Over and over again, we see God ordering people to be marked for salvation or death, but we never see Satan ordering any marks for either death or life. He can't! He is only an angel; he has never had that authority or power. What Scripture shows is that Satan, himself, has been 'marked' for eternal destruction and will be thrown permanently into *the lake of fire*. So, when we ask, 'Who has the power and authority to mark Satan?' We find it is Christ alone who was given the authority from God to judge Satan and all who follow him. No one else has been given the power to 'mark',

> *Satan can't order a 'mark' on anyone.*
>
> *He is only an angel!*
>
> *He doesn't have the authority.*

In Ezekiel, Christ is the man whom God commands to do the marking, for this image cannot represent anyone else. The fine linen he is wearing is symbolic of righteousness, and the writing kit he is carrying is symbolic of the *Lamb's Book of Life*. That he is referred to as *a man* shows it is neither God nor his Spirit choosing who will be marked for salvation, but Christ. Further, it shows that when it comes to the actual destruction, it is not God, his Spirit or Christ who does the destroying, and neither is it an arbitrary act of Satan, for that role has always belonged to the obedient angels of God.

In Exodus, it is only the blood of a sacrificed Lamb that can save from judgment, and in Revelation, it is *the seal of the living God* that protects from judgment. These *marks* of protection from destruction are everywhere throughout Scripture, and they are always authorised by God and delivered through Christ. The judgments themselves are always performed by God's angels.

WHO DOES THE JUDGING?

Modern-day theology abounds with tales of Satanic, end-time, anti-Christ aggression and multiple tales of horror, which terrify believers and non-believers alike. Stories of what will supposedly happen to those in this generation who receive the mark of the beast are horrible and show no respect for the power and authority of our great God or the enormous love and sacrifice of his Son, our hero.

The reality is the judgments of Revelation are not Satan's to play with. He has never had any authority from God to judge mankind. His only role has been to stand before God and accuse us *day and night (Rev.12:10)* so that God will have to judge us. What a tittle-tat! How pathetic! If he had the power to destroy us, he wouldn't be merely telling on us. He would be actively destroying us. But he's not! He can't! The Scriptures below show, without a doubt, who has been given the power and authority to bring judgment to all the people of the Earth, not just to those living in the last days.

The Father judges no one but has entrusted all judgment to the Son. (Jn.5:22)

I did not come to condemn the world but to save it. There is a judge for the one who rejects me and does not accept my words; that very word that I spoke will condemn him at the last day. (Jn.12:47-50)

When he (the Spirit) comes, he will expose the guilt of the world in regard to sin, righteousness and judgment; in regard to sin because men do not believe in me; in regard to righteousness because I am going to the Father, and in regard to judgment because the prince of this world now stands condemned. (Jn.16:8-11)

Scripture is consistent all the way through and confirms that Christ is one who judges in righteousness, only for salvation. Even though he only marks for salvation, anyone not marked by him is subject to judgment and dies at the hands of God's angels. This is an unchanging principle all through Scripture, both in the Old Testament and in the New.

> *Christ is the only one authorised by God to 'mark' people for judgment.*
>
> *And he only marks for salvation.*

The previous three Scriptures show the Heavenly structure of authority in relation to judgment. The first thing we notice is that God, who orders the judgments, does not do any of the judgings himself but has delegated the marking of those who will receive salvation from his judgments to his Son.

Christ, in turn, will not judge the wicked in the world, for his role is to save. He will mark everyone who accepts his salvation with the seal of protection from judgment. Those not sealed for salvation will be subject to the cold, hard judgment of the Law. Without Christ's mark to protect them, they will identify with the beast, that is, with those who reject the Commandments of God and the Testimony of Christ. They will have no protection from God's destroying angels.

As it is the role of the ten-horned beast *to make war on the Commandments of God and those who bear testimony to Jesus (Rev.12:17)*, it is easy to see how the nature of the beast will be seen in those who break the Commandments and mock the Testimony of Christ.

It is also easy to see how those who love Christ will stand with him and overcome as he overcame, *by the Blood of the Lamb and the word of our Testimony to him (Rev.12:11)*.

HOW DOES CHRIST MARK US?

Finally, we see it is the mighty sevenfold Spirit, our gentle helper, who has been given the task of exposing who is marked with sin and who is marked with righteousness, for he, himself, is the 'mark' we receive and therefore he is the 'mark' by which both are judged. If he dwells within us because of the Blood of Christ, we are marked for salvation. If he does not dwell within us, we are marked for death. From these Scriptures, we learn that:

- ♥ God commands the judgment but doesn't do it himself.
- ♥ Jesus brings salvation to those who groan over sin.
- ♥ The presence of the Spirit of God within a person, or not, shows the angels who is marked for salvation or destruction. This is also called the separating of the sheep from the goats.
- ♥ The final judgment of the world and all those not protected by the mark of salvation is carried out by God's obedient, destroying angels.

The Apostle Paul confirms that the *mark of God* is an invisible, spiritual mark, sealed onto our hearts by the Spirit of Christ, and teaches that only those who have their sin covered by the Blood of Christ can receive this indelible *mark of God*.

> *In Him, you also, when you had heard the word of Truth, the Gospel of your salvation, and believed in Him, were marked with the seal of the promised Holy Spirit. (Eph1:13)*

> *Christ has annointed us by putting his seal on us and giving us his Spirit...(2Cor.1:21-22)*

> *Do not grieve the Holy Spirit of God, with which you were marked with a seal for the day of redemption. (Eph.4:30)*

Just as those marked with the invisible Spirit of Christ are sealed for salvation, so those marked with *the mark of Satan,* which is the mark of the beast, do not have the protection of the Spirit of Christ. Whether a person chooses to be marked for eternal life or eternal death, it is evident from Scripture that the mark we receive is a spiritual mark, and the outcome is a spiritual outcome.

IT WILL NEVER BE PHYSICAL

The *mark of Satan* was given to him a long, long time ago, long before the existence of modern technology, before the New Testament was written, and long before banks existed. Therefore his mark can have absolutely nothing to do with modern things like bank cards, computers, microchips or vaccines. There is no way the mark can be physical, for Satan has never had a physical body, which means the mark he received could not possibly be physical. He is a spirit, and he received a spiritual mark that had an eternal spiritual meaning and consequence. Satan's mark of death is simply the absence of God's mark of life. It is not physical; it is 100% spiritual!

A SURE AND ETERNAL PROMISE

Christ *loves* his Bride! He loves us to death! He has slain a dragon, fought beasts and overcome the world for us. He has surrounded us with the most effective protection that can be found in Heaven or on Earth. He has clothed us with robes of righteousness, crowned us with glory and is counting the minutes until he can make us his forever. He has marked us with the seal of his promise, and after all he has done to win us, nothing in Heaven or Earth will now convince him to remove the seal of his promise from us. We are his, forever!

Powerfully protected!

27

WHAT DOES 666 MEAN?

If anyone has wisdom, let him calculate the number of the beast, for it is man's number. His number is 666. (Rev.13:18)

The famous number 666 is a sparkling jewel of Christ's glory. It is not something that will be seen on earth by any human eye, but that doesn't mean we can't understand what it represents. The Scripture above tells us that anyone who has wisdom will be able to calculate the number and understand its meaning, yet many have tried to interpret it from a worldview, and so, of course, can't see what it means. This was God's plan, for he speaks to us in parables.

The only way this number can be understood is by looking at it through the wisdom of God, and who is the Wisdom of God but Christ? In other words, this number needs to be seen through Jesus. Surprise! Surprise! When we look at it through the testimony of Christ, it is easy to understand its meaning. Everyone who values the wisdom of God in Christ will see what I see. This number is not frightening; it is another testimony to Christ's enormous victory. Further, it is not the only number in Revelation that glorifies Christ!

The number 666 is only half the story, for when we see the other half, a number also clearly laid out in Revelation, we get the full picture and understand the meaning of both numbers, which is, of course, the story of the salvation of mankind through Christ! Part of the message of the Book of Revelation is dedicated to revealing how the enemies of God will be marked as goats, while the other part is dedicated to revealing how the righteous will be marked as sheep. The two sets of numbers we see in Revelation represent those two marks. It's not complicated! It's brilliant!

It's not complicated. It's brilliant!

The truth and reality of these two marks are that God's judgment will fall on those marked for eternal death, while at the same time, Salvation from judgment will fall on all those marked by Christ for eternal life. Everyone who joins Satan in his rebellion against God and Christ will receive the same mark for sin Satan has received; the guarantee of eternal death. Everyone who joins Christ in service to God will receive his mark, the guarantee of eternal life.

It's not Satan who issues these marks; it's Christ! They are his righteous judgment in operation, for whether people are marked for eternal death or eternal life, the marking itself has always remained firmly within God's domain. So now, let's look at the two marks and what their numbers mean.

THE NUMBER OF THE BEAST

*And the dragon stood on the shore of the sea. And I saw a beast rising **out of the sea**... (Rev.13:1) ...Then I saw another beast, coming **out of the Earth**. He had two horns like a lamb, but he spoke like a dragon. (Rev.13:11-12)*

Just as sea and land jointly cover the whole of this planet, so here we see the joint influence of these two beasts of Satan also covers the whole of this planet. Their influence is not restricted to one religious organisation, one nation or even one continent but simultaneously affects the whole world, including everyone and everything in it. Since the authority and influence of these two beasts cover the entire world, with no exceptions, then so too does their numbered mark, which is received by those who are contaminated by these two beasts.

It all began back in the Garden of Eden. In Genesis, we see that God gave mankind dominion over everything in the sea and on the land, including the birds that span both earth and sea. *Rule over the fish of the sea, the birds of the air and over every living creature that moves on the ground (Gen.1:28).* The great shame of the fall of Adam and Eve was that they forfeited mankind's God-given authority to rule over the sea and the earth by handing our dominion over to Satan. So, in Revelation, we see that Satan still attempts to use mankind's forfeited authority to try to rule the world.

Satan stole his authority over the land and sea from Adam and Eve.

That Satan calls up these beasts from both the earth and the sea shows they are rising with authority stolen from mankind. This is why the number of the beast is also the number of man. Satan can only call up these beasts because we gave him that authority in the first place. However,

This is why the number of the beast is also the number of man.

since Christ restored dominion to the redeemed, Satan can only access dominion and authority through those who still forfeit the dominion of God; that is, through those who break the Commandments and blaspheme the testimony of Christ.

313

WHAT DO WE CALCULATE?

So far, we have calculated that the mark of the beast, like the beast itself, is invisible, that the number which represents that mark, also invisible, cannot be limited to a person, a religion, a nation, a continent or any technology, because it affects everyone and everything in this world and has done so for a very long time, for this particular number:

- ❤ Is the number that Satan received when he sinned and *fell short of the glory of God.*

- ❤ Is the number that Adam and Eve received when they sinned and *fell short of the glory of Go*d.

- ❤ Is called the number of man, for it is the same number given to everyone who chooses sin over righteousness, and so *falls short of the glory of God.*

- ❤ Is called the number of the beast, for this beast's role is to get us to break the Commandments and blaspheme Christ and so *fall short of the glory of God.*

Scripture shows that the glory of God is seen in his son Jesus Christ; therefore, because Christ is the standard of glory by which mankind is measured, if we *fall short of the glory of God*, we actually fall short of the standard of righteousness shown to the world through the life, death, resurrection and kingship of our Christ.

> *God, who said, 'Let light shine out of darkness',*
> *made his light shine in our hearts to give us the*
> *light of the knowledge of the glory of God in*
> *the face of Christ. (2Cor.4:6)*

Christ's glory has a number, and it can be seen in the Book of Revelation. This is the second set of numbers Revelation reveals; they are the rest of the story.

The number 666 may reveal the sad story of mankind's rebellion and fall, but the number 777 reveals the glory of God, as seen through salvation and redemption. Together these two numbers symbolise the whole Gospel of Christ, both the fall from glory and the return to glory.

It is a simple number with a very simple, uncomplicated message.

THE NUMBER OF CHRIST'S GLORY

Every image in Revelation is a parable that points to the victory and redemption of Christ; this includes the image of the three judgments. Though 777 is not written as a number, it is as easy to see as the sun in the sky, for each of the three final judgments has seven parts, which is why they are called the Seven Seals, Seven Trumpets and Seven Golden Bowls. Simply put, we are shown three judgments, each of which has seven applications, that is, 777.

It doesn't take a rocket scientist to see that Christ's standard of glory is seen in his redemption from the sins which made us all fall short of God's glory in the first place. The number of man, which is also the number of the beast, is simply a number less than 777, which in itself shows that those who receive it have fallen short of the glory of God. The sheep are elevated above 666 into his glory, and the goats continue to fall short. It is a very simple mark with a very simple message.

How brilliant is our God that he is able to capture the entire message of salvation by using just two numbers; 666 and 777. Together, they tell the whole story! Mind-blowing!

Securely Delivered!

28

THE FINAL BATTLE

And they said to the mountains, "Fall on us and hide us from the face of the One seated on the throne, and from the wrath of the Lamb. For the great day of their wrath has come, and who is able to withstand it?" (Rev.6:16)

Now we come to the final battle. Again, this battle reveals the glory and power of Christ's victory at Calvary, but that's not all it shows. It is a kaleidoscope of action so filled with simultaneous activity that several cameo 'snapshot descriptions' needed to be written side by side to explain the enormity of what had just taken place. These few cameo views capture in detail what happened to the two beasts, the scarlet woman and Satan himself, when God suddenly brought an end to the world and the proposed Battle of Armageddon.

Stunningly, for the first time, we also notice there are two wraths at play in Revelation. One is the Wrath of God for sin, which we recognise as the Law of God written by Moses. The other is the Wrath of the Lamb, which instigates and concludes the final, eternal judgment of the great whore, the two beasts, Satan, and the destruction of this sin-saturated planet.

THE WRATH OF GOD

The wrath of God in Revelation is a mirror image of the famine, plague and sword curses described so clearly in God's Mosaic Law. And Jesus confirmed that God's Mosaic Law is the only law by which all people will be judged.

This is proven in Revelation when God hands the Scroll of Judgment to Christ, for the Scroll Christ receives is already written, filled with writing on both sides, rolled up and sealed. This judgment is God's judgment. It is the Wrath of God. And it is placed into Christ's hands for him to execute.

This couldn't happen until Christ returned from Calvary as a Conquering Victor, where he had masterfully wielded the two-edged sword of truth, brought Law into balance with righteousness and put an end to the power of death and hell.

Due to his great victory at Calvary, God promised his Son he would put all his enemies under his feet, and that's what we see happening when the Scroll is handed to Christ.

The Lord said to my Lord: "Sit at my right hand until I put your enemies under your feet. (Mk.12:36)

At that point, Christ is given all the authority of the throne of God until the enemies described in the Scroll are destroyed. Once that is done, Christ plans to hand back the full authority of the Kingdom to his Father. Until then, Christ is the ultimate authority. No one has more power! No one!

Then the end will come, when he hands over the Kingdom to God the Father after he has destroyed all dominion, authority, and power. For he must reign until he has put all his enemies under his feet. The last enemy to be destroyed is death. (1Cor.15:24-26)

318

THE WRATH OF THE LAMB

At Calvary, Jesus conquered death and hell. He conquered Satan and sin. He conquered the rigid power of Law, replacing it with righteousness. And now, he is about to conquer again. This time, not even the echo of sin will survive.

It took the death and resurrection of Christ to strip Satan of his power over mankind. His power has never been any greater than in deceiving people into breaking God's Law so that God's Law itself would spring into action and bring down a curse of judgment on the lawbreaker. Satan's continual deceptions have brought, and continue to bring, untold suffering and harm to God's beloved people.

Now we see in the graphic judgments of Revelation that, because of Calvary, Satan falls victim to the judgment of the very Law he proudly used as a weapon against the Son of God. And so, as soon as the resurrected Lamb is given all authority in Heaven and on Earth, we see him use the Law to destroy the destroyer and all his followers forever. Poetic justice!

> *Don't misunderstand why I have come. I did not come to abolish the Law of Moses or the writings of the prophets but to fulfil them.*
>
> *I tell you, until Heaven and Earth pass away, not the smallest detail will disappear from God's Law until everything is accomplished.* *(Matt.5:17-18)*

The New Covenant ushered in through Christ's Blood does not have any judgments attached. Neither do his two New Commandments. This means the wrath of God for sin that we see written in Revelation can only come through the curses written in the Law of Moses. There are no other curses or judgments for sin written anywhere in Scripture.

A TERRIFYING SIGHT

When Christ opens the Scroll of Judgment, we see the judgments begin to fall on Satan, his beasts and those who follow them, adopt their ways, and in various ways, make themselves enemies of God.

> *The kings of the Earth, the nobles, the commanders, the rich, the mighty, and every slave and free man hid in the caves and among the rocks of the mountains. And they said to the mountains and the rocks, "Fall on us and hide us from the face of the One seated on the throne, and from the wrath of the Lamb". For the great day of their wrath has come, and who is able to withstand it? (Rev.6:15-17)*

Meanwhile, as these judgments of God for sin are falling on the wicked, the Book of Revelation shows who is excluded from the wrath of God and how the righteous who stand with Christ are completely protected from judgment.

> *These are the ones who have come out of the great tribulation; they have washed their robes and made them white in the Blood of the Lamb. Never again will they hunger, and never will they thirst; nor will the sun beat down upon them, nor any scorching heat. For the Lamb in the centre of the throne will be their shepherd. He will lead them to springs of living water, and God will wipe away every tear from their eyes. (Rev.17:14-27)*

All the curses of God, which will destroy Satan and those he has deceived, are written in this Scroll. Yet, we clearly see that they do not fall on the redeemed of Christ.

THE SEVEN SEALS

The first four seals reveal the authority God has given to Christ because of Calvary. The fifth reveals the protection God has put in place for the redeemed, and the sixth shows God's overall plan for the punishment of the wicked. But it's the seventh that makes everyone gasp. The seventh seal opens like a flower to reveal the hidden judgments inside.

The Seven Seals open:

- The first seal: The First Horseman who rides out is the crowned Christ himself, who sets out to *place all the enemies of God under his feet.*

- The second seal: The Second Horseman, holds the sword of Christ, who said, *I have not come to bring peace but a sword.*

- The third seal: The Third Horseman, represents Christ's authority to both bless and curse and commands, *Do not harm the oil or the wine.*

- The fourth seal: The Fourth Horseman, reveals that only Christ is in charge of life, death and hell. *Behold, I hold the keys of death and hell.*

- The fifth seal: Reveals the saints, living and dead, who have endured persecution but are now dressed in white and safe from judgment.

- The sixth seal: Reveals judgment falling on the unrighteous just prior to the collecting of the full number of 'sealed' righteous.

- The seventh seal: The opening of this seal causes silence in Heaven. *The Seventh Seal* opens to reveal the *Seven Trumpets* and the *Seven Golden Bowls* hidden within, and as they open, the final judgment begins.

THE SEVEN TRUMPETS

These curses fall mainly on the Earth rather than on people, affecting trees, grass, the sea, fish, rivers and springs and the sun. One-third of the wicked die from the poison in the rivers, some are made sick by smoke, and some die by war. The most dramatic event happens during the seventh trumpet. This is God's direct judgment on Satan and his followers.

The Seven Trumpets open:

- The first trumpet: causes hail and fire, mixed with blood, to fall from the sky and burn one-third of the trees and all the green grass.

- The second trumpet: causes a volcanic eruption that turns the sea to blood and destroys a third of the ships and a third of all sea creatures.

- The third trumpet: causes fire-filled rocks to fall from the sky. When they hit the Earth, they poison one-third of the rivers and springs, and many people die.

- The fourth trumpet: causes a third of the sun, the moon, and the stars to be darkened, which dramatically shortens daylight hours.

- The fifth trumpet: causes smoke to cover the whole Earth. Out of the smoke, human locusts arise who infect those not 'sealed' with a sickness worse than death.

- The sixth trumpet: causes the Euphrates River area to host the death of one-third of mankind. This is when the two witnesses arise.

- The seventh trumpet: causes Satan to be cast down, the two beasts and the great harlot to be recognised, the true Gospel to be revealed, and sinners to experience 'the grapes of wrath'.

THE SEVEN GOLDEN BOWLS

The curses of festering sores, heat and blindness fall onto those who have received the mark of death. This multitude of people, called the Great Whore, curse God for their sores but refuse to repent. The two beasts lead the Great Whore to the battle of Armageddon. Just as all the armies of the nations gather for battle, the Seventh Golden Bowl is poured out, and God's voice says, "It is done!" This signals the end of the world.

The Seven Golden Bowls open:

- The first golden bowl: is poured out onto the land, causing ugly, festering sores on those who had received the mark of the beast.

- The second golden bowl: is poured out onto the sea until it turns red, and everything in the sea dies.

- The third golden bowl: is poured out into the rivers and springs, which turn to blood.

- The fourth golden bowl: is poured out on the sun, which scorches people with heat so that they curse God for the plagues but refuse to repent.

- The fifth golden bowl: is poured out on the first and second beasts and onto the woman who rides the ten-horned beast, and they are all plunged into darkness.

- The sixth golden bowl: is poured out into the Euphrates River area, which dries up in preparation for the battle of Armageddon - which never actually happens.

- The seventh golden bowl: is poured out into the air, and Christ cries out, "It is done!" This culminates in the collapse of all cities, hail mixed with fire, a monster earthquake, the removal of oxygen and the final destruction of the Earth and of Satan.

PUTTING IT ALL TOGETHER

So much is going on during these three judgments that it is easier to understand when paraphrased like a story...

Despite being cast down to the Earth at creation, Satan has been allowed to visit Heaven to receive commands and seek approval to sift the righteous. That changes at Calvary! Suddenly Satan is permanently evicted from Heaven and locked up. Since he no longer has access to God, he can't get permission to use the Law against people. It's game over!

At this point, angry and seeking revenge, he conjures two beasts to carry on his deceptions and increase his influence. The first beast is given all his authority and power to tempt people to break the Ten Commandments so they will be judged by God's Law, and to blaspheme Christ so they will have no protection from the wrath of God on judgment day.

> *Then there was war in Heaven. Michael and his angels fought against the dragon. And the dragon lost the battle, and he and his angels were forced out of Heaven. (Rev.12:7-9)*
>
> *The dragon was enraged and went off to make war on those who keep the Commandments of God and bear testimony to Jesus. And he stood on the shore of the sea. And I saw a beast rising... (Rev.12:17-13:1)*

The first beast can only tempt those who are not protected by the Salvation of Christ. So, we see Satan conjure a second beast with the ability to deceive the elect. Its role is to use false teaching and false miracles, signs and wonders to trick the elect into inadvertently breaking the Commandments and blaspheming Christ. This beast looks like a lamb but speaks like a dragon. It is the classic 'wolf in sheep's clothing'.

> *Then I saw another beast come up out of the earth. He had two horns like those of a lamb, but he spoke with the voice of a dragon. It exercised all the authority of the first beast on its behalf and made the earth and its inhabitants worship the first beast. (Rev.13:11-13)*

During this time, Satan also creates for himself an anti-Bride. She is described as a whore, dressed in red and drunk on the blood of the saints. She is the exact opposite of the Bride of Christ.

Just as all the redeemed who have ever lived make up the body of Christ in this world, so Satan's whore makes up the body of Satan in this world. She rides on the back of the beast, which shows she represents all the people living and dead of every nation who have ever rebelled against God's Commandments and blasphemed Christ.

> *I saw a woman sitting on a scarlet beast dressed in purple and scarlet and adorned with gold, precious stones and pearls. She held a golden cup in her hand and was drunk with the blood of the saints. (Rev.17:3-6)*

The two beasts hate the humans they deceive and delight in bringing them to 'ruin and nakedness', the result of *famine,* to a place where their 'flesh is eaten', symbolic of *plague,* and to the finality of 'burning with fire', classic *sword.*

> *The waters you saw, where the prostitute was seated, are peoples and multitudes and nations and tongues. And the ten horns and the beast that you saw will hate the prostitute. They will leave her ruined and naked and will eat her flesh and burn her with fire. (Rev.17:15-16)*

It's no surprise that in the judgment of the *Seventh Trumpet,* God brings the first of these three curses down onto those who have chosen Satan over Christ. He brings Satan's mistress to public ruin, writing her abominations, immorality, drunkenness, cruelty and greed in a book called the Book of Revelation, exposing her to eternal shame.

Then we see a plot twist!

During the judgment of the *Seventh Trumpet,* we suddenly understand that Satan's beasts didn't know that the famine, plague and sword curses they wanted so much to fall on the hated whore would actually fall onto them as well. And not only onto them but also onto Satan. As this curse is poured out, God exposes them all!

Further, once their presence, plans and ugly natures are exposed, the people who make up the whore, also referred to as 'goats' and 'tares', are deftly gathered from the Earth in the great harvest of sinners, which is called 'the grapes of wrath'.

The angel swung his sickle and gathered the grapes of the Earth, and he threw them into the great winepress of God's wrath. (Rev.14:19)

These multiple events reveal the first of three curses on Satan, his beasts and the hated whore. The final two curses, of plague and sword, come through the very last judgment, the seventh judgment of the *Seven Golden Bowls.*

So much happens in this last judgment that several events need to be written side by side. Therefore, there are a few cameo shots of extra information written later by the Apostle John to fill in the gaps about what happened to the great whore, the two beasts, Satan, and the redeemed on the battlefield at the moment Christ said, 'It is done!"

What we first see is the end of the world. Islands disappear into the sea, mountains collapse, cities fall, the sky peels back, the Earth quakes, lightning flashes, massive hailstones fall from the sky, and people are terrified.

THE END OF THE WORLD

A voice from Heaven cried, "It is done!" Then there came flashes of lightning, rumblings, peals of thunder and a severe earthquake. No earthquake like it has ever occurred since the beginning of time, so tremendous was the quake.

Jerusalem split into three parts, and all the cities of the nations collapsed.

Every island fled away, and the mountains disappeared. From the sky, huge hailstones, each weighing about a hundred pounds, fell onto people. (Rev.16:18-21)

The sun became as dark, and the moon turned red as blood. Then the stars of the sky fell to the Earth like green figs falling from a tree shaken by a strong wind.

The Heavens receded like a scroll being rolled up, and every mountain and island was removed from its place.

The kings of the earth, the princes, the generals, the rich, the mighty, and everyone else hid in caves and among the rocks of the mountains.

And they cried to the mountains and the rocks, "Fall on us and hide us from the face of the one who sits on the throne and from the wrath of the Lamb." (Rev.6:12-16)

It's clear this is the end of the world. No one can survive beyond this point. There are no mountains left on the earth and no islands. Every city, large and small, is totally destroyed, and there is no air. This is cataclysmic and is confirmed by the Apostle Peter's description of the end of the world.

> *The Heavens will disappear with a roar; the elements will melt in the heat and be destroyed by fire, and the earth and everything done in it will be laid bare. (2 Pet.3:10)*

All these Scriptures describe the big picture of the events of Armageddon, but what about the smaller pictures? We can see what happens to the world, but what happens to Satan, the two beasts, the scarlet woman and the Bride of Christ when Christ says, *"It is done!"*? Like any good storyteller, God does not leave us in the dark. He fills in the gaps with several 'after' stories.

Some biblical scholars insist that Armageddon is not the end of the world, and they use the later events to try to prove that life continues on Earth after Armageddon, but that belief is not accurate, logical or true. John's explanations of this momentous event continue to the end of chapter twenty.

THE SCARLET WOMAN

After the end of the world in chapter sixteen, we are shown the first cameo snapshot, and it begins with the call of an angel to witness the destruction of the Great Prostitute. This angel is the same angel who would later reveal the glory of Christ's Bride.

> *One of the seven angels who had the seven bowls full of the seven last plagues came and said to me, 'Come, I will show you the punishment of the great prostitute'. (Rev.17:1)*

*One of the angels who had the seven bowls full
of the seven last plagues came and said to me,
"Come, I will show you the Bride, the wife of
the Lamb." (Rev.21:9)*

These two announcements, given by the same angel, show that the true Bride and the anti-Bride are just two sides of the same coin, yet total opposites according to their own choices. Together they represent all the people of the world.

What this angel reveals in the next two and a half chapters is a detailed description of the woman who rides the beast to Armageddon and is destroyed almost as soon as she arrives. The angel explains who this woman is, describing her as an army of kings and nations. He exposes what she does and the way she buys and sells souls. He reveals that the redeemed are called by Christ to *"come away from her"* and concludes with the graphic image of her destruction.

*She will be consumed by fire, for great is the
Lord who judges her. (Rev.17:8)*

The *Fall of Babylon* describes the just and righteous punishment of the 'great whore' through whom all the evil of the world has been executed. Her death is not noble. It's not martyrdom. It's the ultimate fruit of foolishness.

When this beastly whore finally understands she has been 'set up' by Satan as his scapegoat to take the blame for the sin he encouraged, it will be too late, for the end will come without warning, sudden, swift and complete. There will be nowhere to hide, no one to turn to, no protection from the judgment of the great and powerful King of kings.

This ultimate betrayal of mankind from the cold heart of Satan, the coward of all cowards, is the sure and definite tragic future for those who reject the loving protection of Christ.

THE TWO BEASTS

The second half of chapter nineteen is a second cameo snapshot of what was happening while the Earth was being destroyed and the armies called 'The Great Prostitute' were being subdued by Christ.

This snapshot begins by showing the beasts with the kings and armies of the earth as they arrive at Armageddon. It clearly explains what happens to the beasts who have dared, along with Satan, to deceive the Great Whore into standing against Christ and his massive army of saints and angles. It will be no surprise that these two beasts also meet a fiery end.

> *Then I saw the beast and the kings of the earth and their armies gathered together to wage war against the Christ and his army. But the beast and the false prophet were captured. The two of them were thrown alive into the lake of fire. (Rev.19:19-20)*

These two beasts are responsible, with Satan, for forcing everyone on earth to make a decision to either support Christ or reject him. The word 'Armageddon' means 'valley of decision', and it is these two beasts who carry, drive, lead, deceive, threaten or coerce everyone on earth to a place of decision. They drive people to choose sides.

These beasts encourage the kings, leaders and people of all the nations of the earth to covet, bribe, lie, steal, blaspheme, kill, torture and persecute the righteous, plus much more. They rejoice with the cowardly, vile, unbelieving and sexually immoral. They applaud drunkness, and Satan worship, and mock everything that is holy (Rev.21:8). The damage they do to the Bride of Christ is the work of sin and is the reason their judgment, when it comes, is just.

SATAN'S DEMISE

Finally, in chapter twenty, we read what happens to Satan. It starts by showing the power of Christ's victory at Calvary, which severely limited his power, chaining him and sealing him in a holding cell while his beasts and whore did his work on earth for him. Then in verse seven, we see him let out so that he can, with his beasts, lead all the anti-Christ kings and nations of the earth to the battle against Christ and his army on the plains of Armageddon. He doesn't know it's a trap!

He proudly overestimates his power and underestimates the breathtaking might of Christ. So, we see that as soon as the kings and nations of the earth surround God's people, fire comes down from Heaven and consumes them. Whoosh! Game over! This is the judgment of the Whore of Babylon, whom we have seen previously is consumed by fire. Fire also destroys the two beasts, leaving Satan alone to face Christ. With one word, Christ authorises his powerful angels to bring an end to Satan forever.

It is clear from these Scriptures that when Christ says, *"It is done!"* there is nothing more Satan can do. His rebellion is over! The Earth he tried so hard to rule is destroyed. His beasts are destroyed. His scarlet mistress is destroyed. It is finished!

> *He will go out to deceive the nations and gather them for battle. In number, they are like the sand of the sea. They marched across the breadth of the Earth and surrounded the camp of God's people, the city he loves. But fire came down and devoured them.*
>
> *And the devil, who deceived them, was thrown into the lake of fire, where the beast and the false prophet had been thrown. And there they will be tormented day and night, forever. (Rev.20:7-10)*

COWARD OF COWARDS

Satan is the epitome of cowardice. Though we would think that the only just judgment for Satan's rebellion against God would be Satan's own death, Satan and his beasts do not die. They are spirits and cannot die, yet God's righteous judgment of 'death for sin' must fall on someone. This is what it means to receive *the mark of Satan*. He is marked for death, but because he can't die, his mark must fall onto others who will die in his place. And it does! His mark falls onto his followers. When the final day happens, the judgment of Satan's beasts and his compliant mistress will show, once and for all, that there is no more apt title for Satan than anti-Christ.

No better title for Satan than anti-Christ!

TOTAL OPPOSITE OF CHRIST

Christ showed his love for mankind by dying in our place, but in total opposition to Christ, Satan and his beasts never die. Instead, they remain alive and watch while those they have deceived into sinning against God take the full force of God's judgment for the rebellion they have promoted and encouraged. The people who follow Satan take the punishment that belongs to him, dying in his place.

Surely this understanding of the final accounting calls for compassion towards those who do not know Christ. Even in the final agonising moments of his own judgment on Calvary, Jesus' heart was full of compassion as he considered the future for so many of God's rebellious children; *Father forgive them; they don't know what they do (Lk.23:34)*. The greatest human tragedy of all time will be seen at the end of days when those who have been deceived into believing they don't need Christ realise, too late, that belief is just not true.

THE REDEEMED

On that day, in an instant, all mankind will suddenly know why Christ is supreme Lord over all. Everyone will understand how his loving death permanently merged the Old and New Laws so that they could now work together to divide the sheep from the goats. The sheer power of the salvation won by Christ at Calvary will be obvious to everyone.

As the final human accounting unfolds, Christ's redeemed will be standing with him, safe, secure and protected. They will be in awe of him, enthralled by his majesty, brimming with the excitement of his victory and fully aware that his judgments are righteous and just. They will bear witness to the last, spine-tingling revelation of Christ's absolute authority and imperial glory on earth. Breathtaking!

Totally free from the judgments of the wrath of God because of Calvary, the Bride of Christ will find herself cheering from the sidelines and crying out with the elders, living creatures and all the angels of Heaven...

> *True and just are your judgments...you have avenged the blood of your servants. (Rev.19:2)*

Then, after all the battles are concluded, and all the judgments are fulfilled, the Bride will hear a decree go out across Heaven, and she will finally step forward into the greatest joy she has ever known.

> *Let us rejoice and be glad and give him glory, for the wedding of the Lamb has come, and his Bride has made herself ready. (Rev.19:7)*

Radiant with jewels!

29

CHRIST'S BEAUTIFUL BRIDE

I saw the Holy City, the New Jerusalem, coming down out of Heaven from God, prepared as a Bride beautifully dressed for her husband... God will wipe away every tear from their eyes, there will be no more death or mourning or crying or pain, for the old order of things has passed away. (Rev.21:2-4)

All the dazzling jewels scattered throughout Revelation sparkle with clarity as they highlight the complex simplicity of salvation. But they fade in comparison to the finest treasure of all. The most precious jewel in our Saviour's crown, huge and central, placed to be the focus of attention and highlighted by the presence of all the other precious stones, is the magnificent glory of the Bride of Christ. This whole story, Christ's entire testimony, is about her, for everything he has done, he has done for his Bride! The last two chapters of the Bible are dedicated to the blessings awaiting the beautiful Bride of Christ. Christ loves his Bride so much we are the first he talks about at the beginning of his testimony, and we are the last he talks about as his testimony ends. What love!

ABUNDANT LOVE

There are so very many blessings our loving Saviour has prepared for his faithful Bride;

- ♥ No more tears or crying,
- ♥ No more death or mourning,
- ♥ No more pain,
- ♥ No more curses,
- ♥ No more nights,
- ♥ No more hunger or thirst,
- ♥ Everything will be made new,
- ♥ Everything will be precious,
- ♥ Everything will shine with beauty.

What an excellent husband! What a marvellous protector! What a great provider! The blessings are not one-sided, though, and this Bride is not a weakling, for just as Christ gives to his beloved, so his beloved gives back to him. Yes, she is glorious, beautifully adorned and radiant, but she has something unusual to give him, something all his riches could not buy! As she acknowledges all he has done for her, she glows with admiration, and this is where we see the blessings become mutual. The one thing God could never do is force his people to praise him, love him, or appreciate his work. Our admiration had to be voluntary. We had to actually fall in love with him and genuinely admire everything about him. This is the gift of the Bride!

An excellent husband!

A marvellous protector!

A wonderful provider!

Our love, appreciation, praise and gratitude are as rare and precious to our beloved Lord as fine gold and sparkling jewels simply because he didn't create them. They are the only things in creation he does not already have. Therefore, even our smallest offerings are received by him as rare and precious treasures, which he, in turn, honours with the highest possible recognition in Heavenly places, highlighting their beauty. Our simple little gifts of praise and appreciation make his heart sing!

A word fitly spoken is like apples of gold in settings of silver.

(Prov.25:11)

THE HOLY CITY

The glorious, richly adorned Bride is described as the Holy City, and this city itself is the most beautiful example of the 'marriage' of the Lamb, for it is through the image of the Holy City that we see how God and man become 'one'.

This city becomes the new and eternal dwelling place of God and the new and eternal dwelling place of man. It shows the mutual nature of the merger of God and man because the gold and jewels of which it is built are supplied to Christ by his perfect Bride, while Christ's life is the light that brings their beauty to life and shows the sparkling clarity of their brilliance. This successful merging of Earth and Heaven into one, through Christ, is the marriage of the Lamb.

This glorious Holy City shines with the light of Christ's love through gold refined to such purity it is as transparent as glass. This image reveals that in the marriage of the Lamb, there will be so many words of unselfish love and adoration spoken by the Bride that the joy of Christ will radiate the glory of God as through transparent gold. There is nothing but ecstasy awaiting the Bride of Christ!

SEEING THE BIG PICTURE

Your eyes will see the King in his beauty and
view a land that stretches afar. (Is.33.17)

The wonderful, encouraging, and enthralling Book of Revelation has been regarded by many as too difficult to understand; a book of symbols, visions and secrets, far too complex for ordinary people to unravel or comprehend, yet that's simply not true. We are supposed to see the vision. We are supposed to understand its meaning.

It is true that the mysteries of Christ's testimony are satisfyingly complex, and an intelligent mind could spend a lifetime exploring the depth and beauty of every nuance, yet at the same time, his testimony can be made so simple it can be understood by a child. Further, I believe that its promises and the comfort it provides need to be shared with children as well as adults.

It seems that's what the authors of most classic children's fairytales tried to do; explain the overall message of Revelation in story form in a way both adults and children could understand. In other words, 'outline the big picture without getting bogged in the details'. I further believe that if most people today could see the big picture, they would then understand all the little details that make the vista so beautiful.

Throughout Revelation, Jesus is the one telling the story, and John is his scribe. Though the Apostle John wrote a serious work, his chapters are laid out like a classic storybook tale. What John saw was *the King in his beauty,* and he was given a panoramic overview of the landscape of a kingdom that *stretches far* across time. In short, he saw Christ as the hero he is, Satan as the villain, the Bride as the damsel in distress, the harlot as the wicked queen, and what he wrote was simply *His*tory!

A VERY FAMILIAR PLOT

Without being flippant, I have dot pointed the main events from their broadly familiar 'story' point of view so that you can see what I mean;

- ♥ John first explains that Jesus is there at the beginning introducing himself as the Alpha and Omega, *the beginning and the end,* of this larger-than-life drama.

- ♥ The story begins as Jesus relates the seven letters of instruction he has written to the seven angels charged with keeping his beloved safe. She has just been rescued, and her prince has no intention of letting her be hurt again. These letters show all the protections he has put in place to keep her safe and the royal authority he has given his future Bride to use at her discretion.

- ♥ Then the scene changes to the throne room of the ancient King, where John sees the recently crowned young King step forward to accept the challenge to bring final judgment to his Father's arch-rival, the dark villain. He is the only one in the Kingdom worthy of leading this final assault because of his knowledge of the enemy and the courage he showed while rescuing his Bride from the villain's stronghold.

- ♥ The next few scenes take us to various battlefields, where John witnesses everything the mighty conqueror does as he fights a dragon, two beasts and three frogs.

- ♥ After that, John is shown how the Bride learns to use her powers to thwart the trickery of the wicked queen. While she is being bombarded with schemes and lured away from her seven protectors, her beloved reminds her to use her royal powers to remove herself from the influence of the evil temptress. Once the Bride is safe, John watches as the wicked queen dies.

- When the victorious warrior returns to his kingdom after the final battle, John is invited to witness the long-awaited marriage of the valiant hero to his beautiful and courageous Bride. A great feast is laid out before them, and everyone is invited to share the joy of this lavish celebration.

- The final scene contains the happy couple beginning their future in a home that can only be described as majestic. So big is this palace it is a city in its own right, with streets paved with gold and building foundations made of precious stones. There is no darkness there, no evil, no sadness, no crying and no villain. It's a place where people live 'happily-ever-after'.

THE GREATEST LOVE STORY

The story of our royal hero's great love for his chosen Bride, the battles he is prepared to fight on her behalf, her dramatic rescue and their happy-ever-after future sounds like every loved fairytale ever written. But his story is not a fairytale! It is a true story! The Book of Revelation, Christ's personal testimony, is saturated with love from beginning to end and has become the most loved story ever told.

Christ is the hero!

The Spirit is his faithful assistant!

The Bride is the damsel in distress!

Satan is the villain and loser!

What Apostle John describes is a king who is splendid in majesty as he defeats his enemy, rescues his beloved Bride and takes her safely to their new home in his magnificent Kingdom. This may seem too simple, but it's not! This is God's book. Christ is the hero. The Spirit is his faithful assistant. His Bride is the damsel in distress, and Satan is the villain and greatest loser in history!

THE VILLAIN IS THE LOSER

All the pictures drawn for us in Revelation, including the most horrible images of Satan's two beasts, his wicked queen and his mark and number, show Satan as the loser and Christ as the victor. All of them! What Revelation teaches from start to finish is that Satan is only a dot in the grand scheme of things. Though he may be God's enemy, his plans to outsmart God fail every time because Jesus is a brilliant tactician and is always ready and waiting for Satan's next move. Isn't it time for believers to throw out the Satan-glorifying horror stories and embrace the beauty and grace of the truth? Jesus is the Truth!

Isn't it time to throw out all those Satan-glorifying horror stories?

Despite what many people teach, Revelation was written to glorify Jesus, not Satan, and there is no image on any page, which gives Satan glory, let alone victory. It is not a horror story, a fairytale, a world history or a crystal ball, and neither is it merely a glimpse into the future or a reminder of the past. Rather it combines both past and future and challenges us to live in the present.

AN ENORMOUS PRIVILEGE

What an opportunity we have been offered to stand in victory with the mighty King of all kings. What a privilege he has bestowed on us to be called his Bride and to share his throne and glory with him. How could a Bride not love to the death such a gentle, loving, generous, protective and mighty conquering hero? Salvation is not a fantasy! Christ and his Bride will indeed live happily-ever-after!

Honoured and regal!

30

AN ENDURING LOVE STORY

Blessed is the one you choose and bring near to dwell in your courts! With awesome deeds of righteousness, you answer us, O God of our salvation, the hope of all the ends of the Earth and of the farthest seas. (Psalm 65:4-5)

Revelation is indeed a book of blessings. *Blessed are those who read and take to heart what is written* (Rev.1:3). The testimony of Christ has so many layers of understanding it is impossible to hold only one view. When we look at Christ, there is so much to see, so much to know, and so much to be grateful for. We are incredibly privileged to be welcomed into his lavish courts, even more so to be called his Bride.

What a thrilling and irresistible love story is the testimony of Christ's love for his Bride. It has captured and held the hearts and minds of people of all ages down through the centuries. It still captures hearts and minds today, whether individuals know our Saviour, the hero of the story, or not. The promise of an attainable, happy-ever-after future is the most compelling message the world has ever known, and whether people know Christ or not, they love this story!

WRITTEN TO REVEAL LOVE

All the other references to our Saviour, in both the Old and New Testaments, talk about the great love he has for the world, but Revelation goes one step further and describes his love in minute detail! These descriptions are brilliantly written and, like a faceted jewel, can be enjoyed from many angles. Even the layout of the chapters, the way they are presented, is brilliant and gives us a completely different view.

The layout of the chapters is a message in itself. It holds the basic storyline, which we can easily recognise as the blueprint for many a fairytale, but there is much more. There are only twenty-two chapters in the Book of Revelation, and when they are laid out side by side and looked at from a writer's point of view, the 'plot' of the entire book is easy to see.

When we look at the plot, it is easy to see what has been added in or taken out.

A plot is like a guideline that holds everything written in place, and writers use the guideline as a reference to eliminate anything that deviates from the intended story. So, when we look at the plot of Revelation the same way, it becomes easy to see what has been 'added' and is, therefore, out of place. For example, a human Antichrist, ruler over the nations, doesn't fit the original plot, and so to 'add' it, the plot has to be adjusted; in other words, every reference to Christ being made ruler over the nations must be removed, and the plot altered, for this addition to fit the new storyline. It's the same with the Rapture Theory. In order to add it, the plot needs to be altered and the Bride removed prior to the beginning of the action chapters. The trouble with that is once you remove Jesus and his Bride, there is no story.

FOLLOW THE PLOT

I have laid out the chapters of Revelation below, the way a writer would lay out the plot or storyline for a novel. It will be no surprise for you to see that I didn't have to change or re-position anything to make the plot work. Looking at the overall plot is basic to understanding any book. The Book of Revelation is no different. When we don't 'add' anything or 'take' anything away, this is how Revelation looks. This is how it was laid out for us centuries ago, written by the King of words, the author of all authors, God himself!

This is how the plot was written centuries ago, by the king of words, the author of all authors, God himself!

CHAPTER 1: The Royal Decree

In the first chapter, God, Christ and the Seven Spirits introduce themselves as the authors of this work and nominate John as their appointed scribe to write down what they show him. Christ further names himself as the Alpha and Omega, beginning and end of the story and tells John that this story is his testimony, the story of his life.

CHAPTERS 2-3: The Royal Bride

The royal 'Bride-to-be' is introduced as a person of position and authority who needs protection and guidance in order to remain safe. Seven agents of the Kingdom are made responsible for her well-being. Christ makes it clear she is the beloved of the Alpha and Omega, for she is the first one he mentions at the beginning of his story and the last one he mentions at the end. This shows she is the focus of his story and that her salvation is the reason he has a testimony.

345

CHAPTERS 4-7: Back At The Palace

The lavish splendour of the vast Kingdom of the ancient King is revealed as we are taken to the throne room, where we find the King waiting for his Son to return from his battle at Calvary. The Son arrives and is crowned as victor and, accompanied by enormous applause, which shows he has the support of the entire realm, takes full authority over the Kingdom. He begins his rule by taking immediate action, with his Father's full support, to bring an end to all enemy-inspired insurrection within the Kingdom.

CHAPTERS 8-16: The King Goes To War

All the enemies of the Kingdom are subdued and either destroyed or permanently imprisoned during this time. The one who stands out more than the others is the wicked queen whom Christ can't touch until his beloved is safely out of her reach. Her schemes and demise are given cameo treatment.

CHAPTERS 17-20: A Victorious Outcome

As the cameo expands, we see the wicked queen, a master at seducing the innocent with trickery, deception and bribes, being given special attention in four chapters. These chapters record who she is, what she has done, her partners in evil and their final demise. Just before she dies, the young King calls his beloved to 'come away from her' so she will not be hurt when the evil queen falls to her fiery death.

CHAPTERS 21-22: The Royal Marriage

The joy in the Kingdom at the return of the victorious hero, the beauty of his Bride, their marriage and happy-ever-after future are all described in these final chapters. Though he is the Alpha and the Omega, he does not hold this role alone! His Bride is with him at the beginning and also at the end. How blessed we are! How loved!

THIS IS GOD'S PLOT!

This is the way the Book of Revelation was written by God. This is the way the plot sits in that most precious and wonderful book. I haven't changed anything! Over the past few decades, a few unscrupulous people have made a lot of money making up lies about this beautiful book, deceiving the elect with stories that have nothing to do with the testimony of Christ. They have deviated so far from the established understanding of Revelation that it has become unrecognisable; a maze of confusion and horror, full of hate and told from the villain's point of view. How horrible! Isn't it time we got back to the truth? Revelation is about the deep and selfless love our Saviour has for his beloved. This has been the normal understanding for hundreds of years! Centuries!

> *Unscrupulous people have made a lot of money making up lies about this most precious book.*

WHAT IS A FAIRYTALE?

Centuries ago, when the stories of *Snow White, Cinderella, Sleeping Beauty* and other similar tales were originally told, they were simply 'folklore'; a way of passing along moral values and belief systems held by communities of people prior to the widespread introduction of books. These stories were told to and remembered by mostly uneducated people, for there were few schools back then, most people couldn't read or write, and the printing press had not been invented. They were not just stories but were told for a purpose; they captured the truth of redemption and the promises of Revelation in the simplest possible way.

347

They were loved, repeated, remembered and faithfully passed down from generation to generation because their intrinsic moral codes reminded people they could choose to be either good or evil and would be rewarded according to their choices. 'If the shoe fits…' is a classic moral from folklore that comes directly from the story of Cinderella. Are you a kind-hearted person whom the prince would love? Or are you an evil step-sister whom the prince would shun? Folklore stories were filled with easy-to-remember moral values, which gave people a reason to aim for the moral high ground.

'FOLKLORE' BECAME 'FAIRYTALE'

The first time these and other folklore stories were collected and put into handwritten form was in the mid-1600s by French academic Charles Perrault, a devoted Christian. His first written collection was introduced to the academic world under his newly created literary genre, 'fairytale'. Though that was when the classic understanding of fairytales began, the stories were nevertheless folkloric in origin and had already been around for a long, long time. It would be another 200 years before the Grimm Brothers of Germany, also strong Christians raised as Calvinists, would publish many of the same tales, plus more. As academics, the Brothers Grimm established a methodology for the collecting and recording of folklore stories to be used as the basis

The fairytales that everyone loves today started out as moral roadmaps.

for folklore studies, which is today known as Folkloristics. These studies have established that folklore tales were not written just for children. They were systems of belief which contained morals for living. The fairytales that everyone loves today started as moral roadmaps for Christian communities.

The morals and beliefs contained in the stories of *Snow White, Cinderella, Sleeping Beauty* and similar tales clearly reflect the great love of a royal hero for his beautiful Bride-to-be, who is always in need of rescue. They also show the battles he is prepared to fight to bring her safely to their happy-ever-after future. Can children understand Revelation? Yes!

FOLKLORE IS STILL ALIVE

I am not glib or clever when I say that many folklore stories are a strong and accurate reflection of the promises of Christ revealed to the world in the Book of Revelation. God is well able to ensure his Son's remarkable story is passed down from generation to generation to people all over the world, whether they read the Bible or not. He is, after all, God!

The story of Salvation cannot be confined to preachers in pulpits, or the educated, or readers of books. God himself spread it to the general population!

The overwhelming enormity and power of His Son's rescue of humanity is not something which can be confined to preachers in pulpits, or to the educated, or to readers of books. God himself made sure it spread out into the general population of the world. Over hundreds of years, the truth about *the hope of salvation* has entwined itself into the general human psyche, and its promise now drives much of the hope found in ordinary people and in ordinary lives, whether they believe in God or not.

For the Earth will be filled with the knowledge of the glory of the LORD as the waters cover the sea. (Hab.2:14)

Millions of people all over the world, who would never dream of going into a church, nevertheless know and love these folklore tales and yearn for the promise of unfailing love and eternal happiness without knowing why. But we know why! *Deep calls to deep (Ps.42:7),* and God himself has ensured down through the ages that the message of his Son's deep love for mankind reaches the deep places in the hearts and minds of ordinary people, even if they don't understand the message of the Gospel.

The remarkable hold folklore tales about the Royal Hero of Revelation have had on societies for centuries is enormous, and it hasn't diminished over time. In fact, it can't be quenched, and its influence continues to widen. We have a current example in society today!

GOD IS STILL USING FOLKLORE

There is a folklore tale still being passed down from generation to generation throughout most of the world, yet its origin might surprise you. The story of Santa Claus is folklore, and it is taken straight from the Book of Revelation. Consider these few questions;

- ♥ Who is coming to town?
- ♥ Who sees us when we're sleeping?
- ♥ Who's keeping a naughty and nice list?
- ♥ Who's bringing gifts to those who are good?
- ♥ Who's going to put on a great feast?
- ♥ Why do we all wear paper crowns at Christmas?
- ♥ Who has an unlimited number of willing helpers?

The celebration of Christmas is not only about remembering Christ was born but is also about remembering his return as a mighty King and judge.

Everything about the folklore tale of Santa Claus reflects the power and authority of the unstoppable return of Christ laid out for us in the Book of Revelation.

- ♥ Our Saviour is coming back,
- ♥ He is the one who sees us awake or asleep,
- ♥ He is writing names in his Book of Life,
- ♥ When he returns, he will bring rewards,
- ♥ When he returns, there will be a great feast,
- ♥ He will give out crowns of victory,
- ♥ He has billions of angels at his beck and call.

How do we not know, as Christians, whom Santa Claus represents? Why are we not screaming this truth from the rooftops? We have the opportunity to do so every Christmas. Why are we not giving our great conquering Redeemer the glory he deserves? Why are we not reminding the world each Christmas of the truth of his amazing promises?

THE GREATEST HOPE

The Book of Revelation holds the greatest hope the world has ever known. It is the stuff of fairytales and every child's Christmas dream, yet the reality is Revelation is not a fantasy or a child's whim; it is the Gospel! It is the truth about Jesus, the most captivating, evocative, influential and compelling love story ever told. There has never been any other testimony that can and does capture the hearts and minds of people all over the world the way the story of the Book of Revelation captures them. The story of Revelation is *HIS*tory! And it is brilliant!

About the Author

Monica Bennett-Ryan

Hi! I'm Monica. Thank you for reading this book. Writing it has been one of the greatest joys of my life.

I've been a believer most of my life, since the age of seven, and currently live in Australia. I am the mother of three adult children, two boys and a girl, and the grandmother of eight beautiful grandchildren. As you can see, I absolutely love the Book of Revelation.

For decades I listened dutifully as prophets of doom expounded the Book of Revelation with cries of 'disaster', 'horror' and 'quick, let's escape', and I could never, ever agree with their interpretations. Their views and what I was reading in Revelation didn't match at all. In fact, they clashed terribly!

I couldn't stand seeing Christ's amazing, eternal victory over Satan at Calvary being tossed aside as irrelevant to Revelation, and so I wrote this book.

It has allowed me the opportunity to refute the claims of the prophets of doom and explain why I believe Christ is the Champion of Heaven, how safe and protected his Bride is from the tribulation of the last days, and why their scary end-time predictions of Satanic power on Earth can never happen.

Be careful when you read this book.

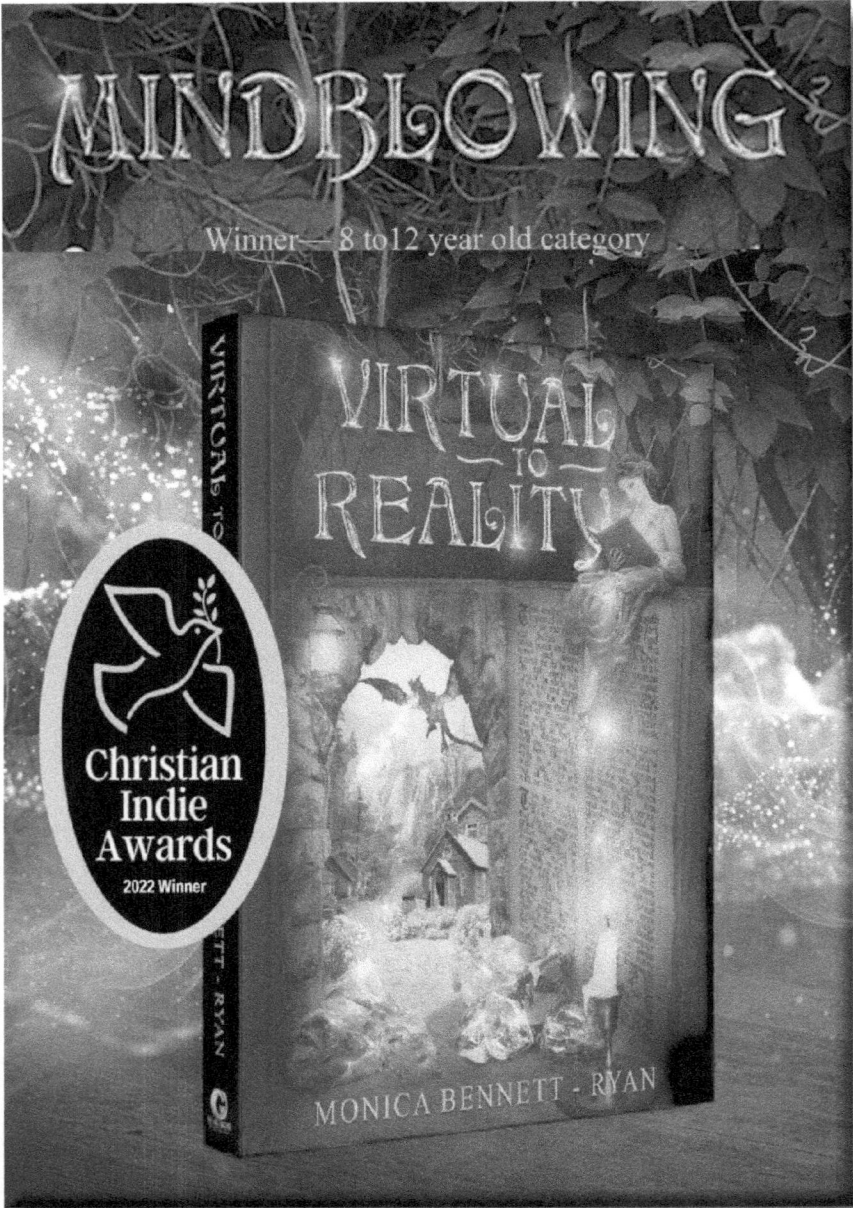

You could become part of the story!

2022 AWARD-WINNING BOOK

There is enormous encouragement for believers in Revelation, and believers include children, so I've also written a book on Revelation in a way that children can easily understand. It uses a realistic virtual world to bring the spiritual to reality.

The novel-sized book is called VIRTUAL to REALITY and is a delightful read for anyone from 9 to 90 who would like to understand the general message of Revelation.

An Age-Old Story!

After the royal hero saves a girl and her village from a vicious dragon, he returns home for a time, leaving his new love in the care of his seven most trusted helpers. As soon as the hero leaves, the evil ones set about making the girl and her friends believe the dragon is still in control of them and their village. They deceive leaders, poison people, cause division between friends and families, destroy traditions and threaten war.

Enter the seven mighty Fire Lords! Using the gifts the Fire Lords give her, and with their powerful assistance, the girl gradually changes from a simple villager to a radiant princess as she overcomes all the nasty traps and attacks of the wicked queen and the dragon's two beastly pets. Finally, the royal hero returns to find a strong and confident bride, ready to take her place beside him on his throne.

A world in crisis!

This book gives children and teens much-needed hope. It shows that Christ is trustworthy and his mighty Spirit will powerfully help them overcome every sneaky, evil influence in this world and ensure they are prepared for the next.

You can read more about my books at:
www.inhisname.com.au

www.ingramcontent.com/pod-product-compliance
Lightning Source LLC
Chambersburg PA
CBHW021959090426
42811CB00001B/85